# Great Gardens

## of the National Trust

Stephen Lacey

National Trust

ibraries

# To the gardeners of the National Trust

This edition published in the United Kingdom in 2014 by
National Trust Books
10 Southcombe Street
London W14 0RA

An imprint of Anova Books Ltd

Based on *Gardens of the National Trust* (revised edition), 2011

ISBN: 9781849941549

A CIP catalogue record for this book is available from the British Library.

10 9 8 7 6 5 4 3 2 1

Printed in China by 1010 Printing International
Colour reproduction by Rival Colour Ltd, UK

# Picture Credits

# Contents

# Introduction

Much has happened in the gardens of the National Trust in recent years. The most remarkable development is the resurgence of fruit and vegetable gardening, which, because of its high labour demands, the Trust had little opportunity to champion in the past. Today, largely thanks to the small army of volunteer and community gardeners who now work alongside the Trust's own staff, this deficiency has been comprehensively addressed, and kitchen gardens have been restored and revitalised in nearly 50 properties.

This is allowing the Trust not only to assist in the conservation of heritage fruit and vegetable varieties and traditional, even esoteric, cultivation techniques such as pineapple-growing, but also to convey a truer and more rounded picture of the life of a country house – for without their kitchen gardens, these properties, which were often far from centres of commerce, would scarcely have been able to function. Some of the newly revived kitchen gardens, such as at Knightshayes Court, Tatton Park and Wimpole Hall, are on an astonishing scale.

Wildflower and wildlife gardening has also been gathering momentum, with, for instance, often just simple changes in mowing regimes producing orchid-studded tapestries. Sheffield Park, Wakehurst Place, Tyntesfield and Packwood House are prime examples of this, but in a large number of gardens the promotion of organic and more environmentally sensitive methods is reaping rewards. Restoration work continues apace – notably at Hidcote Manor, Croome Park, Tyntesfield, Stowe, Dyrham Park, Prior Park, Cliveden, Osterley Park, Kingston Lacy and Canons Ashby, but with changes and additions also in a great many others.

For me, travelling the length of Britain, meeting the head gardeners and tapping into the story of each garden's evolution and idiosyncrasies has again been an adventure and an education. The diversity of the Trust's gardens is immediately apparent from the photographs. They range from landscape park to walled town garden, box parterre to rhododendron woodland, Derbyshire hilltop to Cornish coombe. Lakes, temples, herbaceous borders, Japanese gardens, conservatories, pinetums, daffodils, roses, regional apple varieties and eighteenth-century statues, views of sea, moor and motorway, yew trees clipped as pointed Welsh hats, it is all here.

The gardens engage you on many levels. There are the straightforward pleasures of seeing, smelling, touching, listening and exploring. For home gardeners, there are ideas and plant names to pick up. But go deeper and invariably you tap into a story, perhaps of great individuals and family successions, designers and plant hunters, period politics and preoccupations, changing fashions, destructions and restorations.

The landscape movement spelled destruction for many of the great formal gardens, but those at Ham House, Westbury Court, Powis Castle, Erddig and Hanbury Hall survived in large part, or have been resurrected by the Trust, and show the European-inspired styles of the late seventeenth and early eighteenth centuries. The story of the subsequent departure from these enclosed and geometric patterns and the evolution of the landscape style through its Arcadian, Brownian and romantically Picturesque phases is recounted, in whole or in part, at Claremont, Stowe, Fountains Abbey and Studley Royal, Wimpole Hall, Prior Park, West Wycombe Park, Croome Park, Stourhead, Petworth House and Scotney Castle.

The early nineteenth century's renewed enthusiasm for formality and self-consciously artful gardening is marked at Calke Abbey and Peckover House, with grand revivals of earlier styles displayed at Oxburgh Hall, Montacute, Blickling Hall and Belton House. The innovation, ingenuity and derring-do that became the order of the day is revealed in the fantasy evocations at Biddulph Grange, the engineering feats at Cragside and the multi-coloured parkland and bedding schemes at Ascott, while Waddesdon Manor, Tyntesfield, Lyme Park, Tatton Park and Polesden Lacey give a varied and luscious insight into country-house living and gardening in their Victorian and Edwardian heyday.

The influx of new trees and shrubs from the Americas, the Far East and Australasia through the nineteenth and early twentieth centuries fuelled the development of exotic woodlands, and at Mount Stewart, Killerton, Glendurgan, Nymans, Wakehurst Place, Bodnant,

Rowallane, Trengwainton, Trelissick and Winkworth Arboretum, we have supreme displays – equalled later at Knightshayes Court --and Greenway.

Simultaneously, architectural gardening was evolving, and in time became coupled with some dreamy and painterly herbaceous planting. Gertrude Jekyll's influence pervades the gardens at Barrington Court and Lindisfarne Castle as Sir Edwin Lutyens' does at Castle Drogo and Coleton Fishacre, while in the crisp compartments and sophisticated colour schemes of Hidcote and Sissinghurst the marriage of plantsmanship and formal design reaches a new twentieth-century zenith.

It is a rich legacy, but also a dynamic one. The gardens come to the Trust already many-layered – often, as in the case of Cliveden, Dunham Massey, Kingston Lacy or Shugborough, shaped by activity (destructions as well as embellishments) over many generations. Restorations by the Trust – invariably based on fragmentary evidence, and with the degree of finish and style of upkeep modified to suit the available resources – add fresh layers.

And thereafter the gardens continue to change. Plants grow and die; Mother Nature unleashes her storms, wood-boring beetles, honey fungus and, more recently, the devastating pathogen *Phytophthora ramorum*, or Sudden Oak Death, which is having a far greater impact on plants than any previous disaster. The Trust's response has been to launch the largest plant survey ever undertaken in the UK, using maps and GPS technology to record each specimen in 80 of its most important plant collections. Only now is the scale and importance of the Trust's plant collections being understood – rarities it never knew it had are being discovered.

Year by year, there is also change initiated from within the gardens which, happily, the Trust recognises as essential if a garden is to be kept alive and pulsing, and for staff to develop and demonstrate their skills. This may be a variation in bedding schemes or border planting, the continual enrichment of tree and shrub collections, or the sudden annexation of unemployed areas for new pursuits, such as winter gardening at Anglesey Abbey and Dunham Massey. Restoration always brings opportunities for innovation. And, particularly where the donor family is still in residence, the gardens may even be carried forward by bold new work from contemporary designers and artists, as at Ascott and Plas Newydd.

Overall, the Trust's gardens seem to be in very good fettle and with ever-increasing visitor numbers. The tone of my descriptions will reveal which of them I have found particularly exciting and which have left me cool or puzzled; I hope there will be plenty of opportunity for you to see and judge them for yourself.

# Anglesey Abbey

**LODE, CAMBRIDGESHIRE**

AREA 49ha (120 acres) • SOIL good loam on clay base • ALTITUDE 30m (100ft)
AVERAGE RAINFALL 533mm (21in) • AVERAGE WINTER CLIMATE cold

What is one to make of this extraordinary twentieth-century garden? It is the product of one man's vision, Urban Huttelston Broughton, 1st Baron Fairhaven, who, with grand gestures and a breathtaking sense of scale, transformed an unpromising piece of fenland into a landscape which, as Arthur Bryant has described, 'can compare with the great masterpieces of the Georgian era'. It is a garden of broad avenues, immense vistas and 12ha (30 acres) of mown lawn, decorated with extravagant flower gardens and classical statuary of the best quality, all maintained to the highest standards.

When Lord Fairhaven bought this former Augustinian priory in 1926, he inherited a small garden, laid out by Rev. John Hailstone in the 1860s, and some fine trees, including the cedars and weeping silver lime. From this nucleus he gradually expanded into 36ha (90 acres) of surrounding pastureland. The network of avenues and grass walks do not radiate from the house, but are part of a series of surprises and enticements within an independent garden design. Walking west along Coronation Avenue, you come upon a dramatic cross-vista, culminating in a marble urn, framed at one end by a triple semi-circle of fastigiate Dawyck beech (formerly Lombardy poplars) and, at the other, by silver birch. As you emerge from the beech, you are then offered a view, between island beds of coloured-leaved shrubs, towards a circle of Corinthian columns that houses a replica of Bernini's *David* and is guarded by eighteenth-century lead lions.

Statuary is often the reward for exploration, for Lord Fairhaven was an energetic and discerning collector. Many pieces date from the eighteenth century; some are much older. The Emperors' Walk, on the eastern edge of the garden, is especially richly endowed. It takes its name from the twelve eighteenth-century marble busts of Roman emperors displayed along its 401m (440yd) length, but there are also lead figures within a central circle of copper beech, pairs of bronze and copper urns, a bronze version of the Versailles Diana and of Silenus holding the infant Bacchus, and an open temple sheltering a Roman urn made of Egyptian porphyry.

The displays of bulbs and border plants are as extravagant as the avenues and statues are impressive. Lord Fairhaven chose plants for their impact *en masse*, and several enclosures focus on individual species. Dutch Elm Disease killed 4,000 trees here, and much of the garden has been replanted by the Trust. The new hornbeam avenue was initially underplanted with a ton of white poet's daffodils, *Narcissus poeticus* var. *recurvus*, and N. 'Winifred van Graven'. As this area became more shaded, an additional 10,000 bluebells, *Hyacinthoides non-scripta*, were planted in the autumn of 2002 to take over from the narcissus. Ten thousand summer snowflakes, *Leucojum aestivum*, grow in the grass of Warrior's Walk.

The rose garden beside the house was one of Lord Fairhaven's favourite areas, and contains a range of modern bush roses. The Hyacinth Garden beyond, one of the garden's most photographed features, is a sea of 4,000 scented white 'Carnegie' and 'Blue Star' hyacinths in spring, followed in summer by 1,500 red 'Madame

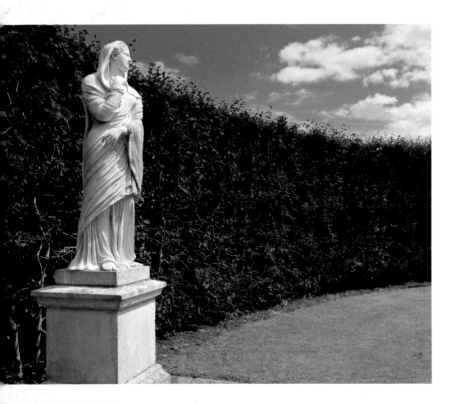

**LEFT** Copper beech hedging creates a striking foil for some of the statuary in the Anglesey Abbey garden.
**RIGHT** The open temple with its Neo-Classical columns is one in a series of surprises throughout the garden. It shelters a Roman urn of Egyptian porphyry.

Simone Stappers' and gold 'Ella Britton' dahlias. The Dahlia Garden is also filled with these potent performers. Delphiniums are a feature of the vast curved border in the Herbaceous Garden, although here not in solitary splendour but accompanied by a variety of other plants, including peonies, geraniums, campanulas and *Crambe cordifolia*, with its giant sprays of white blossom; heleniums, achillea and eupatorium help to carry the colour throughout the summer. At its peak, this is perhaps one of the most impressive herbaceous borders in the country.

In 1998, a 1ha (2$\frac{1}{2}$ acre) Winter Garden was opened to commemorate the centenary of the 1st Lord Fairhaven's birth. The winding route provides a succession of brilliantly coloured barks, bulbs and scented flowers, a complement to the extensive collection of snowdrops (some 240 varieties), which draws crowds of visitors in January and February. Such spectacles contrast with the dark evergreen passages of yew, ruscus, box and ivy, and the open swathes of grass and trees (including huge areas of carefully managed wildflower meadow and woodland), creating not only a stimulating pattern of light and shade, rest and drama, but also startling juxtapositions of style. In the end, Anglesey Abbey remains a triumphant anachronism; a garden to make you gasp.

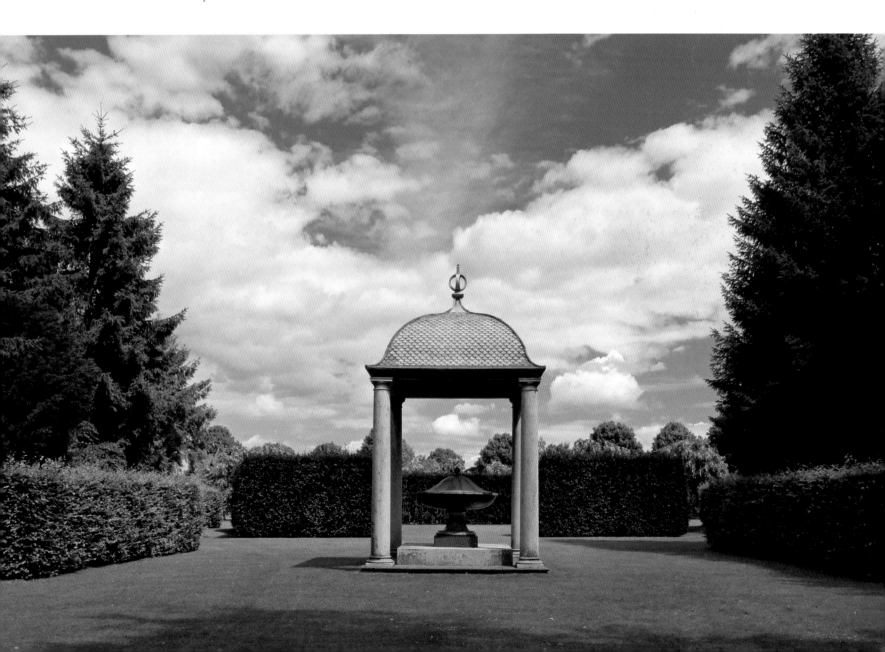

# Antony

**TORPOINT, CORNWALL**

**AREA** 14ha (35 acres) • **SOIL** medium loam on shale • **ALTITUDE** 30m (100ft)
**AVERAGE RAINFALL** 1,016mm (40in) • **AVERAGE WINTER CLIMATE** mild

As you turn into the approach drive at Antony, a prospect of Plymouth across the estuary is a final reminder of twenty-first century bustle and congestion. The limes now lead you into parkland and woods, back into a more elegant and spacious age.

The silver-grey house was completed for Sir William Carew in 1724, though Antony had been home to his family for 250 years previously, and the garden and park radiate from it in a pattern of formal walks and enclosures and soft-edged avenues. The present design has evolved at a leisurely pace, but was much influenced by the great landscape gardener Humphry Repton, who was consulted by Reginald Pole-Carew in 1792. You can feel his hand in the uninterrupted, undulating sweeps of grass and trees, and in the gentle drama of the main views.

But other features pre-date Repton's involvement, including the terrace, the circular dovecote and the groves of holm oaks which frame the fine views from the house to the River Lynher; these were planted in the 1760s. By 1788, Reginald Pole-Carew had himself already embarked on an extensive programme of ornamental tree planting; the immense black walnut in front of the house and the cork oak at the end of the Yew Walk may date from this period.

The gravel terraces in front of the house and the formal walks and gardens to the west reveal layers of Victorian, Edwardian and more recent planting by subsequent members of the Carew family. The broad paths, high yew hedges and abundance of substantial trees continue the generous scale, but there are more intimate touches in Lady Pole-Carew's early twentieth-century Japanese garden at the east end of the terrace and in the enclosed Summer Garden and Knot Garden begun in 1983 by Lady (Mary) Carew Pole.

The planting themes at Antony tend to be focused on favourite genera. There are two magnificent rows of large, free-standing magnolias, the evergreen *M. grandiflora* 'Exmouth' and the deciduous *M. × soulangeana*; at the end of the former, overhung by an old mulberry, is the splendid Mandalay Bell brought back as booty from the Second Burmese War by General Sir Reginald Pole-Carew in 1886. Hoherias and eucryphias, which provide a mass of

white blossom in summer, set new themes for the west end of the garden. Around the walls, beneath tender climbing plants such as *Acacia pravissima*, *Senna corymbosa* (syn. *Cassia corymbosa*), *Sophora tetraptera* and various wall shrubs, is a National Collection of daylilies (*Hemerocallis*), including many American varieties, assembled and hybridised by the late Lady (Cynthia) Carew Pole between 1960 and 1977.

A romantic escape from order and elegance is offered by the 24ha (60 acres) of woodland, wilderness and wildflowers between the house and the river. This is actually outside the Trust's domain, and run by the Carew Pole Garden Trust, which allows the Trust's visitors to explore it on the days the house is open. Paths take you past an eighteenth-century bathhouse (owned by the National Trust), mature rhododendrons, long-needled pines, birches, Asiatic magnolias, and, most memorably, a long valley of pink, red and white camellias which now number over 2,000 varieties – Sir John Carew Pole's plantings being continually enhanced by those of his successors, Sir Richard and Lady (Mary) Carew Pole, with many plants grown from wild-sourced seed.

**ABOVE** The Summer Garden in late May.

# Arlington Court

BARNSTAPLE, DEVON

AREA 12ha (30 acres) • SOIL acid/light, sand overlying slate • ALTITUDE 244m (800ft)
AVERAGE RAINFALL 1,524mm (60in) • AVERAGE WINTER CLIMATE moderate, occasional frost

The green combes and woods of this 971ha (2,400 acre) estate were conserved by Miss Rosalie Chichester as a wildlife sanctuary, with a lakeside nature reserve at its heart. Her domestic menagerie of dogs, canaries, budgerigars and parrots has gone, but peacocks still strut over the grass and her beloved Shetland ponies and Jacob's sheep still graze the parkland on the garden's fringe.

The house, a sober Georgian mansion, stands among trees, lawns and shrubberies, looking out over the Yeo valley. In high summer, only hydrangeas – mostly an electrifying blue, but pink-tinged where they make contact with the limestone chippings of the curving carriage drives – interrupt the greens. Earlier in the year, the grass sprouts bluebells, primroses, violets, daffodils, Siberian claytonia and, beside the main drive, colonies of cerise-pink Japanese primulas. At the same time, the rhododendrons are in bloom; like the primulas, they appreciate the high rainfall. Hidden in the south-east corner of the garden is an atmospherically Victorian wilderness pond where they grow with ferns, gunnera and pampas grass, backed by the grey stone tower of the parish church.

The moist, clean air fosters the growth of mosses and lichens and, with ferns, which also colonise the branches and trunks, they give some of the trees a jungle flavour. The backdrop is ever-changing, with the native oaks, beeches and sycamores joined by sweet chestnut, cut-leaved beech, tulip tree, redwood, hemlock, fir, cypresses, a varied collection of ash and numerous others; the walk to the lake takes in an avenue of monkey puzzles. Miss Chichester could not bear to fell trees – neither would she interfere with the advance of invasive Pontic rhododendron – with the result that the Trust inherited large tracts of derelict and senescent woodland. Much clearance and replanting has been required to rejuvenate these areas and to reopen the garden glades for wildflowers.

The chief surprise, as you stroll through the buxom plantings of these informal pleasure grounds, is suddenly to come upon the manicured terraces of the Victorian flower garden of 1865, neatly packaged in walls and grey railings. The Trust's restoration has included the rebuilding of part of the conservatory, the garden's centrepiece, which now displays plumbago, agapanthus, tibouchina, *Daphne odora* and potted azaleas and lilies, against crisp white woodwork and a slate- and tile-patterned floor. Circular beds cut into one of the grass terraces have been enclosed in authentic, basket-weave ironwork frames to re-create a quaint, early nineteenth-century feature, the basket bed. Cobaeas are encouraged to ascend the handles in summer, and the baskets are filled with colourful ephemera. The looped pattern is echoed by the arches of common honeysuckle – alternately, the Early Dutch cultivar

**BELOW LEFT** Sweet peas in July.
**BELOW** Heleniums and Shasta daisies contribute to the lively palette of summer colours.

'Belgica', and the redder-budded, Late Dutch cultivar 'Serotina' – which stand either side of the goldfish pool on the platform below.

The upper borders are very delicate (too delicate to pass as Victorian creations) in their fresh blue, yellow, green and deep pink colour scheme, with geraniums, alchemilla, irises, osteospermum, kniphofia, phlox and filipendula among the company. With the conservatory as their centrepiece, and the bowed, whitewashed façade of the adjoining rectory to punctuate the view, they are very photogenic.

Since 1990, the Trust has also been bringing the adjacent walled Kitchen Garden back to life. The greenhouse has been rebuilt, vegetables and cut flowers have been returned to the beds, and an array of fruit trees has been trained on the walls. These include a number of local apple varieties, such as 'Devonshire Quarrenden', 'Star of Devon', 'Devonshire Buckland' and 'Lucombe's Seedling'.

**BELOW** The wilderness pond in autumn, overlooking the parish church of St. James.

# Ascott

**WING, LEIGHTON BUZZARD, BUCKINGHAMSHIRE**

**AREA** 19ha (46 acres) • **SOIL** acid to neutral • **ALTITUDE** 76m (250ft)
**AVERAGE RAINFALL** 660mm (26in) • **AVERAGE WINTER CLIMATE** moderate

Ascott is a spectacular illustration of the great reversal of gardening taste that took place during the nineteenth century, when, in response to technological innovation and a new celebration of the creative mind, art and artifice became the dominant forces, with colour, bedding, exotic foliage and formality replacing the predominantly green, naturalistic landscapes of the Georgian era.

Leopold de Rothschild acquired the property from his brother, Baron Nathan Meyer, in 1876, and engaged the architect George Devey to transform the seventeenth-century farmhouse into the present black-and-white residence, strung together like a row of Tudor houses and cottages and once romantically shrouded in ivy and other creepers. The task of setting out the garden was entrusted to the renowned Chelsea nurserymen James Veitch & Sons, with Rothschild closely involved. The principal ingredients are presented as soon as you walk down the curving entrance drive towards the house's north front: fine trees, neat lawns, pristine gravel, the splash of water from a fountain and patterns of clipped evergreens, in this case Portugal laurels pruned into umbrella shapes.

Added to this are colourful and curious specimen plants: the autumnal flame of the large-leaved vine *Vitis coignetiae* and the female form of *Garrya elliptica*, producing its green and red fruits on one side of the house door while its partner drips grey catkins on the other. A quirky contoured walk, featuring serpentine hedges of beech, leads to a skating and waterlily lake, fringed in weeping willows, bold-leaved gunnera and darmera, and appointed with a thatched changing hut. Yet all this is merely a taste of what awaits as you follow the meandering path down slopes and steps, through scented and shady shrubberies, to the main south garden. Here, the grounds open out into an extensive arboretum, the foreground to a sweeping panorama across the Vale of Aylesbury to the Chiltern Hills. Although there are acres of lawn, groves and avenues of green trees, it is the wealth of ornamental incident that immediately strikes you. Everywhere, there are trees of eccentric habit and hue: weeping, cut-leaved and copper beeches, blue, golden and weeping cedars, variegated sweet chestnut, purple maple, cut-leaved alder, yellow catalpa – the scene further enriched in autumn by the potent tints of

scarlet oak, red maple, tulip tree and liquidambar. In spring, waves of yellow and white daffodils wash over the slopes, followed by colonies of snakeshead fritillaries and native wildflowers.

Most arresting of all are the clipped and coloured evergreens. Hedges, tumps and topiaries, including yews of an electrifying yellow, are strung through the landscape, contrasting abruptly with the relaxed mood of woodland and meadow, and signalling the presence of a series of impressive formal enclosures.

The Sundial Garden is one of the first you come upon, a fine period piece made entirely out of topiary, with the gnomon in green and golden yew (the one grafted onto the other, and aptly described in an article by Arthur Hellyer as like a giant egg in an eggcup), the Roman numerals in green box, and the quotation 'Light and shade by turn but love always' (with accompanying hearts) again in golden yew. In recent years, Sir Evelyn de Rothschild, the present tenant, has added further features including, opposite the sundial, a sunken box parterre by Arabella Lennox-Boyd patterned with circles and squares and with a central bubble fountain. These features have introduced a late twentieth-century flavour, but the creativity and panache echo that of Leopold de Rothschild's gardening a hundred years before.

Below the house, a long, straight run of golden yew shelters double borders of spring and summer bulbs and herbaceous plants, in a repeated pink, blue and silver colour scheme (penstemons, sedums, delphiniums, eryngiums and artemisia among the cast) that is a little subtle for the garden, perhaps. The low wall behind is topped with a hedge of yellow holly and supports a range of frost-tender, winter-flowering and other shrubs and climbers, giving this garden the name Madeira Walk. It is when you enter the circular garden opposite that you receive your first taste of High Victorian flower gardening in all its shocking splendour. Here, a bronze Venus rises from the sea in a great marble shell-chariot, drawn by winged horses and with cherubs in attendance – a work by the American sculptor Waldo Story. Enclosing it is a radiant hedge of golden yew, and in the box-edged borders there is a changing display of rich seasonal bedding.

Passages of grass and trees allow the eye some respite before a second, still more lavish scene is revealed. This is the Dutch Garden, a strip of lawn presided over by Eros atop a slender fountain (also by Story), nestling below a high shrubbery ridge, and backed by a rock and tufa grotto with a mysterious dripping cavern and eruptions of hart's tongue and other ferns. The beds cut out of the grass are stocked with flamboyant nineteenth-century favourites, including coloured-leaved coleus and cabbages, cannas and castor oil plants – all to provoke squeals of delight or horror, depending on your sensibilities.

# Attingham Park

SHREWSBURY, SHROPSHIRE

**AREA** 20ha (50 acres) • **SOIL** sandy, clay • **ALTITUDE** 40–85m (131–279ft)
**AVERAGE RAINFALL** 711mm (28in) • **AVERAGE WINTER CLIMATE** moderate

Attingham, in an advanced stage of restoration by the Trust, has been gradually regaining the elegant finish imposed by Humphry Repton. In its overall design it has changed little since the early 1800s, and offers much insight into Georgian landscaping. There is a fine view of the grand Neo-classical mansion from Tern Bridge on the A5, which was decorated at the 1st Lord Berwick's expense, and from the house makes an important landscape feature; reverse views take in the Wrekin and the south Shropshire hills. However, Repton was not the first landscape designer on the scene. A lesser-known practitioner, Thomas Leggett, was employed here between 1769 and 1772, before the present mansion was built, and his tree planting was extensive; a single bill of 13 February 1770 reveals that 7,000 trees were bought from Messrs Williamson of London for £42 11s 1d. Many of Repton's proposals, contained in his Red Book of 1798, consisted of alterations to this earlier work.

The tour centres principally on the mile-long ambulatory walk – a popular mid-eighteenth-century garden feature. It begins above the cedar grove and leads off, between meadow and water, through a succession of stands and groves of different trees, shrubs and native daffodils. A number of species, notably rhododendrons and azaleas, were added early in the last century, but in its replanting programme the Trust is attempting to follow Leggett's original lists wherever this is possible. A splendid cedar of Lebanon presides over the north-east curve of the circle, behind which a secondary path meanders through a willow carr and across the river into the deer park. As you continue around the circumference, you pass a circle of honey locusts (*Gleditsia*), and a sombre stretch of giant fir (*Abies grandis*) before the trees suddenly part and a broad expanse of mown grass, framed by a nuttery and a high south-facing wall, carries the eye to the eighteenth-century Bee House, where the skeps are still occupied.

The wall is clad in peaches, nectarines and apricots and belongs to the 0.8ha (2 acre) kitchen garden, which pre-dates Repton's involvement but which he included in his circuit walk. It is currently being refurbished. Around the centrepiece of a brick-lined well and dipping pond, there will be a traditional quartered design planted with many heritage varieties of fruit and vegetables, with further espaliered fruits on the walls. The peach house on the south wall has long gone, with only its footprint remaining, but the melon, pine and tomato houses in the adjacent frame yard have been restored and are accompanied by cut flower beds. There are also plans to open up some of the impressive range of mushroom, fruit and root storage sheds at the rear of the garden. Here also is a 0.8ha (2 acre) orchard, planted with old and local tree varieties, including *Prunus insititia* 'Prune Damson' and the cooking apple 'Shropshire Pippin'; in the past, the apple trees would have been carefully selected to provide the family with a full year's supply of fruit.

There is further ornamental planting to the south-east of the hall, comprising rhododendrons (surrounding a brick ice-house), and a Spring Garden of trees and shrubs. The remains of formal yew and knot gardens, made in the 1920s in front of the hall, were removed by the Trust in 1976. This is now restored to grass and Reptonian tranquillity, the principal animation being provided in summer by the huge colony of resident house martins collecting mud from the riverbank.

**ABOVE** The River Tern divides the parkland of the Attingham Park estate in two.
**RIGHT** The circular pool in the kitchen garden at Barrington Court.

# Barrington Court

**ILMINSTER, SOMERSET**

**AREA** 4.5ha (11 acres) • **SOIL** neutral/lime, loam over clay • **ALTITUDE** 20m (65ft)
**AVERAGE RAINFALL** 762mm (30in) • **AVERAGE WINTER CLIMATE** mild

Gertrude Jekyll was in her late seventies and had very poor eyesight when she was approached by architects to the Trust's tenant, Colonel Arthur Lyle, to undertake the planting at Barrington Court. The plans were submitted to her with biscuit boxes of garden soil. Although only half her schemes were put into practice, those that were rank among her finest work. Their structure and style – familiar to all students of gardening from the black-and-white photographs in her many books – remain evocatively intact, as does the warm Arts and Crafts detailing of the different outdoor rooms. In fact, the garden at Barrington Court is one of the best preserved of her gardens.

The introduction is grand. Long avenues of trees (previously of horse chestnuts, which as a result of canker have now been replaced), punctuated with 1920s farm buildings, give way to closely mown lawn, high, dark hedges (Lawson cypress as well as yew), canal ponds and scrolled stonework. Ahead is the Tudor honey-coloured mansion, and beside it an equally large stable block, built in 1674 of red brick, and known as the Strode House. The two buildings are a curious pair, particularly on the south side, where they are in alignment in the midst of open lawn and park – the house here showing its Elizabethan E-shape, and skyline of gables, finials and twisted chimneys.

Away from the house, the grandeur quickly melts into the traditional and the rustic. Cider orchards, some grazed by sheep, fringe much of the garden and are once again being harvested, producing award-winning apple juice and cider. Clipped mushrooms of Portugal laurel sprout in front of a line of thatched cottages, and runs of hurdle fencing provide makeshift pens. In spring, there are welcoming bursts of daffodils in the rough grass, and in summer, an assortment of wildflowers, including spotted and twayblade orchids.

This blend of the grand and formal with the homely and vernacular, the essence of the Arts and Crafts style, also characterises Gertrude Jekyll's flower gardens. The display begins to the west of the Strode House, with borders of predominantly pink and purplish shrubs and perennials – wisteria, buddleja, claret-leaved smoke bush and clove-scented *Daphne × burkwoodii* with the glossy, evergreen leaves of bergenia and *Acanthus mollis*, both much favoured by her as punctuation marks – alongside one of the most beautiful paths to be seen in this country: a straight run of mellow Tudor brick, its pattern changing every few paces, from diamond to herringbone, circle to basketweave to square.

However, it is in the adjacent Lily Garden that her influence is most keenly felt. Here, steps lead down from the Strode House's west terrace to a rectangular lawn and waterlily pool, surrounded by raised rectangular beds and, across the patterned paths, richly coloured mixed borders. In the raised beds, only the crinums, with their bold strap-like foliage and pink trumpet flowers, remain from the original scheme. Miss Jekyll's hydrangeas have been replaced with salmon-, apricot- and flame-coloured azaleas (growing in imported lime-free soil) in partnership with the early yellow daylily, *Hemerocallis dumortieri*. The inner beds echo these tones and generous stands of orange alstroemeria, helenium and lilies, scarlet crocosmia and fuchsia, and yellow hypericum and rudbeckia are blended into powerful harmonies. Miss Jekyll's supreme legacy to modern gardening is, of course, her colour teaching and this is a wonderful demonstration of her principles. The shrubs and perennials are also interwoven, as she advocated, with splashes of spring and summer bedding, including wallflowers, marigolds, snapdragons and dahlias, to disguise gaps and prolong the display.

Bergenias mark the corners again, and the foliage of tropical canna lilies helps the crinums and daylilies to provide definition and contrasting structure. It is an appealing composition.

Beyond, through another of the garden's handsome, faded oak doors, is the Rose and Iris Garden, cleaned of perennial weeds and replanted in the mid-1990s along the lines of Miss Jekyll's original scheme, with the surrounding box hedge rejuvenated from cuttings. Following rose sickness, her Rose and Peony Garden changed more dramatically; it was redesigned by Colonel Lyle's grandson Andrew in 1986 as a White Garden, such as Jekyll suggested in *Colour Schemes for the Flower Garden*. It is still strongly Edwardian in character, and the plantings of longstanding annual and perennial border favourites such as phlox, crambe, alyssum, cineraria, cosmos and silver stachys are marshalled within Jekyll's formal circular design.

The patterned brick paths run between and around these gardens, bordered by hedges of bulging boxwood and Munstead lavender, fringed by beds of catmint and pink penstemons. In one part, there is the shade of a long pergola (recently erected, but strongly Jekyllian in flavour), clad in vine, wisteria, jasmine, clematis and golden hop, and underplanted for early summer with geranium, alchemilla, aubrieta and Solomon's seal. Until 1920, this was all a cow yard, and on the north side, the calf sheds, or bustalls, are still standing, picturesquely hung with Climbing roses.

Further stretches of the canalised stream which serves the Court as a moat skirt the outer walls of the flower gardens, and you leave by way of an oak bridge, back into the cider orchard. A final surprise is sprung, another sudden change of scale: a long, deep, buxomly planted herbaceous border, designed by Colonel Lyle's wife Ronnie, containing massive swathes of achilleas, hollyhocks, salvias, helianthus and other flowers for cutting. Behind it is the huge walled kitchen garden, which has been in continuous production since the 1920s. Built of local stone, and with flower borders down its centre, this presents a panoply of wall fruits, from peaches and nectarines to figs, plums and gages, beds of vegetables ranging from asparagus and sea kale to aubergines and peppers, and a further scene of plump Somerset abundance. A local school has a plot within the garden.

**LEFT** Wisteria climbing the walls of the Walled Garden.
**RIGHT** The early nineteenth-century Italian Garden from the north at Belton House.

# Belton House

**GRANTHAM, LINCOLNSHIRE**

**AREA** 14ha (35 acres) • **SOIL** neutral/sandy loam • **ALTITUDE** 52m (170ft)
**AVERAGE RAINFALL** 686mm (27in) • **AVERAGE WINTER CLIMATE** cold

This elegant composition of green and gold takes its cue from the honey-coloured mansion which presides over its level acres with the serenity of a French château. It was built for Sir John Brownlow in the 1680s, and its architect is thought to have been William Winde, who may also have been responsible for the elaborate geometric gardens that once accompanied it; Winde designed the grand terraces at Cliveden and, probably, Powis Castle. Most of this early formality has gone, a victim of the dramatic change in gardening taste that occurred in Britain during the eighteenth century. Avenues, however, continue to radiate from the house: a spectacular lime avenue to the east, punctuated with statues, sweeping up to the Bellmount Tower, constructed *c.*1750 to provide a prospect of the park and surrounding landscape; another of Turkey oak, leading south to the Lion Gates; and a shorter lime avenue leading west, reinstated by the Trust and framing a view of the clocktower. A

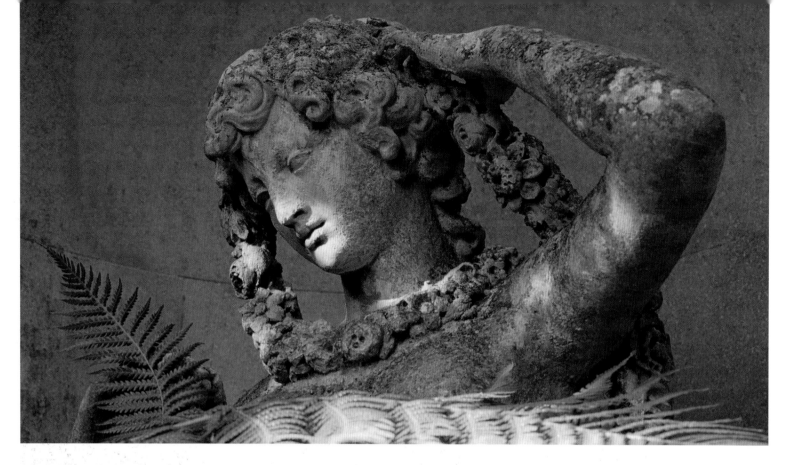

mirror pond, north-east of the house, also remains, reflecting a statue of Ceres and a small Palladian temple in its water.

The linear framework therefore survived the 1740s, when the picturesque Wilderness, with its Gothic ruin, cascades, shrubberies and flower-rich meadows, was added, and the late 1770s, when the parkland planting suggested by William Emes was pursued. The resulting blend of styles is one of extreme beauty, and in the late nineteenth century when the flowing lawns were studded with specimen beech and oak, cedar and wellingtonia, the harmony merely deepened.

The Dutch Garden, a reproduction of the Georgian layout, was created by the 3rd Earl Brownlow in the 1870s. Its theme of green and gold is taken up by alternating green yew pillars and golden yew globes, the pattern complemented by honey-coloured gravel, urns and statuary. 'Iceberg' roses, lavenders, catmint and sea-green cedars provide scent and cool contrast. The sunken Italian Garden, designed by Jeffry Wyattville, dates from the early nineteenth century, its central axis adorned with a large fountain pool, an Orangery to the north, and an exedra with lion fountain to the south. The Orangery itself, restored and now one of the finest in the Trust's hands, contains a host of exotic plants, including palms, tree ferns, Norfolk Island pine, *Passiflora* × *exoniensis*, and *Tibouchina urvilleana*; in Edwardian times, it housed a flock of free-flying budgerigars. The walled garden behind it shelters roses, sweet peas and herbaceous plants, with 'Nottingham' medlar trees set around a stone ornament, the Brownlow Basket.

Paths wind from the formal gardens and lawns to the wilder pleasure grounds, where much restoration has been taking place. You are now led through woodland gardens, full of spring colour, to a recently reopened maze, and on to the shore of the lake. The handsome architectural feature here is the chalet-style boathouse from the 1820s. Designed by Anthony Salvin, it has a fishscale slate roof and basketweave plasterwork, and was used by the family for picnics and fishing parties. The paths and terraces by the cascade have also been uncovered and planted up once again, reopening a lost world.

**ABOVE** Statue in the Dutch Garden, created in the 1870s by the 3rd Earl Brownlow.

# Beningbrough Hall

SHIPTON-BY-BENINGBROUGH, YORK, YORKSHIRE

AREA 2.8ha (7 acres) • SOIL neutral/silty loam • ALTITUDE 15m (50ft)
AVERAGE RAINFALL 762mm (30in) • AVERAGE WINTER CLIMATE cold

By the time restoration of this Baroque house, standing among water meadows in the Vale of York, began in 1977, the gardens too were declining. The estate records were lost and there were no clear historical guidelines for the Trust, but there had been especially active passages in the evolution, and it was decided to anchor the garden in these periods. The hall itself seems to cry out for a simple uncluttered setting that conveys a flavour of eighteenth-century elegance. Early maps show it at the centre of a formal landscape of radiating avenues, but the eighteenth-century tide of opinion against formal landscaping gathered momentum, and at Beningbrough a more natural landscape of open parkland and irregular clumps of trees replaced the avenues. Today the south front of the hall, flanked by trees, including an unusual variegated oak, surveys a pristine gravel walk and velvet lawn and, across the ha-ha, a relaxed prospect of the water meadows bordering the River Ouse.

The first Ordnance Survey map of 1852 shows the two wings of the garden, the Wilderness and the American Garden, well furnished with trees. The latter takes the form of an open glade encircled by a shady walk of trees and shrubs. Spring is its high season, when the ground is smothered with daffodils and there is

BELOW The parterre in the West Formal Garden which was redesigned in the style of a sixteenth-century knot garden with low-growing plants between dwarf box hedges.

blossom on cherry and amelanchier. Rhododendrons tolerant of a little lime take over in early summer – *Rhododendron* 'Cunningham's White', *R.* 'Cunningham's Blush' and *R. catawbiense*.

From 1827, Beningbrough benefited from an outstanding head gardener, Thomas Foster, and during his time the Walled Garden must have been a model kitchen garden. The walls still shelter a range of pears, apples and figs, and the original pear alley remains as a centrepiece, with the varieties 'Black Worcester', 'Beurré Hardy' and 'Pitmaston Duchess' underplanted with herbs. Foster's home-raised grape varieties, 'Lady Downe's Seedling' (still rated one of the finest, late-keeping grapes) and 'Foster's Seedling' (one of the best early-fruiting vines) have been returned to the vinery. Among the accompanying beds of soft fruits, vegetables and cut flowers is a collection of northern rhubarb varieties and a large patch of liquorice, a plant long associated with Yorkshire. Recently, an orchard has also been planted south of the Walled Garden, featuring a collection of Yorkshire apple varieties. Now, much of this produce feeds visitors in the restaurant rather than the family.

The Victorian pleasure grounds at Beningbrough featured formal touches, and formality returned to the Park when the Lime Avenue was installed some time after 1913. Although this feature is being retained, the broad-leaved limes (*Tilia platyphyllos*) are gradually being replaced with common limes (*T. × europaea*), which are more tolerant of the high water table.

In 1916, the estate was bought by the 10th Earl and Countess of Chesterfield. Their main interest was racing and their main enterprise their stud, so they orchestrated the long South Border, below the Walled Garden, to peak during the week of the Doncaster St Leger meeting in late September. It now features buddlejas, hardy salvias and other plants attractive to bees and butterflies. To the west of the Walled Garden are further planting schemes. The double borders feature an Edwardian theme of cool midsummer tints. 'Iceberg' roses, purple berberis, philadelphus and deutzias are repeated down their length, along with standard wisteria and varieties of clematis. In front are waves of catmint, purple sage, salvia, alchemilla and *Geranium* 'Russell Prichard', with pink and white Japanese anemones to take over later, and tulips and anemones as an appetiser for spring.

The East Formal Garden has a ground cover of cobbles and Yorkstone flags, and also a rectangular pond surrounded by clipped box and lavender, while the West Formal Garden, adjacent to the restored nineteenth-century conservatory, is filled with richly coloured bedding plants. To reflect the architecture of the hall, a new development has been the Italianate Baroque garden, which features a small palm grove, silver-leaved plants, bulbs, annuals, and quiet sitting areas. Altogether, this now adds up to a garden of great charm.

**ABOVE** The pear arch in the kitchen garden spans borders of catmint, alchemilla, red monarda and silver-leaved stachys and artemisia.
**RIGHT** The thatched summer-house at Benthall Hall with the woodland wilderness beyond.

# Benthall Hall

**BROSELEY, SHROPSHIRE**

AREA 1.2ha (3 acres) • SOIL alkaline/clay • ALTITUDE 189m (620ft)
AVERAGE RAINFALL 686mm (27in) • AVERAGE WINTER CLIMATE cold

Benthall Hall is tucked into well-wooded countryside close to the Severn Gorge. The approach is unassuming, along a lime-edged lane and past a whitewashed church, and suddenly the sandstone hall is revealed, flanked by topiary and softened by a sweep of flowers.

In gardening history, Benthall is most famous as the home of George Maw, the bulb and alpine specialist, who lived here for a period of 35 years from 1853. Maw, a manufacturer of ornamental tiles, travelled extensively, especially in the Alps, Pyrenees and Mediterranean region, and brought a great many plants back to Shropshire, including the familiar glory of the snow, *Chionodoxa luciliae*, which bloomed for the first time in Britain at Benthall in 1877. He researched his great work *A Monograph of the Genus Crocus* here, and the garden's self-sowing carpets of spring-flowering *Crocus tommasinianus* and *C. vernus*, and autumn-flowering *C. speciosus*, *C. pulchellus* and *C. nudiflorus*, are another of his legacies. In the June 1872 issue of *The Garden*, the thunderous Victorian gardening writer William Robinson stated that 'for the culture and introduction of valuable new and hardy plants, there is not a more noteworthy garden'. Robinson was particularly impressed by Maw's collection of saxifrages and by his method, now commonplace, of displaying alpines in broad, shallow pans instead of small pots. Sadly, the only remaining evidence of the rockery is some large rocks beneath hollies and beech trees to the east of the lower lawn, and a strange hollow in the grass, which was once an extensive run of cold frames.

In the hands of his successor, Robert Bateman – son of James Bateman of Biddulph Grange – the nucleus of the garden shifted to the west side of the house. Bateman, a sculptor and painter, built the dovecote here and with his wife, Octavia Caroline, laid out the Rose Garden beneath it. It is a romantic Arts and Crafts composition with a pond and symmetrical rosebeds sheltered by walls, dissected by narrow paths and foaming with mixed beds of choice plants, many inherited from George Maw. Against the walls are the late-flowering *Clematis tibetana*, *C. viticella* subsp. *campaniflora*, *C. × jouiniana* and others. A mixture of English roses has recently been planted in the beds, accompanying magnolias and tree peonies, including the white, maroon-blotched *Paeonia rockii*. Scillas, narcissi, sisyrinchiums, hardy geraniums and dianthus are part of the varied carpet beneath them, and homage is paid to George Maw through the inclusion of a scree bed which is home to a number of alpine plants, including a collection of saxifrages.

There is a flavour of Biddulph Grange in the shady rockery behind this formal area, where you must squeeze along stone paths, mount stone steps and duck under cherry branches. Hellebores, pulmonarias, comfreys and arums make a leafy contrast to the garden below. The plantsman's theme is also carried on to the rock banks and shrubberies that frame the sweep of terraced lawn to the front of the house. Roses and brooms are here interspersed with stands of devil's walking stick, *Aralia elata*, mats of mouse plant, *Arisarum proboscideum*, and drifts of an unusual form of bear's breeches, *Acanthus balcanicus*.

The old kitchen garden, with only two of its four walls now standing, features plums, damsons and gages, together with an unusual orchard of crab apples. However, it is mostly used for flowers, with roses and sweet peas trained on decorative supports and cut flowers grown for the house.

The relaxed and painterly style of today's garden is due in large part to members of the Benthall family, who reclaimed their ancestral home in 1934 after a gap of a hundred years. Their continuing presence and enthusiasm for Benthall and its pastoral setting ensure a homely mood. Brash blocks of plants and excessive neatness are eschewed, and a liberal view is taken over the colonising activities of ferns, campanulas, Welsh poppies and the ubiquitous *Geranium nodosum*.

# Berrington Hall

**LEOMINSTER, HEREFORDSHIRE**

AREA 4.7ha (11½ acres) • SOIL clay/silty loam • ALTITUDE 76–137m (250–450ft)
AVERAGE RAINFALL 635mm (25in) • AVERAGE WINTER CLIMATE cold

The diarist Viscount Torrington, visiting in 1784, refers to Berrington as 'just finish'd and furnish'd in all the modern elegance, commanding beautiful views, a fine piece of water, and … throughout a scene of elegance and refinement'. Although they are now accompanied by the rumble of the Hereford road, the views remain pastoral. A circuit walk, opened up by the Trust in 1993, takes you across the park, fashioned by 'Capability' Brown some time after 1775, to the 5.7ha (14 acre) pool with its 1.6ha (4 acre) island. It allows the visitor the equally fine reverse views, back between the oaks, limes, beech and ash to the portico and pediments of the red sandstone hall.

The garden thus sits within an important Georgian framework, complete with ha-ha (recently reconstructed by the Trust), elegant stable block and office pavilions, and a grand triumphal archway as the entrance lodge. Around the west front of the hall, the open lawn rolls away into the park, and to the north, there is a shady shrubbery walk (the shrubbery expanded into a protective wood in 1906), offering views out over Bircher Common. Elsewhere, the Brownian scheme has been subjected to a more ornamental overlay, applied from the mid-1840s onwards.

South-east of the hall, a medley of flowering trees and shrubs now border the curving entrance drive. Bladder nut (*Staphylea colchica*), Persian lilac (*Syringa × persica*), Chinese tulip tree (*Liriodendron chinense*), *Lonicera involucrata*, *Magnolia wilsonii* and several ginkgo trees are among the company, many of which were introduced by the 3rd Lord Cawley. An avenue of clipped golden yews, planted in 1901, processes from the Triumphal Arch, and an assortment of shrubs and climbers flank the wisteria pergola on the south-facing wall of the Walled Garden, including yellow *Rosa banksiae* 'Lutea', red *Buddleja colvilei*, white-flowered *Crinodendron patagua*, and the very unusual (and invasive) yellow-flowered climbing marrow, *Thladiantha oliveri*. Until recently, a further 36 flower-beds adorned the east lawns and their departure has rather stranded the remaining stone fountain.

All this jollity certainly counters the rather sombre look of the hall, but, of course, it also confuses one's initial taste of the eighteenth-century composition. The colour is much more readily appreciated in the Walled Garden, now replanted around patterns of fruit trees: medlars, mulberries, figs and, in the main grass plots, a large collection of pre-1900 apple varieties raised in Herefordshire, such as 'Doctor Hare's', 'Warner's King' and 'Ashmead's Kernel'. These are accompanied by a lavender-edged sundial lawn, cutting beds, a herb garden, double herbaceous borders of mixed colours and the camellias and climbing plants in the adjacent laundry-drying ground. There is a further concentration of flowers behind the curtain of weeping ash to the north-east of the hall, where the woodland path meanders between handkerchief trees, maples, and a large collection of azaleas and rhododendrons, including hybrids raised by Lord Cawley. Hydrangeas give a later wash of summer colour, together with daylilies, crocosmias, and, back along the north front of the hall, past the clipped tumps of holly, rhododendron and laurel, a pool of pink and white cyclamen in the grass. There is a fine show of snowdrops here in winter.

# Biddulph Grange

BIDDULPH, STOKE-ON-TRENT, STAFFORDSHIRE

AREA 6ha (15 acres) • SOIL acid/loamy clay • ALTITUDE 145–195m (475–640ft)
AVERAGE RAINFALL 914mm (36in) • AVERAGE WINTER CLIMATE cold

Gardens do not come more ingenious or entertaining than Biddulph. The meandering paths have you squeezing between rock faces, crossing water by stepping stones and plunging down dark tunnels; you enter a half-timbered cottage and find yourself in an Egyptian tomb, clamber through a Scottish glen and come out in a Chinese water garden; at every turn, there are strange beasts, flamboyant flowers, eruptions of rock, or soaring exotic conifers in ambush. The genius behind it all was the Victorian plantsman James Bateman, aided by his wife Maria and their friend Edward Cooke, the marine artist. The estate, in cold hilly country below Biddulph Moor, was bought by Bateman's grandfather for its coal-mining potential, with the family living at nearby Knypersley Hall. James and Maria Bateman moved here in 1840, two years after their marriage, and soon began transforming the vicarage into an Italianate mansion and commissioning for the grounds some mind-boggling feats of earth-moving, contouring and stonework.

When the garden came to the Trust in 1988, it was in serious decline. However, the superstructure remained and, thanks to good documentation and on-site archaeology, a very precise reconstruction was possible. An appeal was launched and the immense and labour-intensive programme of work began.

From the south-west corner of the house, the starting point of the tour, the view is of an intimate garden, with foreground terraces, a small lake below and a heavy fringe of yews, hollies, rhododendrons and evergreen trees. There are lively splashes of colour, as you would expect, but no jarring contrasts of style. Bateman avoided falling into the trap set by Victorian eclecticism by subdividing the garden into different compartments, each with its own theme and screened from one another by a unifying framework of hedges and walls, trees and rocky mounds. It was an innovative and influential approach. The terraces extend the width of the house. At the west end, the door opens onto an Italian garden of stone platforms, stairways and balustraded walls. To the east, within a framework of yew hedges, a range of nineteenth-century plant novelties and artful styles of cultivation is displayed. There are parterres devoted to verbenas, hybrid China roses and the quirky

monkey puzzle tree (reintroduced to gardening by William Lobb in 1844). An ornamental orchard features clipped double Morello cherries, planted on raised mounds and associated with *Cotoneaster microphyllus*, pruned as bells, and various clematis, grown up posts and trained along chains. Hardy herbaceous plants, in the form of peonies, *Iris pallida*, phlox and delphiniums – favourites of Maria Bateman – also appear. Running almost the length of the terrace, is a kaleidoscopic walk of hybrid dahlias, whose tropical colours were enthusiastically embraced by many a Victorian gardener.

Earlier in the year, it is the shrubberies around the lake that steal the show, for they are stocked with rhododendrons of every hue. At the head of the lime avenue marking the garden's western boundary, they were arranged by Bateman in rainbow bands around a stone seat. Beside the water, they are loosely dispersed – flashes of yellow from the scented yellow azalea *Rhododendron luteum* and mounds of pink, purple, white and cherry-red from the Hardy Hybrids. Rhododendrons also once filled the adjacent stream-fed glen. These were the new species collected by Joseph Hooker on his

ABOVE LEFT The Walled Garden in May at Berrington Hall.
ABOVE The gilded water buffalo sculpture by Waterhouse Hawkins in a part of the garden named China.

expeditions to Sikkim, Nepal and Bhutan in 1849–51, but their reluctance to bloom here, in spite of the provision of moist, shady pockets of peaty soil, persuaded Bateman to move them under glass. Instead, the glen was stocked with ferns, another fashionable tribe of plants to which both Bateman and Edward Cooke were devoted.

Cooke's major contribution to the garden was the architectural features, both ornamental buildings and rockwork. Here in the glen you see the results of his careful study of rock formation for his paintings: spectacular outcrops and massive boulders of locally quarried gritstone, with every crack and cascade geologically justified. Wild heather and bilberries, collected on the moor, contribute to the realism, with weeping holly added for picturesque effect and native and foreign water plants strung along the stream. From the lakeside shrubberies, you pop down a tunnel to emerge in the Pinetum, among redwoods, hemlocks, cedars and pines. The range of conifer species had been boosted by David Douglas's plant-hunting on the west coast of America in the 1820s and 1830s, and here Bateman prepared ideal conditions for them; many are planted on mounds to give improved drainage and a better display. In late spring, bluebells lap the curving walk between the grassy banks and there is carefully contrived contrast from variegated oak, golden yews and hollies – many added by Robert Heath, who bought Biddulph from the Bateman family in 1871.

The focal point of the walk is the half-timbered façade of a Cheshire cottage, sporting the date 1856 and the intertwined initials 'J & MB'. Inside, there is no cosy welcome, only a squat, subhuman creature (the Ape of Thoth, an associate of the Egyptian god of botany) bathed in bloody light by a pane of red glass in the roof. You are inside a pyramid, and you emerge from the dark into its open court to see a stone arch set into a slab of clipped yew, guarded by two pairs of sphinxes. This stands at the opposite end of the terraces from where you began, and the main path continues east behind it, through a rough arboretum, planted with autumn-colouring North American red maples and liquidambar, gorse and other heathland shrubs, and pampas grass and osmunda fern set beside a small pool, then on to a long avenue.

To the north, the Woodland Terrace has recently been restored to the 1862 plan, one of the relaid paths leading to Bateman's Geological Gallery, laid out to reflect his belief in the Genesis story of creation. The principal avenue tree was intended to be the most

**RIGHT** Leading away from the Shelter House, stepped yew hedges divide the Dahlia Walk into compartments.

majestic of the newly introduced conifers, the wellingtonia (brought in by William Lobb in 1853, and immediately obtained by Bateman through Messrs Veitch). He interplanted his specimens with deodar cedars for quick effect – and gave them an interesting backing formed by lines of white briar rose, red horse chestnut and Austrian pine – but unfortunately, when the time came to thin, his successor Robert Heath decided to retain the cedars instead. The Trust has returned to Bateman's original plan and in time the wellingtonias will assume their rightful dominance. From here, the sandy path leads upwards to the moor through heath and woodland, gradually narrowing as it rises to give the appearance of a natural obelisk; this land is now a country park, belonging to the local district council.

Where is the Chinese garden? So well concealed is the prize exhibit that it is possible to complete the circuit without encountering it, yet it stands at the garden's very heart. There are two points of entry: one is via a cleft in the Scottish glen and along a dark tunnel and grotto, while the other is below Egypt. This latter route takes you through one of the most curious of Victorian garden features, the Stumpery. This involved excavating tree stumps and upturning them to create a framework for woodland perennials like ferns, ivies, hellebores and epimediums. The path descends between rocks and shrubs and then you are inside the Great Wall. There is a watchtower high on the north-east bank and a joss house

to the south, above a winding flight of steps. The flora of the Far East is all about: Japanese maples, bamboos, cryptomeria, paulownia, tree peonies, hostas and a golden larch – again, many of these were collected by contemporary plant-hunters, particularly Robert Fortune, who explored China and Japan in the 1840s and 1850s. Irish yews, weeping trees and coloured foliage strike contrasting notes.

Behind a stone doorway, you come upon the gilded head of a water buffalo – a Chinese idol, sculpted by Waterhouse Hawkins – and further along, an enormous stone frog. Dragons are carved out of the lawn, and more dragons and grebes perch on the corners of the temple's upturned eaves. The central water scene will look familiar, for it is based on the willow pattern featured on countless household plates, with its hump-backed footbridge joined to a zig-zag railing, and waterside rocks and plants. The pagoda is the predominant structure, a glorious flight of fancy but, as always, with its surprises: one tunnel leads to the Scottish glen and the other to an ice-house. These buildings were among the last expressions of the fashion for chinoiserie, and, painstakingly restored and freshly painted in their original livery of scarlet, buff and blue-green, are once again a sparkling contrast to the black waters and coniferous backdrop.

**ABOVE** The Rhododendron Ground around the lake at Biddulph Grange.

# Blickling Hall

BLICKLING, NORWICH, NORFOLK

AREA 22ha (55 acres) • SOIL acid/loam • ALTITUDE 30m (100ft) • AVERAGE RAINFALL 635mm (25in) • AVERAGE WINTER CLIMATE cold

The sudden prospect of this beautiful Jacobean mansion, with its turrets and gables and salmon-red brickwork, is arresting. It sits square to the road, separated by simple railings, backed by trees and flanked by Dutch-style service ranges and ancient hedges of yew. It is a complete picture, with which horticulture does not interfere. Only as you walk up to the house do you take in the globes of *Magnolia grandiflora* either side of the stone bridge, and the shrubs and climbers in the dry moat below. These are an hors d'oeuvre to the gardens awaiting you through the arch in the east wall.

Of the early seventeenth-century design to accompany Sir Henry Hobart's house, there remains only an outline. Before you is the product of the three subsequent centuries, each layer building on the bones of its predecessor. The central axis, the vista uphill to the Doric Temple, is the work of the 1st Earl of Buckinghamshire, who swept away his great-grandfather's garden in the early part of the eighteenth century. The present grid pattern is a Victorian evolution carried out between 1861 and 1864 by the 8th Marquis of Lothian. It is a much grander and more intricate design than was here previously, with radial walks, each of a single tree species – Turkey oak, beech and lime – infilled with mixed deciduous trees with a shrubby understorey of evergreens, and leading to circular clearings. The hurricane of October 1987 wreaked havoc here but the area is now regaining a sense of maturity.

In front of the hall is the 0.8ha (2 acre), flower-filled parterre, its rich colours playing against the shadowy topiary. It, too, is Lord Lothian's creation and part of the garden's momentous return to Jacobean formality. It was excavated for him from the sloping lawn by Markham Nesfield, son of the garden designer William Andrews Nesfield, the great champion of parterres. However, the planting that colours it today is the work of Norah Lindsay, who was associated with some of the best country gardens in the 1920s and '30s, including Hidcote and Chirk Castle. Indeed, her dreamy planting style – a relaxed and billowing interpretation of Gertrude Jekyll's painterly approach, ordered by hedges and topiaries – influenced a generation of garden-makers. She was commissioned by the 11th Marquis to simplify the elaborate Victorian pattern of beds and ribbon borders, which she achieved by clearing the centre of everything but its seventeenth-century fountain and joining the corner flower-beds into four large squares. She retained the yew topiary, including the famous Blickling topiary grand pianos. To each square she gave a two-tone fringe of roses – pink and crimson Floribundas 'Else Poulsen' and 'Kirsten Poulsen', or red and orange 'Locarno' and Polyantha 'Gloria Mundi' – and underplanted them with catmint. She then filled two with herbaceous plants in tints of pink, white, violet and blue, including monkshoods, bellflowers, globe thistles and delphiniums, and the remaining two with glowing yellows, oranges and reds in the form of achilleas, heleniums, rudbeckias and the apricot Nankeen lily, *Lilium × testaceum* 'Apricot'. Since the gardener's palette becomes hotter as the summer advances, it is inevitable that the cooler beds should peak slightly earlier than their neighbours, soon after midsummer; nevertheless, it is a triumphant composition.

Over the past few years, further extensive planting in Norah Lindsay's style has taken place on the raised south side of the parterre, where a flower garden existed in Jacobean times. As they recede from the house, these new box-edged double borders warm in colouring through daylilies, crocosmias, purple berberis and striped miscanthus grass, until finally concluding in a garden of black-red dahlias, heuchera and ophiopogon. Behind them runs a border of pale and silvery plants such as artemisia, *Salvia sclarea* var. *turkestanica* and *Lilium regale*, equally handsomely composed and textured.

The subterranean world of the dry moat must certainly have appealed to Norah Lindsay's romantic temperament. It is a world of old walls and arched bridges, and she caught its spirit well in her plantings of dripping fuchsias, ferns and ghostly Japanese anemones. The shelter has since been exploited to grow a range of wall shrubs and climbers that you might not expect to see in this hostile Norfolk climate of dry summers and cold, windy winters. These include spring-flowering *Buddleja crispa* var. *farreri* and autumn-flowering *B. auriculata*, ceanothus, camellia and variegated *Trachelospermum jasminoides* with flowers scented of orange blossom.

Penetrate the formal woods above the parterre, or turn the corner towards the north front of the hall, and suddenly you see a further layer of the garden's history – for here is the parkland landscape moulded in the late eighteenth century by the 2nd Earl of Buckinghamshire. Living through the golden era of the English landscape garden, he set his father's classical ornaments in this more natural setting of rolling pasture, broken by groves and stands of oak, beech and sweet chestnut. There are fine elevated views of the park behind the Temple, where the remnant of an earlier fortification serves as a broad terrace and provided the 2nd Earl with a ready-made ha-ha. At one end of it he built the handsome Orangery. Probably designed by Samuel Wyatt, it was completed in 1782 and is now once again housing citrus fruit, including oranges, lemons, limes and grapefruits. Behind it, new areas of garden have recently been developed; 0.8ha (2 acres) have been planted for winter and early spring interest, with double-flowered hellebores, including yellow forms, grouped among mahonias, viburnums, *Daphne bholua* and the coloured stems of willows and dogwoods. A pedimented, rustic pavilion, topped with carved pine cones, now looks over a shady dell that includes a fine stand of tree ferns; the pavilion is a copy of that designed by John Adey Repton, who was employed extensively at Blickling after 1823, designing trellis, arbours and furniture. Hereabouts, as elsewhere along the radial walks, vast numbers of snowdrops, crocus and white *Narcissus pseudonarcissus* flood the ground beneath the trees and shrubs.

On the south side of the woods, tucked under the oaks, hollies and sweet chestnuts, is the Secret Garden. With its 'profusion of Minionet Roses, mirtles and honeysuckles' (sic), this was the principal flower garden in the late eighteenth century and the domain of Lady Buckinghamshire, with John Adey Repton's father, Humphry Repton, offering suggestions on its improvement. The garden took on its present shape and reduced size in the 1860s, and is now a quiet green retreat of grass and beech hedge, brick paths and sundial. The cool shrubbery, fronted with hostas and daylilies, by which it is approached, is the work of Norah Lindsay (although largely supplemented by the Trust), and is quite a contrast to her plantings near the house. The soil is more acidic here and joining the laurel, philadelphus, bamboo and dogwood are rhododendrons and blue-flowered hydrangeas.

The centrepiece for the 2nd Earl's park was the great lake, which comes into view suddenly as you walk from the parterre to the north front. It makes a dramatic moment, linked in my mind to the scent of the vast Oriental plane trees growing on this corner, whose leaves, on the right day, infuse the air with sweet resin. The ancient Turkey oak is also a major feature, and in spring both it and the plane trees are knee-deep in bulbs and wildflowers.

**BELOW** The Jacobean-style parterre is a nineteenth-century recreation, with later planting schemes around the topiaries designed by Norah Lindsay.

# Bodnant Garden

**TAL-Y-CAFN, COLWYN BAY, CONWY**

**AREA** 32ha (80 acres) • **SOIL** acid/clay • **ALTITUDE** 52m (170ft) • **AVERAGE RAINFALL** 1,016mm (40in) • **AVERAGE WINTER CLIMATE** moderate

The scale, grandeur and scenic beauty of this garden are nothing short of stupendous. Set on a west-facing slope, 52m (170ft) above the tidal River Conway, the massive granite house (privately owned) commands panoramic views of the eastern edge of the Snowdonia range. Below, a series of five gigantic Italianate terraces anchor the house majestically in its mountainous setting. To the south, the precipitous-sided valley of the River Hiraethlyn is embraced, manipulated and coloured to make a woodland garden of epic proportions. And furnishing and overlaying each part of the composition is a plant collection to excite expert and layman alike.

The estate was bought by Henry Pochin, the late Lord Aberconway's great-grandfather, in 1874. There was little garden here then, apart from lawns and shrubberies, but when the house was built in 1792, a large number of native trees – in particular, beech, oak and chestnut – were planted. With the help of landscape architect Edward Milner, Pochin began laying out a 'reposeful garden' comprising a spacious terrace, grass banks and spreading trees. On the valley floor, he planted the conifers which are now one of Bodnant's chief delights, and in succeeding years continued to expand the bounds, adding features such as the Mausoleum and the Laburnum Arch in 1878.

The leap of imagination that transformed Bodnant into the garden we see today was made by his grandson Henry, 2nd Lord Aberconway. It was he who in 1902, with his mother's encouragement, conceived the great terraces and supervised their construction, and who, in 1908, encouraged a sceptical head gardener called Sanderson to try his hand with Chinese rhododendrons. Subsequently, he subscribed to many plant-hunting expeditions and, after 1920, engaged Bodnant in an extensive programme of rhododendron hybridisation, under his skilled head gardener Frederick Puddle. The evolution continues today under the Hon. Michael McLaren, whose father, Charles, 3rd Lord Aberconway, guided the garden from 1953 to 2003, and was a former President of the Royal Horticultural Society. The garden has also benefited from a remarkable partnership between the family and their head gardeners, since the post was handed down through three generations of Puddles.

A tour of Bodnant traditionally begins with the East Garden and terraces, where the emphasis is on a summer show to succeed the woodland shrubs. Hot-coloured herbaceous plants in the broad entrance border hold the eye before it is carried off, across the gentian bed, by the sweep of smooth lawns. Among the many trees and shrubs to admire in this area are some fine paperbark maples, *Acer griseum*, one of which has its flaking chestnut trunk memorably backlit by orange azaleas.

The drama of the view greets you as you approach the front of the house, though the scale and contents of the terraces below are cleverly concealed. Each is intended as a revelation. You descend alternately by the sides and the centre to savour the full size of the composition, and each set of steps opens onto a vast empty stage of grass or water, flanked by plants and architectural ornament.

The staircase from the Rose Terrace to the Croquet Terrace, hung with white *Wisteria brachybotrys* 'Shiro-kapitan' and

**ABOVE** The Pin Mill over a swathe of white cosmos.

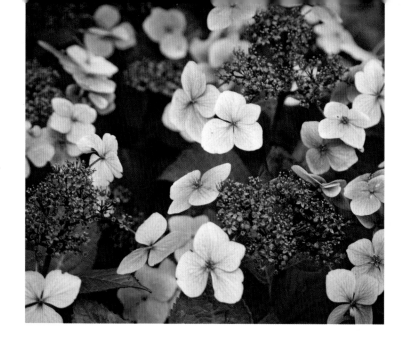

*W. floribunda* 'Alba', curves around a Baroque sandstone fountain, and water flows underground and through basin and rill into each of the platforms below. The high, grey-blue retaining walls are home to many slightly tender shrubs, including *Crinodendron hookerianum, Eucryphia lucida, Buddleja colvilei, Ceanothus × lobbianus* 'Russellianus' and scented white rhododendrons. Carpenterias, blue hydrangeas and wall-trained *Magnolia grandiflora* 'Goliath' and *M. delavayi* ensure later colour.

The great cedars on the Lily Terrace are a legacy of Henry Pochin and account for the asymmetry of the terraces in relation to the house. To adorn the Canal Terrace, the 2nd Lord Aberconway had parts of an eighteenth-century mill, once used for the manufacture of pins, dismantled and transported from Gloucestershire. The rebuilding was completed in 1939 and makes a romantic reflection between the rafts of waterlilies. The tree and shrub borders to the north and west of the terraces provide the first hints of the spectacle awaiting you in the Dell. Here are camellias and tree magnolias, including *M. sargentiana* var. *robusta, M. × veitchii, M. campbellii* 'Charles Raffill' and *M. sprengeri* var. *diva*; and a host of rhododendrons, including cream 'Penjerrick', blue *R. augustinii*, the deciduous *RR. albrechtii, quinquefolium* and *schlippenbachii*, and some of the famous blood-red Bodnant hybrids. In August, the large group of *Eucryphia glutinosa* in the North Garden is a vision of white.

Behind the Pin Mill a path leads past further banks of camellias and rhododendrons and through a stream-fed rockery before arriving at the famous vantage point over the Dell. Well over 15m (50ft) beneath you is the River Hiraethlyn, lushly edged by ferns, hydrangeas and large-leaved bog plants, studded by moss-covered boulders and the haunt of dippers and wagtails; to your right is the old stone mill; and ahead, a long linear prospect of woodland shrubs, speared by rocket-shaped conifers and bare-trunked pines. In spring, it is a riot of colour, in summer, a valley of cool greens.

The conifers on the east side of the river were planted ten years before those on the west, in 1876. They include immense specimens of fir, cedar, hemlock and redwood, and from the shrub borders above the valley you gain the rare opportunity of viewing their cone-studded tops. The rich, alluvial soil and moist atmosphere of the Dell suit the larger-leaved rhododendrons well, though frost can be trapped here and many plants were lost in the severe winter of 1981–2. Accompanying them are belts of Japanese and deciduous azaleas, the fruity scent of the latter flooding the valley in early June. Magnolias, including the Bodnant-raised *M. sprengeri* var. *diva* 'Claret Cup' and the potently fragrant *M. obovata*, are also a feature.

The shrub borders provide an additional tier of entertainment. Japanese cherries, viburnums and shrubby magnolias are succeeded in May, in spectacular fashion, by the suckering stands of Chilean fire bush, *Embothrium coccineum* var. *lanceolatum* 'Norquinco'. The hardiest form, this was collected in the wild by Harold Comber in an expedition organised and part-financed by the 2nd Lord Aberconway (see *Nymans*). The flame red of the flowers has few rivals among woody plants. Later performers here include *Cornus kousa* var. *chinensis* and the handkerchief tree, *Davidia involucrata*.

At the end of the year there is a panoply of autumn colour from birches, rowans, liquidambar and Japanese maples. Visitors to Bodnant at the end of May have an additional treat, the Laburnum Arch, where saplings of *L. × watereri* 'Vossii' – which have, incidentally, been replaced many times since the arch was first planted – are forged into a long, glowing tunnel of brilliant yellow. As a feature, it epitomises the spirit of Bodnant: generous in concept, stunning in decoration, and, with its raised sides and twisted passage, ingenious in design.

**ABOVE** A blue lacecap hydrangea blooms in August.
**RIGHT** The River Hiraethlyn runs through the Dell Garden past the old mill.

# Buscot Park

**FARINGDON, OXFORDSHIRE**

AREA 25ha (62 acres) • SOIL acid, alkaline/clay, sandy, loam • ALTITUDE 100m (328ft)
AVERAGE RAINFALL 762mm (30in) • AVERAGE WINTER CLIMATE cold

Towards the end of the nineteenth century, the great gardens of Renaissance Italy began once again to exert their influence on garden designers. Buscot boasts one of the finest designs from this period, by one of its leading exponents, Harold Peto. He was commissioned in 1904, and again in 1912, by the financier and connoisseur Alexander Henderson, later 1st Baron Faringdon, to create a water garden that would connect his Neo-classical house to the 8ha (20 acre) lake below. It was meant to appear suddenly between two elm trees to the north-east of the house, but sadly one of the elms fell almost immediately and the other died some years later. Nevertheless, the drama of first seeing the long, narrow vista cut through the tall, dense woods framed by box hedges and terminating in the temple on the other side of the lake remains intense. The stone steps lead first to a circular pool containing a statue of a dolphin embracing (or strangling) a boy, and the water then flows off, via canals, rills, still pools and rushing cascades until it reaches the lake. Much of this is revealed only as you descend, which you must do on a serpentine line, skirting the different shapes of the basins, with the invitation to cross sides by means of a small hump-backed bridge. Roman herms and other statues embellish the design, and Irish junipers and yews furnish sharp verticals.

The theme of dynamic formal avenues slicing through the woods below the house was pursued further by the 2nd Lord Faringdon. A *patte d'oie*, or goose foot, of avenues, constructed of fastigiate oak and beech, cherry and poplar, is centred on the Theatre Pavilion arch. Along one of these rides is a sunken garden, where citrus trees are set out each summer.

Always there is the backdrop of the park. It was the first owner of the house, Edward Loveden Townsend, who landscaped the grounds with two lakes and dense belts of trees, but many more trees were planted subsequently. The ravages of Dutch elm disease necessitated an extensive programme of replanting and thinning by the present Lord Faringdon, and many young oaks and beeches are now swelling into position for the future.

A second, distinct portion of garden lies to the west of the house. This centres upon Townsend's walled kitchen gardens, which have been redesigned and replanted over recent years as formal flower, fruit and vegetable gardens. The powerful contrasts of the Parent's Walk borders were devised by Peter Coats in 1986. The path, like the avenues on the other side of the garden, plunges and ascends dramatically. It leads to the orchard, where many old varieties of apple and pear are assembled, some espaliered on the walls. The main section of walled garden has a formal groundplan, revolving around a central fountain and quartered by alleys of Judas tree and hop hornbeam. The walls are concentric, to take full advantage of the sun's warmth, but although fruit and vegetables are still grown here, the emphasis is now on shrubs and old roses. Statues of the Four Seasons by Frank Forster, cast in fibreglass, set the theme, and the planting of each corner, designed originally by Tim Rees, is anchored in winter, spring, summer or autumn flowers, with roses, potentillas, hellebores and rosemary acting as unifying links. The entrance to the walled garden is guarded by fifteen life-size terracotta warriors, while opposite the descending stairway Buscot's Italianate water features have a contemporary echo in a new water feature by David Harber, comprising panels of highly polished stainless steel.

**ABOVE** The water garden created by Harold Peto.
**RIGHT** Terracotta warriors guard the entrance to the walled garden.

# Calke Abbey

**TICKNALL, DERBYSHIRE**

AREA 8ha (20 acres) • SOIL acid, alkaline/clay • ALTITUDE 91m (300ft)
AVERAGE RAINFALL 635mm (25in) • AVERAGE WINTER CLIMATE cold

In 1985, the Trust lifted Calke's veil and exposed an estate that had hardly been disturbed for a hundred years. The grey Baroque house is well sited for seclusion, concealed between deep folds of a large and hilly park, and a succession of idiosyncratic and reclusive members of the Harpur Crewe family, owners of the estate since 1622, ensured it remained a private, self-contained world. The Trust's restoration has been unusual, for the temptation to spruce up the house and garden has been vigorously resisted. Rough grass and the colonising activities of wild yellow mimulus between paving and walls preserve the air of a house lost in time and shrouded in mystery.

The flower and kitchen gardens are hidden. They were moved up the hill from the house in the late eighteenth century, following the conversion of the park to a more natural landscape. You can still see vestiges of the earlier formal layout, such as sections of avenues that used to carry the geometry of the house into the park and fragments of the former walled orchard, but the house's present tranquil setting of trees, pasture and lakes is one of curves and undulations. The heart of the woods is ancient, confirmed by the rich population of beetles associated with an unbroken continuity of decaying trees stretching back many centuries.

A shady Pleasure Ground of trees and evergreen shrubs has been renovated after years of damage by Calke's herds of red and fallow deer, which have now been fenced into the north-east section of the park. The plantation is lightened by wildflowers and bulbs, and in one of its secret hollows there is a mineral-lined grotto.

The invisible rebuilding of the gate piers that lead into the walled gardens has left the old rust stains on the brickwork. Between the piers, the path leads past summer borders of sweet peas and dahlias to the fruit store and gardener's bothy, still with its old tools and seed cabinet leaning against walls washed a surprisingly opulent blue. They form part of a very fine collection of garden buildings that includes an ice-house dating from 1810.

The flower garden to the west has been reconstructed as a rare example of a mid-nineteenth-century villa flower garden and given the same polish as the best-kept rooms in the house. The basketweave ironwork that encircles the pond is a typical feature of the period, as is the elaborate, labour-intensive and, to modern eyes, rather eccentric pattern of small beds cut out of the lawn. There are 23 of these, and each is bedded out brightly with wallflowers in spring and a mixture of annuals and exotic feature plants, such as cannas and Chusan palms. The herbaceous planting that laps the surrounding walls is in Loudon's 'mingled style'.

However, the most exciting feature, for garden historians and plant enthusiasts alike, is in the north-west corner. Here, along from the stove house and aviary, is a theatre for displaying auriculas and summer pot plants, possibly the last original structure of its kind in existence. Auriculas, cousins of the primrose, have enjoyed waves of popularity since Elizabethan times, and the idea of showing them off on covered staging, which exposes them to the air but protects them from rain and midday sun, was recommended as far back as 1717. The Calke gardeners have now built up a large and fascinating collection.

To the east of the bothy is the Physic Garden, which has been restored as a working kitchen garden. As far as possible, old varieties are grown here, and its 0.6ha (1½ acres) are divided into rotating beds for potatoes, brassicas, legumes such as 'Bunyard's Exhibition' broad bean and root crops such as 'Long Red Surrey' carrot; permanent beds for asparagus, globe artichokes, rhubarb and soft fruit; a herb border; strips for cut flowers; and an orchard of local apple varieties including 'Newton Wonder' and 'Beeley Pippin'. In addition, there are frames and hot beds, productive glasshouses and a vinery. The 1.6ha (4 acre) Upper Kitchen Garden over the wall, once a model Victorian working kitchen garden, is now largely a sheep-grazed paddock, and the glass-domed conservatory is elegantly mouldering.

**ABOVE** Vegetable beds and runner bean tripods in the Physic Garden.
**LEFT** Salvias bloom in the Walled Garden.

# Castle Drogo

DREWSTEIGNTON, DEVON

**AREA** 4.9ha (12 acres) • **SOIL** acid/stony shale over rock • **ALTITUDE** 263m (862ft)
**AVERAGE RAINFALL** 1,143mm (45in) • **AVERAGE WINTER CLIMATE** cold, wet

Castle Drogo – the name sounds a bass note of foreboding, which reverberates when, from the road, you first catch sight of the granite fortress sprouting from its rocky spur, high above the bleak expanses of Dartmoor. Even as you climb towards it, it stretches out no welcoming hand; the long drive has no entrance lodges or banks of flowers, only dark clumps of yew and evergreen oak, and belts of beech trees framing dramatic views of the wild Devon landscape. And when you finally arrive, you are confronted by hostile, defensive walls, with battlements and few windows, silhouetted starkly against the sky. Edwin Lutyens entered fully into the spirit of his unusual brief when he designed this Norman fantasy for Julius Drewe, founder of the Home and Colonial Stores.

The contrast with the wilderness behind is intentionally abrupt. Drewe wanted his castle to appear to rise directly out of the moors and the suggestion by Gertrude Jekyll for elaborate terraced gardens directly below the house was rejected in favour of untamed vegetation lapping the precipice. The only garden connected to the house is the small, draughty Chapel Garden, planted with patio roses and wall shrubs, including a cordon-trained *Viburnum plicatum*. Julius Drewe decided to locate his main flower gardens beyond the drive, to the north-east. Echoing the castle, they are potently architectural, generous in scale and solidly walled in yew, but it is likely that they owe more to the Kent-based garden designer George Dillistone than to Lutyens. The centrepiece is the Rose Garden, planted as a series of square and rectangular beds chequered into a velvet lawn. The soil being naturally poor, hungry and stony, rose cultivation is a labour-intensive business, but both old and modern Shrub roses and floribundas are here in a variety of colours.

The highlight of the composition is on the terrace above, where the contributions of both Dillistone and Lutyens are clearly defined. The paths follow an intricate Indian motif that Lutyens, then at the height of his international career, imported from Delhi, and conclude in yew pavilions, roofed originally in weeping elm but now in Persian ironwood, *Parrotia persica* 'Pendula'. Into this crisp

pattern, Dillistone, a knowledgeable plantsman, wove gorgeously hued and textured plantings of tree peonies, agapanthus, crinums, daylilies, phlox, delphiniums, bearded irises and the glaucous-leaved *Kniphofia caulescens*. The result is as imaginative a herbaceous garden as you are likely to see.

In the centre of the terrace, steps rise between spiky yuccas and dripping wisterias to a fragrant garden, and thence via a gravel corridor between shrub borders, foaming with azaleas, cherries and magnolias in spring and hoherias, eucryphias and lilies in summer, to a further flight of steps guarded by erect cypresses. Here is the greatest surprise of all, for you enter into a huge circle of yew, empty of all but a smooth expanse of shaven grass – a silent counterweight to the bulk of the castle and busy detail of the flower gardens below.

The ever-present backdrop to all this is the trees: beeches marshalled into avenues and flooded in spring by wood anemones and daffodils, and woods of oaks, beeches, Scots pines, tree magnolias and birches, with their understorey of ferns and bluebells. Among these, on the steep slope north-west of the house, meandering paths entice you down into a rhododendron valley, created by Basil Drewe, second son of Julius Drewe, and now in a lively phase of redevelopment. Blue *Rhododendron augustinii* 'Electra', pale yellow 'Lionel's Triumph', pink *R. racemosum* and rose-magenta *R. albrechtii* pull the eye this way and that, while tactile snakebark maples tempt the fingers and heavy lily scents of 'Loderi' rhododendrons excite the nose. Nearby, a new orchard of Devonian apples and plums, underplanted with snowdrops and daffodils, is also being developed. Like the rest of the grounds, these areas simultaneously defy the raw, windswept terrain and merge scenically with it, comfortably adding to what is one of the most extraordinary flights of fancy of the last century.

**RIGHT** The Terrace Garden has paths on an Indian motif, designed by Edwin Lutyens, with texured plantings by George Dillistone.

# Chirk Castle

CHIRK, WREXHAM

AREA 2.2ha (5¹/₂ acres) • SOIL neutral-acid/sandy loam • ALTITUDE 213m (700ft)
AVERAGE RAINFALL 1,016–1,143mm (40–45in) • AVERAGE WINTER CLIMATE cold

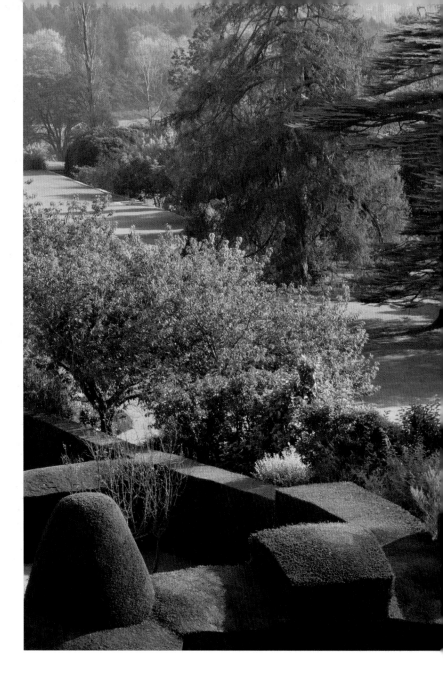

The gentle folds of oak-studded pasture through which you climb to reach Chirk Castle lull you back into the luscious decades of the eighteenth century. It comes as quite a shock when a massive medieval fortress rears up on the horizon, its high walls joined to heavy drum towers and topped with battlements. For Chirk, completed by 1310, is one of the chain of great border castles built at the command of Edward I to survey the defeated Welsh tribes. It is the transition from military stronghold into a comfortable and splendid home, and the fact that the changes – sometimes subtle, sometimes dramatically abrupt – have been effected since 1595 by a single family, that give Chirk such powerful character. Add to this its stupendous hilltop views, topiary and richly planted shrub borders, and you have one of the Trust's most exciting little-known gardens.

It is an exposed site and the great oaks help to filter the wind through the gardens. As the late Lady Margaret Myddelton once explained to me, 'Without them it would be impossible to stand up.' The yew hedges and shrubberies provide further barricades. However, a hilltop location has many advantages. The panorama from the Terrace, looking out over the Ceiriog Valley towards the hills of Shropshire, is said to encompass fourteen counties; there is a pavilion by William Emes, who landscaped the park after 1764, from which to savour it. The falling ground also accentuates shapes. This is a garden of spectacular silhouettes, cast against a broad sky. Among the most striking is the long topiary hedge beneath the castle, whose black-green battlements create a further defensive courtyard beyond the grey walls. On the terraced lawns within them are many more yew specimens, a double row of large cones and 'Welsh hats', and a magnificent giant crown resting on a cushion. These were all planted in the late nineteenth century, but allowing them to grow to their present size and plumpness was the suggestion of the celebrated garden designer Norah Lindsay, a close friend of Lord and Lady Howard de Walden, who leased the castle from 1911 until 1946. The task of pruning the Chirk yews takes three gardeners from mid-August until mid-October.

The sunken Rose Garden, filled with old Hybrid Tea and Floribunda varieties, is a softening influence on the scene, as is the lavish assortment of shrubs and climbers against the castle walls, including *Hydrangea anomala* subsp. *petiolaris*, roses, clematis, and, for its autumn colour, *Celastrus orbiculatus*. The climate being relatively mild here, half-hardy plants such as *Luma apiculata* can also be risked in the more sheltered niches. Alpines such as lewisias and campanulas grow in the dry-stone walls.

Pass between two hefty yew buttresses and their accompanying graceful bronze nymphs – yet another disarming juxtaposition – and you step onto a long, linear sweep of lawn, flanked by fine trees and flowering shrubs. In spring, sheets of daffodils swirl towards the great larch and cedar in the rough grass; and in early summer, it will be the scarlet flowers of *Embothrium coccineum*, backed by the purple leaves of beech, that catch your eye.

The undulating, 274m (300yd) border on the north side has recently been refurbished, its four bays planted for the four seasons with a cast including magnolias, azaleas and Shrub roses interplanted with hellebores, peonies, heleniums and other herbaceous plants. The luxurious planting of the rock bank, flanking Lord Howard de Walden's thatched Hawk House and the

Shrub Garden opposite, is by Lady Margaret Myddelton. In late spring, the fiery trusses of rhododendrons and azaleas blaze against the whites and pinks of pieris, magnolias, dogwoods and the handkerchief tree, *Davidia involucrata*. Later, near the newly extended waterlily pond, white-flowered *Eucryphia glutinosa* glows above pools of blue hydrangeas. February sees a sheet of snowdrops under the woodland canopy, and May a haze of bluebells.

**ABOVE** Gateway to the upper lawn with silver weeping lime and cedar.

# Claremont

**ESHER, SURREY**

**AREA** 20ha (49 acres) • **SOIL** acid/sandy loam • **ALTITUDE** 30m (100ft)
**AVERAGE RAINFALL** 635mm (25in) • **AVERAGE WINTER CLIMATE** moderate

The restoration of this landscape garden, once praised as 'the noblest of any in Europe', began in 1975, thanks largely to a generous grant from the Slater Foundation. The task facing the National Trust was monumental, since 20 years of neglect had turned the entire site into an impenetrable evergreen jungle.

Today, you can see just how much the clearance revealed: contributions by a succession of the eighteenth century's greatest gardeners, each building on (and only occasionally destroying) the work of his predecessor, the whole encapsulating the early evolution of the English landscape movement. A place of varied beauty was awoken, a composition of framed views, dramatic eye-catchers, open arenas and meandering lakeside and woodland walks; the greens complemented by the changing trees and seasonal surges of colour from bluebells, daffodils, purple rhododendrons and yellow azaleas.

The Belvedere Tower, crowning the ridge above the garden, is the obvious place from which to embark on the historical tour, though it stands just a few metres outside the Trust's boundary; the adjoining part of the estate still belongs to the house, now a school, with limited opening since 1995 in conjunction with the Trust. Equipped with a banqueting room and viewing platform, the Belvedere, designed by Sir John Vanbrugh, was the place from which the landscape was to be surveyed, and was the first building erected in 1715 by the garden's creator, the Duke of Newcastle (then Lord Clare: hence, Clare Mount). From this battlemented pavilion, a long grass corridor channels the eye downhill, over Vanbrugh's accompanying bastions (reconstructed by the Trust) and between beech hedges to a rectangular bowling green. The corridor extends into a lime avenue introduced in the 1730s, and replanted by the Trust. Following this around to the left, you suddenly arrive at the vantage point over the next feature to be installed by the Duke, the 1.2ha (3 acre) grass amphitheatre – Claremont's masterpiece.

The designer of this stupendous earthwork, a reference to ancient Rome and, perhaps, an idea borrowed from the gardens of Renaissance Italy, was Charles Bridgeman, the foremost landscape gardener of the time, and a colleague of Vanbrugh at Stowe. The Duke had been consulting him since 1716, and he is thought to have built the amphitheatre not long after the *Vitruvius Britannicus* plan of 1725 was drawn.

Scenic rather than thespian drama was the amphitheatre's purpose, and from the vantage point you have a fine panorama of trees and water. The view below, however, is not of circular pond and plantations, but of informal lake and woods. This change took place in the early 1730s, under the supervision of a second celebrated gardener, William Kent, who would now use the natural contours to create scenes evocative of landscape painting, complete with curving lines and architectural eye-catchers.

The next architectural structure you come upon as you round the south-west corner of the lake is the grotto. Constructed of sandstone and chalk conglomerate, it is probably the work of Joseph and Josiah Lane, the builders of the splendid grotto at Painshill. Behind the lake, the path entices you up a mound, thickly covered in beech, chestnut, oak and bracken. This land, formerly severed from the garden by the main Portsmouth road, was landscaped and brought into the composition after 1768, when, on the Duke of Newcastle's death, the estate was bought by Clive of India.

The bold, sweeping style of Lancelot 'Capability' Brown was now the prevailing fashion, and Clive turned to Brown to build him a crisp new Neo-classical house in place of Vanbrugh's low-lying, castellated palace and to expand and further deformalise the garden. Part of this work involved the smothering of Bridgeman's amphitheatre (which had become far too artificial a feature for contemporary taste) with cedars, deciduous trees and evergreen shrubs. Skirting the north side of the lake, past the laurel shrubberies, through the rhododendron tunnels, and following the line of Brown's brick ha-ha, you come to open meadow, sheeted with native Lent lilies (*Narcissus pseudonarcissus*) in spring and spangled with other wildflowers in summer, and then back up the ridge to the sites of the nineteenth century's architectural additions.

In 1816, the estate was purchased as a home for Princess Charlotte, the only daughter of the Prince Regent, and her husband

Prince Leopold of Saxe-Coburg, and it remained a royal residence until 1922. Several buildings were erected in this period, but apart from the Thatched House (a replacement for the thatched building put up by William Kent, and now a dovecote), they survive only as foundations. Above the amphitheatre you can see the vestiges of Princess Charlotte's Gothic tea house, which became a mausoleum after her death in childbirth. Just below the Belvedere, framed by an ironwork balustrade, are the remains of the camellia house, built in 1824. The bushes of *Camellia japonica*, hardier than the Victorians suspected, now grow in the open.

**ABOVE** The informal lake and surrounding plantations, devised by William Kent in the 1730s.

# Cliveden

TAPLOW, MAIDENHEAD, BERKSHIRE

AREA 73ha (180 acres) • SOIL neutral-alkaline/gravel overlying chalk • ALTITUDE 75m
(246ft) • AVERAGE RAINFALL 686mm (27in) • AVERAGE WINTER CLIMATE moderate

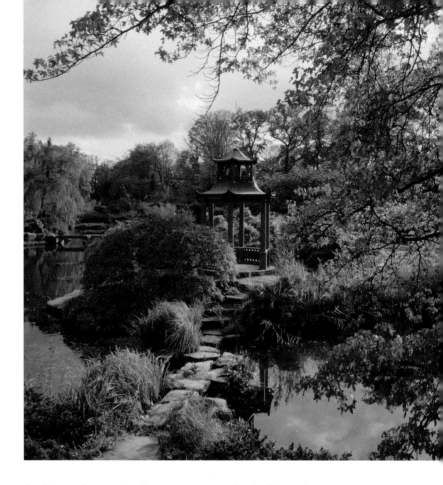

An opulent marble fountain by Thomas Waldo Story, which has
water pouring from a giant shell between female figures intoxicated
by the elixir of love, meets you in the drive; you turn to the south to
find yourself looking down a long, broad lime avenue at an ornate
Italianate palace. It is a grand, theatrical opening scene. The house,
one of the masterworks of Sir Charles Barry, was built in 1850–1 for
the 2nd Duke and Duchess of Sutherland. As you approach, you
pass between two forecourt borders of herbaceous plants laid out by
the Trust. Planned primarily for seasonal colour rather than for
textural contrast, they reach a climax in high summer – after displays
of tulips, geraniums and early daylilies – with massed phlox,
Japanese anemones, macleaya, achillea, rudbeckia and much else.
The scale is suitably impressive and the colours are founded in one
border on the yellow end of the spectrum and the other on the pink.

Cliveden's two earlier houses were both destroyed by fire, but
when you emerge beside the garden front – having passed further
planting in the Edwardian fashion of roses and fuchsias – you
discover the first has left a magnificent legacy, a brick terrace in the
French Baroque style with arcades, balustrades and a central double
stairway. It stands as a podium below the house, and from it you
look out over a sweeping platform of lawn and a landscape of
plunging beechwoods and still largely pastoral valley, centred on a
glistening stretch of the Thames. There are miles of hill and
riverside walks to explore in this panorama, the eastern route taking
you through a landscaped valley, much admired by the influential
Victorian garden writer William Robinson, and offering superb
views back to the house.

The first house and the terrace, both designed by William
Winde for the 2nd Duke of Buckingham, were built in the 1660s
and 1670s. The plateau of lawn, levelled for the Duke, was
extended and given its terminating raised circle after 1695 by his
successor, the Earl of Orkney, and then, in the early 1850s,
decorated with the present pattern of wedge-shaped parterre beds.
The gardener at the time, John Fleming, is credited with being the
first to use spring-flowering bulbs and other plants, bedded out in
the autumn, to follow up the summer annuals and tender exotics

(earlier gardeners relied upon evergreen bushes), and he wrote an
account of his experiments in *Spring and Winter Flower Gardening*,
published in 1870. Over the past few years, the Trust has begun
reintroducing such planting to the beds, having previously opted for
a more labour-saving scheme. Now spring sees bright, ever-
changing mixtures of forget-me-nots, tulips, bellis and pansies,
followed in summer by pelargoniums, ageratum, verbena and
marigolds. Groups of hot-coloured Ghent azaleas are also included,
as they were by Fleming, whose varied plant palette also embraced
hollyhocks and gladioli.

The other notable feature directly beneath the terrace is the
Baroque balustrade brought from the Villa Borghese in Rome.
This was installed by William Waldorf (later 1st Viscount) Astor,
who bought Cliveden in 1893. This introduction to the south
garden indicates that the composition was shaped over many
years and involved a succession of owners, not least the Trust.
Much of the framework, however, is due to Lord Orkney, and the
early eighteenth-century mood becomes strong as you turn to the

ABOVE The water garden with its Chinese pagoda.
RIGHT A wintry scene, looking at the house from the great plateau of lawn where
elaborate bedding schemes are played out in spring and summer.

north-west and exchange the open plateau for the shady, wooded bank that runs high above the river. Here, you come to an octagon temple with a copper-domed roof, designed for Orkney by Giacomo Leoni – later transformed into a chapel and mausoleum by Lord Astor – and pick up traces of the earlier landscape. Orkney's garden designer, probably recommended by their mutual friend Alexander Pope, was Charles Bridgeman, the leading practitioner of the day and a key figure in the transition towards the more naturalistic gardening style shortly to come into fashion.

The combination of straight walks, many bordered by large yew trees, and prospects of the countryside beyond give the flavour of Bridgeman's work, even if much of it has evolved subsequently. In the north-west corner, you come upon the most remarkable remnant, a turf amphitheatre (*c*.1723), a miniature version of that at Claremont (*qv*), carved into the slope. Further straight drives cut through the woods, one leading to a triumphal pedimented pavilion, also by Leoni, commemorating the Battle of Blenheim (Lord Orkney was one of Marlborough's brigade commanders), and another leading to a stone urn, said to have been presented to Orkney by Queen Anne.

These enclosed spaces play against the views out over the countryside, and much work is taking place at the moment to re-create them. At the same time, *Rhododendron ponticum* is being removed, and light welcomed in. The short grass sward, especially in the Blenheim Lawn, supports an array of chalkland wildflowers. In one of the glades, the swirling lawns are filled with clouds of evergreen oak, *Quercus ilex*, probably planted by Lord Orkney. In another, you enter a circular garden of sinuous beds of roses and other plants, gravel paths, and arches – a secret and soothing refuge shortly to be restored by the Trust to the original cabbage rose design by Sir Geoffrey Jellicoe of 1959. There is also a memorial garden to the soldiers who died in the Canadian Red Cross hospital on the estate.

The Astors have contributed two further gardens. To the north of the woodland, the 1st Viscount set out a formal garden, echoing the parterre below the house. A great collector of classical and Renaissance art, he introduced the many urns, well-heads, statues and sarcophagi you encounter in various parts of the grounds, and here you find a group of eighteenth-century figures, placed within a linear composition of box-edged beds. Topiary adds additional verticals, and within the box is a 200m (656ft) long double herbaceous border, arranged according to the plan produced for the Astors by the garden designer Norah Lindsay. It was

intended to climax in Royal Ascot week. Following a Jekyll sequence, the colours are graded and become warmer near the centre of the garden, the cast including campanulas, lupins, delphiniums and anthemis. Flowering shrubs such as lilac and laburnum have been planted in front of the yew trees behind, and lavender, rosemary and other low shrubs grow by the south-facing brick wall on the other side, accompanied by roses and shrubs including *Umbellularia californica* and *Dipelta floribunda*.

The other Astor garden is in complete contrast. It is an informal water garden, begun by the 1st Viscount and developed by his son and latterly the Trust into a rather magical landscape with an oriental flavour. It is also undergoing comprehensive restoration, helped by family records and an early *Country Life* article. The centrepiece is a painted pagoda, made for the Paris Exhibition of 1867 but bought later from Bagatelle. This is set on an island amid a pool of waterlilies and golden orfe, and reached by stepping stones. The marginal plants and ornamental trees and shrubs are mainly Chinese, and include primulas, water irises, azaleas and rhododendrons, witch hazel, white cherries, and wisteria grown as shrubs. Nearby is the recently replanted yew maze. Occupying a third of an acre, it was created by Lord Astor in 1894 but taken out in the mid-twentieth century. There are scenes at Cliveden for every taste.

# Clumber Park

**WORKSOP, NOTTINGHAMSHIRE**

AREA 11ha (26 acres) • SOIL acid/sandy • ALTITUDE 30m (100ft)
AVERAGE RAINFALL 610mm (24in) • AVERAGE WINTER CLIMATE cold

Enter the park under the Apleyhead arch, and you will drive through one of the most impressive lime avenues in England, over 3.2km (2 miles) in length; the grease bands on the trunks are to fend off egg-laying moths, whose caterpillars have ravaged the foliage in the past. The avenue is purely a landscape feature, planted in the 1830s by W.S. Gilpin, the pioneer of Picturesque gardening, to enliven an otherwise featureless stretch of approach road and to indicate the magnitude of the domain through which it leads.

At its heart is the great serpentine lake created in the mid-eighteenth century by damming the River Poulter. This provides the setting for a long terrace walk, adorned with specimen trees and shrubberies, urns and a temple. The transformation of the site was effected from about 1760 by successive Dukes of Newcastle, to whom the estate, then adjacent to Sherwood Forest, had been granted some 50 years earlier. Although 'Capability' Brown was working nearby and may have contributed, it seems most likely that the principal influence on the landscape was Joseph Spence, a tutor and man of letters widely consulted on garden matters by northern landowners.

The surprise is that there is no great mansion to give the park its *raison d'être*. The first house burned down in 1879, and its replacement, by Sir Charles Barry, was demolished in 1938 as a drastic tax-saving measure. Adjoining estate buildings, including the stable block and clock tower, however, remain. The treatment of the ground fronting the vanished house poses rather a dilemma for the Trust, since evocation of the earlier formal garden by intricate horticulture only emphasises the void, but as you move away from the buildings, along the lakeside walk, this sense of absence gradually wanes. The entire scene is framed in oaks, limes and other broad-leaved trees, sheltering the garden from the north wind, shading the lawns, furnishing the distant banks and reflecting in the water.

The paths meander through stands of willows, past dense island beds of conifers and Hardy Hybrid rhododendrons, and under some impressive specimen trees. Mediterranean species, in particular cedars, sweet chestnuts, Turkey and Algerian oaks, prove themselves well suited to Clumber's poor sandy soil. Quite a diverse collection of rowans (*Sorbus*) is also growing here. The mood is strongly Victorian, and the design is likely to be the work of Gilpin. In the late 1880s, the ornate Gothic chapel, by G.F. Bodley, was added to the Pleasure Ground and, in the absence of the house, now serves as the core of the garden.

The formal path leads to the Lincoln Terrace, designed by William Eden Nesfield in 1861, a promenade ornamented with splendid stone seats, and concluding in a narrow dock where a pleasure boat was once moored. North of the chapel, an avenue of cedars leads to an absolutely magnificent 1.6ha (4 acre) walled garden, dating from the 1770s and now almost fully restored. The range of produce grown is mind-boggling, including no fewer than 90 varieties of rhubarb. The lower section is subdivided by numerous additional walls for fruit production, and pre-1910 varieties of peach, nectarine and apricot, together with other crops such as pears, gages, cherries and damsons, are once again being cultivated on them. The grass orchard plots feature apple varieties associated with Nottinghamshire and the north-east Midlands. Soft fruit sections include marionberry, black raspberry, Siberian kiwi fruit and 'Mara des Bois' and 'Cambridge Late Pine' strawberries, while in the vegetable beds grow countless heritage seed varieties such as 'Prince of Prussia' pea and 'Major Cook's Bean'. There are beds for asparagus and Mayan potatoes, and for curious herb and salad crops such as golden purslane, saltwort, red spring onion, and the lettuce 'Drunken Woman'.

To enhance the garden's decorative quality, a double herbaceous border runs 122m (400ft) down its central axis, and this has been planted in graded colours to give a *trompe l'oeil* effect. Beginning with plants such as crambe, cardoon, pale sweet peas and white cosmos, the scheme warms through delphiniums, alliums and phlox to reach a sweltering climax among dahlias, daylilies and crocosmias. Here you are outside the central door of an impressive range of Edwardian glasshouses, the thirteen sections of which lead you past peaches, aubergines, melons, vines such as 'Madresfield Court' and 'Foster's Seedling', and an array of ornamental plants from palms and pelargoniums to fuschsias and tender scented rhododendrons. Beyond them, you gain a glimpse into the range of fruit stores and potting sheds, one of which presents a collection of early garden implements such as a cucumber straightening jar and a pair of leather horse slippers to prevent hoof prints on the lawns.

This restoration has made Clumber Park a truly fascinating horticultural destination and given it something of its soul back.

# Colby Woodland Garden

AMROTH, PEMBROKESHIRE

AREA 8ha (20 acres) • SOIL acid/mineral rich over coal seams • ALTITUDE 15–46m (50–150ft) • AVERAGE RAINFALL 1,143mm (45in) • AVERAGE WINTER CLIMATE mild

The wooded slopes of this hidden Pembrokeshire valley are dotted with small, open-cast mine-workings, and it was this iron ore and anthracite that attracted the industrial entrepreneur John Colby to settle here and commission his Nash-style villa in 1803. Before you plunge into the garden proper, it is worth a wander through the oaks and beeches on the eastern flank of the valley, especially in spring when the ground is white with wood anemones. The climax is a pale obelisk, a monument to Peter Chance, a former chairman of Christie's, who owned and developed much of the garden from 1965 until his death in 1984, when he left it to the Trust.

From here, to the sounds of the birds, including sometimes the wood warbler, you can survey the shape of the garden. Its heart is the meadow, which rolls down the valley bottom in front of the house to, a mile or so away, the sea and the village of Amroth. Bisected by a meandering trout stream, and colonised by violets, primroses, buttercups and meadowsweet, it is a rich habitat for butterflies, dragonflies and damselflies.

On the opposite flank of the valley, the woodland displays a quite different character – a confection of flowering trees and shrubs, especially rhododendrons. This exotic planting began in the late nineteenth century, when Colby was bought by Major Samuel Kay. This was continued by his daughter, Mrs Crosland, and her husband, and then really gathered momentum in the hands of his niece, Miss Mason. By recent times, the planting had become somewhat overgrown and congested, so a programme is under way to marshal the shapes and colours into more scenic thickets and glades, to expose the natural contours and to open up breathing spaces for the bluebells, daffodils, ferns and other wildflowers. It has been dramatically ravaged by recent plant disease.

Periodic storms have done some damage in the past, but generally this is a mild, moist, sheltered site that is ideal for the cultivation of Chinese and Himalayan plants. As you follow the paths up the hillside, an extensive collection of species and

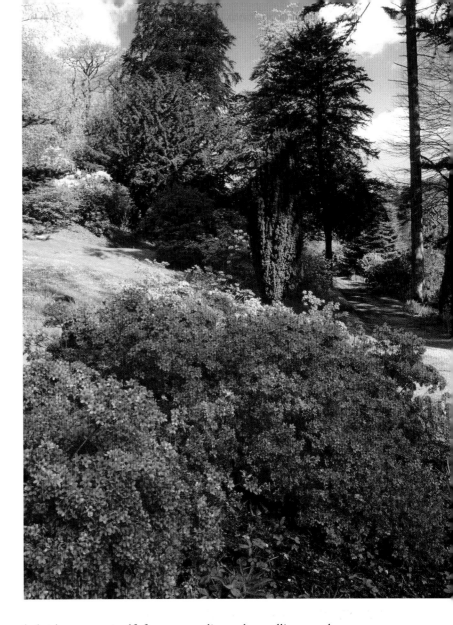

hybrids presents itself, from magnolias and camellias to red-bracted pieris and drifts of blue and white hydrangeas. Among the panoply of rhododendrons, you will find everything from towering pink *R. arboreum*, pale yellow *R. lutescens*, blood-red *R. thomsonii* and some luxuriant, giant-leaved *R. sinogrande* and *R. maccabeanum* to a vast assortment of hybrids, from the pastels of 'Alison Johnstone', 'Lavender Girl' and 'Moonshine Bright' to deep yellow 'Crest', scarlet 'The Hon. Jean Marie de Montague', white 'Peace', wine-crimson 'Moser's Maroon' and hot pink Japanese azaleas.

From South America comes monkey puzzle, the scarlet bottle brushes of embothrium, white-saucered eucryphia and the red

ABOVE Japanese azaleas in one of the woodland's sunny glades.

lanterns of crinodendron. And it is South Africa we can thank, or curse, for the orange montbretia (*Crocosmia*), which has naturalised itself along the grassy fringes of Colby's pathways, as it has done all along Britain's western seaboard. Here and there you pick up the sound of water splashing down mossy rocks, and at one point it collects into a contemplative pool. The reward for climbing to the top of the woods is the view from the summer-house, out over the sea to the Gower Peninsula, but equally absorbing is that from Pamela Chance's memorial on the lower path, back over the meadow to the house and its adjacent walled garden.

The walled garden has been leased out to the Trust's tenants, Anthony and Cynthia Scourfield Lewis, who open it to the public. They have redesigned it as an intricate plantsman's garden, with sinuous paths, lawns and island beds, and a formal fuchsia garden.

Yellow New Zealand *Sophora tetraptera*, crimson *Acca sellowiana* syn. *Feijoa sellowiana* from South America and South African *Melianthus major* are among the original cast savouring the warm micro-climate, supported now by numerous other shrubs and perennials, from indigo-berried *Dichroa febrifuga* to the scintillating blue domes of *Scilla peruviana*. The white gothic gazebo in its top corner, built by Chance and with a *trompe-l'oeil* painted interior, is a landmark across the garden, and below it, a rill has now been constructed to bring the sound of water to another part of Colby.

**BELOW** Pink hybrid rhododendrons bloom along a shady pathway.
**RIGHT** The stream in the Rill Garden at Coleton Fishacre. The clear water is bordered by hostas, azaleas and bluebells.

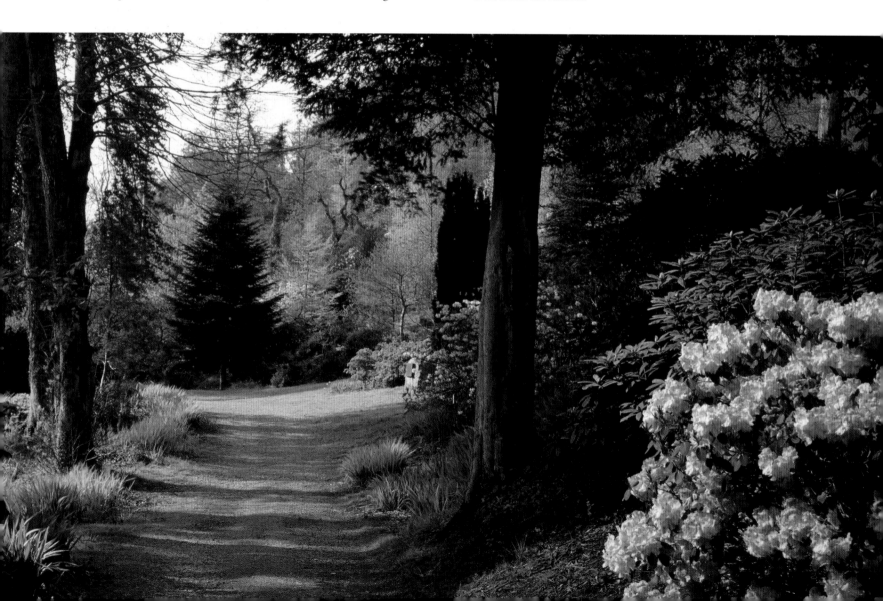

# Coleton Fishacre

**KINGSWEAR, DARTMOUTH, DEVON**

**AREA** 12ha (30 acres) • **SOIL** acid/shaly loam; pockets of silty clay • **ALTITUDE** 100m (328ft) • **AVERAGE RAINFALL** 914mm (36in) • **AVERAGE WINTER CLIMATE** frost-free, mild

The plunging sides and deep bowl of this south-facing valley garden offer near-perfect growing conditions. Cold air flows away quickly through the combe, and the shelter belts of Monterey pine and holm oak limit the impact of the salt-laden winds. Humidity is high, thanks to the proximity of the sea, while the abundance of underground springs, coupled with the shaly soil and precipitous terrain, provide that ideal but elusive combination of constant moisture and sharp drainage.

Rich and extensive as its collection of rare and tender plants may be, the mood at Coleton Fishacre is not, however, exotic. Rather, true to the spirit of the Arts and Crafts Movement, the house and garden maintain a strong bond with their Devon setting. Walls and terraces are built of stone quarried on site, and their vernacular construction, incorporating steeply pitched roofs and curved walls, enables them to blend easily with the contours of the land. The spirit of Edwin Lutyens is pervasive, though this is the work of his pupil Oswald Milne, commissioned by Rupert D'Oyly Carte, son of Gilbert and Sullivan's business partner, and his wife Lady Dorothy, soon after they purchased the estate in 1924.

A generous leavening of native and traditional plants also helps to mellow the impact of rarified horticulture, but between the cherries and chestnuts, rosemary and wisteria, banks of daffodils and wild garlic, there is rich fare indeed to be discovered. Following a long period of inactivity, the golden opportunities the site offers have again been seized as the Trust advances its programme of restoration and improvement.

As you walk into the garden past suede-trunked *Luma apiculata* and various *Prunus*, you are immediately diverted by the Seemly Terrace. Early in the year it will be hellebores, euphorbias and scented daphnes, such as *Daphne bholua* and *D. acutiloba*, that catch your eye and draw your nose, as you pass the polished mahogany trunks of *Prunus serrula*; later, perhaps, it may be brightly hued crocosmias and hedychiums.

The Rill Garden below, with its canalised stream and horizontal patterns of stone, is strongly redolent of the great formal gardens of the Lutyens-Jekyll partnership. Originally planted with roses, which struggle to thrive in the humid maritime atmosphere, it is now bolstered with unusual and tender perennials in pink and other pastel shades, including salvias and rehmannia. Beds near the house, and along the walk to the Gazebo, shimmer in the richer colour of plants from the hotter and drier parts of the world, such as kangaroo paw, cuphea and king proteas, while fascicularia, aloes and aeoniums contribute an array of spiky and succulent foliage.

The views from the Gazebo towards the Blackstone rocks and wide expanse of sea allow a pause from this intensive horticulture. But then, taking a deep breath, you must choose your descent into the combe. The sunny terraces now give way to the dappled shade of woodland, and stone-edged rill and basins become burbling stream and natural pools. In spring and early summer you are submerged in colour from camellias, magnolias, rhododendrons, embothriums and dogwoods, with azaleas and tender white-flowered rhododendrons, including *RR. maddenii* ssp. *crassum, burmanicum, johnstoneanum* and *lindleyi*, providing pools of scent. Hydrangeas, eucryphias, orange-flowered *Lomatia ferruginea*, melon-scented *Magnolia × wieseneri* and self-seeding *Cornus capitata* extend the season through the summer, while providing a backdrop of subtle green delight are bamboos and tree ferns, nothofagus and *Pinus radiata*, glossy-leaved *Gevuina avellana*, a large tree of heaven (*Ailanthus altissima*) and a magnificent tulip tree (*Liriodendron tulipifera*).

Numerous paths snake their way between the shrubs and trees, and as you swing sideways up the combe's high flanks, the scale and drama of the terrain becomes thrillingly apparent. The reward for this slow descent is the sheltered, rocky inlet of Pudcombe Cove, and in late spring your arrival is sweetened by thickets of scented *Elaeagnus umbellata*. No lover of plants will be disappointed by this garden.

# Cotehele

**ST DOMINICK, SALTASH, CORNWALL**

AREA 6.9ha (17 acres) plus 4.9ha (12 acres) of orchard • SOIL acid/loam • ALTITUDE 76m (250ft) • AVERAGE RAINFALL 1,143mm (45in) • AVERAGE WINTER CLIMATE mild

Here is an estate full of Cornish character. The approach is along narrow, plunging, high-banked lanes, affording sudden views across the Tamar Valley over the hilly expanse of Dartmoor. Below is the tidal river itself, punctuated by Cotehele quay, once busy with traffic transporting copper and other minerals downstream to Plymouth, but now the tranquil mooring for the last of the Tamar barges, *Shamrock*. Cream teas are served in a former hostelry, the Edgcumbe Arms.

The house and its outbuildings are at the head of the wooded combe high above. In spite of the towers and battlements, they are a snug and welcoming collection of buildings, low-lying and warmly constructed of brown and grey slate. Of medieval origin, the property was remodelled and enlarged in Tudor times by Sir Richard and Sir Piers Edgcumbe, whose family were to own Cotehele for nearly six centuries.

The garden, divided into a series of intimate enclosures and sheltered walks, is equally inviting. An avenue of young sycamores opposite the old barn take up the colour of the walls in their clean grey trunks, and in spring this opening scene is cheered by a swathe of daffodils growing on the bank. Later in the year, there will be autumn crocuses and cyclamen flowering under the sycamores. Beyond the two cobbled courts, one with walls hung with wisterias and *Rosa bracteata* and lapped with Algerian iris, and the other flaunting myrtle and camellias, is a gateway leading into an enclosed acre of sloping meadow. Here daffodils grow in their hundreds between the well-spaced trees – simple, old varieties, in clumps that are seldom disturbed. The grass is not cut until the middle of June, by which time orchids and other wildflowers have completed their cycle. It is a timeless picture.

A white-painted gate leads into the Upper Garden, a large enclosure of sloping lawns with, as its centrepiece, a pool of pink and white waterlilies. Scattered trees, including tree of heaven (*Ailanthus altissima*), a superb tulip tree (*Liriodendron tulipifera*) and a fine yellow-twigged ash, *Fraxinus excelsior* 'Jaspidea', preserve an informal character, while on the south side, a border of tall shrubs screens the garden from the estate cottages and the old orchard. Through a yew arch, you come into a small garden that

reflects Cornwall's long history of horticultural commerce. The traditional crops – daffodils, irises, strawberries and eucalyptus – grow in a series of raised and sloping borders, and in one corner stands a replica of one of the corrugated metal packing sheds that were once a common sight in this area. Apple trees also have a long association with the Tamar Valley, and in the winter of 2007–8 the 'Mother Orchard' was planted up with 270 traditional varieties, the trees widely spaced to allow them to grow large and the grass between them managed as hay meadow.

Accompanied by a burbling rill, the Upper Garden's beds and borders are at their most colourful in summer and autumn. On one side, a striking scheme of silver and gold, designed to counteract the many overcast Cornish days, consists of cardoons, daylilies, kniphofias and an assortment of daisy-flowered plants. Elsewhere, tulips and peonies are succeeded by fuchsias, agapanthus, *Eucomis bicolor* and tender perennials, while from the cut-flower garden nearby some 30,000 flowers are harvested and dried for use in the Cotehele Christmas Garland displayed in the Great Hall.

Early in the year, as you walk back into the daffodil meadow along the top path, you will catch the scent of *Acacia pravissima*, foaming with bright yellow flowers. It vies for attention with one of the garden's young cork oaks, standing in the grass above the squat grey tower of the house. To the left, another path beckons, leading you through a gate and over parkland to the three-sided Prospect Tower and its panorama of Plymouth and the rolling fields, woods and moors of the Cornish-Devon border.

The top path now descends between camellias and aucuba, through a bowl of Japanese maples, under the drooping branches of *Erica arborea* var. *alpina*, casting vanilla scent in spring, and across the gravel drive, past crimson *Rhododendron russellianum* and a weeping silver lime (*Tilia tomentosa* 'Petiolaris') to bring you out onto the stone terraces below the east front of the house. This is the most formal part of the garden, constructed in 1862 to complement the house's rebuilt façade, but even here the character is modest and mellow, with cool pink, white and silver-leaved perennials presented against a relaxed and varied backdrop of magnolias, white wisterias, green-tasselled *Itea ilicifolia*, a bower of *Robinia hispida* and a spectacular pink *Clematis montana* scrambling up a laurel.

The views over the stone balustrade, down into the combe and across to Calstock village and the railway viaduct, were opened up by the severe gales of January 1990. This is not the first time a storm has blasted the woods; Calstock and Cotehele were also rudely revealed to each other in 1891. But although privacy has been lost from the terraces, the gales did not disturb the sense of secrecy within the combe itself, a feeling heightened by the dark stone tunnel that serves as its entrance.

The slopes and fringe woodland, boosted by the Trust, provide the shelter required to exploit Cornwall's mild maritime climate to the full. The tree and shrub planting is exciting and diverse, but so interwoven with the native trees as to appear natural and homely. Self-sowing bluebells, primroses, foxgloves and red campions form an unpretentious carpet, and on the shady slopes, ferns, especially lady ferns, grow in abundance.

Presiding over the valley is the handsome domed dovecote and stewpond, relics of medieval days when they would have provided meat and fish for the house. From this pond, water splashes down the combe in a series of pools and runnels, increasing the humidity and supplying damp ground for primulas, marsh marigolds, wild mimulus, *Darmera peltata* (formerly *Peltiphyllum peltatum*) and giant-leaved *Gunnera manicata*. The ornamental tree and shrub planting appears to have begun at the head of the valley in 1867, while the building of the viaduct in 1907–8 may have prompted the addition of screening conifers. Much of the present planting, however, is the work of the Trust, including the establishment of a new arboretum on the land known as Nellson's Piece.

**ABOVE** The terrace and east front of Cotehele are the most formal parts of the garden.

Early in the year, rhododendrons are prominent, including large stands of *Rhododendron arboreum* and *R.* Smithii Group ('Cornish Red' as it is known in Cornwall, 'Devon Pink' over the border) and an extensive range of azaleas. But they are not grown to the exclusion of other shrubs: camellias, enkianthus, kalmias, embothriums and magnolias are also well represented, with eucryphias, hoherias, hydrangeas and Japanese maples providing later colour. Hemlocks, firs and the unusual *Sciadopitys verticillata* are among the comparatively modest conifer population. Striking an exotic note is the Chusan palm, *Trachycarpus fortunei*, which produces panicles of yellow flowers in early summer, followed by great bunches of black fruits that persist throughout the winter and spring. Towards the bottom of the combe, the vegetation reverts to native woodland and a footpath leads to Sir Richard Edgcumbe's chapel and the River Tamar.

# The Courts

HOLT, BRADFORD-ON-AVON, WILTSHIRE

AREA 2.8ha (7 acres) • SOIL alkaline/loam • ALTITUDE 61m (200ft)
AVERAGE RAINFALL 762mm (30in) • AVERAGE WINTER CLIMATE moderate

This is a garden in the Hidcote tradition, full of charm and variety, and deserving to be far better known. The house, described by Christopher Hussey as 'an early Georgian gem', was built for one of the area's prosperous cloth manufacturers, and had a mill adjacent, powered by the stream that flows from Great Chalfield Manor. The mill was demolished in the third quarter of the nineteenth century.

The bones of the present garden were set out by Sir George Hastings, who owned The Courts between 1900 and 1910, and the design was elaborated and given its rich overlay of plants by Lady Cecilie Goff after 1921. It is a compartmented garden, not as severely delineated as Hidcote, but each section has a formal structure and its own rather imaginative blend of colours. Generally, it is a quirkier composition: Lady Cecilie loved springing surprises. You enter from the village along a walk of pleached limes (formerly of pollarded poplars), emerging opposite the east front of the house onto wide lawns, framed by assorted hedges and topiaries. Though planted symmetrically, each seems to have its own idiosyncratic bulging or lop-sided shape, immediately setting the relaxed mood. Pillars and cones of common yew, fringes and slabs of green box, domes of holly and giant buns of golden yew are part of the scene, supported by a backdrop of fine trees.

Into this are inserted the self-contained planting schemes. There are hedged semi-circles of pink, lilac and white (limonium, galtonia and pink old-fashioned roses among them); a pair of blue and yellow borders featuring thalictrum, asters and achillea; a long fuchsia border, brightened with white Japanese anemones; and a small fernery. The most exciting colouring is in the Mediterranean-style walk, flanked by sentinel yews, down which scarlet, orange and pale yellow flowers (zauschneria, crocosmia, cephalaria and others) crackle among the silver mounds of santolina, artemisia and the perennial wallflower *Erysimum* 'Jacob's Jacket'. It is a superb piece of planting. All is in contrast to the pale stone of the house and its loggia, the terraces and paths (the slabs gleaned by Lady Cecilie

from the demolished Devizes gaol), and the various ornaments – a large dog, a column surmounted by a Roman bust, pillars hung in vines and much else – many of the grander pieces being copied by Sir George Hastings from those at Ranelagh House, Barnes.

The greenhouse, kept frost-free and stocked with exotics like aloes, tender nerines and *Passiflora × exoniensis*, is similar to the pastiche Georgian orangery Sir George created at Ranelagh. And at the head of a long, straight grass walk below the house, now flanked by borders with a pink and yellow colour scheme (phlox, crinums and Japanese anemones, partnered with golden-leaved *Cornus alba* 'Spaethii' and physocarpus, and the curious evening-opening daylily, *Hemerocallis citrina*), he installed a classical temple.

We are now in the lower garden. Water sets the theme here, and at various points you cross the trickling stream by little bridges. A large rectangular pool, created by Lady Cecilie and restored by the Trust, is framed by beds of Siberian iris and dierama and covered by vast rafts of pink, crimson, yellow and white waterlilies. It lies parallel to the temple walk, and below it is the informally shaped Dye Pool, fringed with giant gunnera and other bog plants. Everywhere, there are thickets of trees and shrubs. The range should inspire all visitors who share a heavy, limy soil, especially in autumn, when the leaf colours are quite as brilliant as those to be seen in acid woodlands. Paperbark and Nikko maples (*Acer griseum*

LEFT The former stew pond in the Upper Garden at Cotehele blooms with water lilies.
RIGHT Mediterranean style planting with silver santolina, verbena and kniphofia around topiary yews at The Courts.

and *A. maximowiczianum* syn. *nikoense*), *Viburnum carlesii*, cotinus and Sargent's cherry (*Prunus sargentii*) are among those contributing reds and oranges, and there are major displays from the various cultivars of guelder rose (*Viburnum opulus*), the native wayfaring tree (*V. lantana*), and the thorn *Crataegus persimilis* 'Prunifolia', all of which partner their tinted leaves with coloured fruits.

There is more drama in the arboretum, an extensive area of pasture developed by Moyra Goff in 1952, and a welcome change from the intimacy and formality of the rest of the garden. Pink-candled horse chestnuts, limes, walnuts, a fine cut-leaved beech, Turkey oak and catalpa are among the contents, with daffodils appearing beneath them in spring, followed by snakeshead fritillaries – a native plant that once carpeted many an English water meadow. The recently restored Kitchen Garden includes herb borders, an apple arch and an apple orchard framed by espaliered pears.

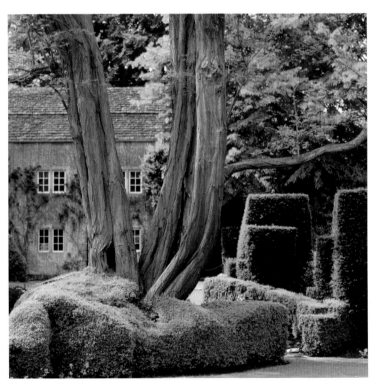

**ABOVE** Autumn reflections across the Dye Pool, interspersed with rafts of water lilies at The Courts in Wiltshire.
**RIGHT** Trees are complemented by formal evergreen shapes to striking sculptural effect.
**FAR RIGHT** The steep valley running down to Debdon Burn divides the Cragside garden in two, linked only by the recently restored footbridge.

# Cragside

ROTHBURY, MORPETH, NORTHUMBERLAND

**AREA** 405ha (1,000 acres) • **SOIL** acid/sandy moorland • **ALTITUDE** 152m (500ft)
**AVERAGE RAINFALL** 813mm (32in) • **AVERAGE WINTER CLIMATE** cold

Here is the rugged and mystical landscape of the Gothic novel and
Wagnerian opera, a landscape of dark conifer forests, boulder-
strewn hillsides, lakes and waterfalls. The estate encompasses over
688ha (1,700 acres), 405ha (1,000 acres) of which are owned by the
Trust, and in its midst, on a site blasted from the cliff face, stands
the massive frame of the Victorian *schloss*. It is all the work of the
1st Baron Armstrong, inventor and armaments manufacturer, who,
from 1864, began harnessing in earnest his great wealth, ingenuity
and engineering skill to create an extensive picturesque retreat out
of the empty moorland. The transformation involved much of the
male population of Rothbury and included the planting of seven
million trees and shrubs, the laying of 50km (31 miles) of road and
pathway and the digging of four large lakes.

There is no tame garden around the house. The stupendous
rockery that anchors it to the steep, west-facing slope running down
to Debdon Burn looks as if it has been created by an avalanche.
Before the Trust began its restoration, there was hardly a rock
showing; gaultheria had run rampant, and *Rhododendron ponticum*
swept in from the surrounding woods. Now, thanks partly to the
help of volunteers, the giant stones are again revealed. Alpine and
moorland plants, including saxifrages, sedums, *Hypericum
olympicum*, heathers and vacciniums, have been reintroduced into
the crevices and bays, with phormiums and hebes in the hotter
spots. A gentle transition from wilderness into garden has been
allowed by planting a range of shrubs and trees that furnish splashes
of contrasting colour without being overly ornamental. These
include a wide range of Hardy Hybrid rhododendrons, evergreen
and deciduous azaleas, brooms, berberis and some beautiful
Asian rowans, including orange-berried *Sorbus sargentiana*, pink-
berried *S. hupehensis* and the seldom-seen whitebeam *S. vestita* syn.
*S. cuspidata*.

This same transition takes place rather more dramatically
nearer the burn. Here, on the lower banks and floor of the valley,
the black woods of pines and firs break into an open arboretum of
conifers. The cool, moist atmosphere promotes tremendous growth,
especially in North American species, and many trees have reached

champion size. There are soaring specimens of Douglas, Caucasian, and noble fir, western hemlock and Nootka cypress, and, as at Bodnant, the terrain allows you to both stand among their trunks and to view their crowns from above. Dippers and grey wagtails can often be seen braving the fast-flowing water, and beyond the arched iron footbridge the paths entice you into many more acres of wooded pleasure ground, through plantations of autumn-tinting trees, past drifts of foxgloves and rustic bridges, and on towards Tumbleton Lake.

In 1991, the Trust acquired the missing part of the picture, the terraced formal gardens, 800m (½ mile) from the house, the restoration of which is almost complete. The Orchard House, with its quirky system of turntables for rotating the pots in order to promote balanced growth, has survived intact and is once again filled with figs, grapes, peaches, citrus and other fruits. Early crops of vegetables are cultivated in front of it, with other produce such as tomatoes and broad beans grown in pots nearby. Other houses have disappeared, but exotic-looking hardy plants and summer bedding are being cleverly used to convey their former character. *Lobelia tupa* is a feature in what was once the Palm House; unusual shrubs grow in the Display House; and an assortment of hardy begonias and crested and fancy ferns filter between the boulders in the Temperate Ferneries.

A display of Victorian carpet bedding – one of the most intricate examples in the Trust's gardens – is part of the colourful fringe to the lawns, which also includes a walk of double-flowered dahlias. The Italian Terrace has also been restored: centred on a quatrefoil pool and water spray, the borders have been replanted with striking foliage, scented flowers, and plants considered half-hardy in Victorian times, such as fuchsias, nerines and kniphofias. The fine clematis collection mentioned in the *Gardener's Chronicle* of 1880 has also been reassembled. It is all in striking contrast to the rest of this wild estate.

**ABOVE** Fruit trees and vegetables line the shelves in the greenhouse at Cragside. They are grown in large pots before being planted out on the estate.
**ABOVE RIGHT** A peaceful lakeside scene at Croome Park designed by 'Capability' Brown.

# Croome Park

HIGH GREEN, SEVERN STOKE, WORCESTERSHIRE

AREA 283ha (700 acres) • SOIL neutral/silty loam, some clay • ALTITUDE 20–33m (65–108ft)
AVERAGE RAINFALL 635mmn (25in) • AVERAGE WINTER CLIMATE moderate

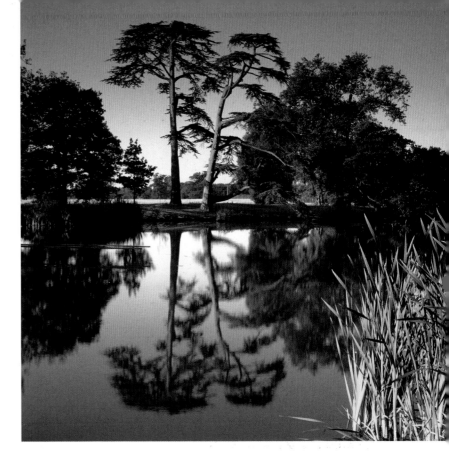

From high ground beside the church of St Mary Magdalene, you look down onto a wide bowl of open park and farmland, scattered with trees. A river curls across the valley, leading the eye to the presiding ornament, a large, pale Palladian house. It is an uncluttered scene, rising in the middle distance into a ring of hills. The confident hand of Lancelot 'Capability' Brown is unmistakable. Brown was still at Stowe, and just establishing an independent design practice, when he was approached by George William Coventry, later 6th Earl, to undertake the grand and expensive transformation of Croome. He worked here for over 30 years, intensively between 1751–6 and 1762–6. It was his first complete landscape, and cemented his reputation, while Croome itself became hugely influential as the first landscape in which the existing topography was harnessed and perfected in the new 'natural' style.

However important Croome has been in the history of gardening, it has not been spared from indignity. In the 1940s there was an RAF base here, with attendant runways; in 1948 the house was sold off; and in 1962 the M5 motorway sliced through the estate. Over the years, grazed parkland turned into arable farmland, the river silted up, and there was even a proposal for a golf course. So the National Trust, which acquired the heart of the park in 1996 with the help of a grant from the Heritage Lottery Fund, has embarked upon a major restoration project. While the buildings and contours are emerging again in pristine order, the extensive replanting now gives the sense of a landscape in the making, much as it was 250 years ago – the accuracy of the project assisted by comprehensive historical records.

The Gothic exterior of the church, like the exterior of the house itself, was designed by Brown, and both form part of the succession of architectural eye-catchers, changing views and set-piece scenes that are revealed on the circuit tour. There was no river here before the 1740s. This was one of Lord Coventry's first projects, which he undertook with advice from a friend, the architect and landscape gardener Sanderson Miller, before Brown's arrival. Brown curved it – echoing the course of the River Severn on the boundary of the estate – and extended it into a lake, as well as

completing the extensive network of drains required to convert the marshy ground into fine grassland.

Following the paths down the hill, you exchange the unimpeded prospect of the house – to which the grass is intended to flow seamlessly, across an unusual inward-facing ha-ha – for meandering shrubberies. By the church, the shrubbery is sombre and melancholy, thick with evergreens such as box, yew, privet and ruscus growing under pines and ash; concealed among them is a thatched ice-house. Elsewhere, the shrubberies are cheery with Shrub roses, philadelphus and much else besides, for Croome was at the forefront of new plant introductions in the eighteenth century, its collection said to be rivalled only by Kew's. Some of the most prized plants would have been grown in the shrubbery near the house, which is starting to be planted up again, having recently been acquired by the Trust, together with its Rotunda ringed by cedar trees. The Trust has also acquired the lease of the house, offering visitors the important reverse views over the landscape.

Opposite the house to the north, you are led down a long mingled thicket of shrubs such as daphne, rhododendron, rosemary, variegated holly, viburnum, wintersweet and yellow broom, each variety often represented by a single specimen, which is very strange to modern eyes. A restored statue of Pan, dating from about 1800, presides over a glade, and here and there are small island beds, or flowering studs, of shrubs, roses, and herbaceous plants such as monkshood and astrantia.

The route takes you to the magnificent Temple Greenhouse, designed by Robert Adam, who joined Brown in producing buildings and interiors for Lord Coventry after 1760. Protected by glass in winter and warmed by a furnace, it provided the opportunity to display a rich assortment of tender plants behind its Doric portico. After this diversion, the path continues under oaks and chestnuts, past a Coade stone statue of a druid and under a stone bridge – designed by Brown and sporting the heads of river gods between vermiculated decoration – to the lake. Here, a grotto, designed by Brown, is encrusted with shells, fossils and crystals, and features Sabrina, goddess of the Severn, pouring water from her urn to feed it. This stands in contrast to Adam's elegant temple, presiding over one of the lake's two islands, supported by Corinthian columns and decorated with Coade stone reliefs. Collections of trees including planes, thorns and cedars of Lebanon provide the sylvan setting.

A further array of architectural eye-catchers draws the eye into the wider reaches of the park and landscape, blending the garden with the countryside and rewarding the eighteenth-century visitor who took the longer tour. To the south, 1.6km (1 mile) away, is Dunstall Castle, built by Adam as a Gothic ruin, while another sham castle, Pirton Tower, to the north and the Panorama Tower to the west were completed some years later by James Wyatt.

The debt owed to Brown is expressed in the monument by the lake, erected by Lord Coventry some years after Brown's death in 1783, which bears the dedication 'To the Memory of Lancelot Brown Who by the powers of His inimitable and creative genius formed this garden scene Out of a morass'.

**ABOVE** The lake at Croome Park has been extensively dredged as part of the ongoing restoration of the landscape.
**RIGHT** Skunk cabbage and other leafy plants border the canal at Dunham Massey.

# Dunham Massey

ALTRINCHAM, CHESHIRE

AREA 10ha (25 acres) • SOIL severely acid/loamy sand • ALTITUDE 25m (82ft)
AVERAGE RAINFALL 889mm (35in) • AVERAGE WINTER CLIMATE mild to moderate

Thanks to the bequest of the 10th Earl of Stamford, one of the most generous in the Trust's history, these 1,214ha (3,000 acres) of farmland and woods will be a permanent green oasis between the conurbations of Manchester and Liverpool. At their heart is a predominantly early eighteenth-century brick mansion, tactfully described by the landscape architect Dame Sylvia Crowe as one of 'beautifully proportioned austerity', richly planted gardens and a wooded park of great historic and scientific interest.

Dating back to medieval times and still roamed by a large herd of fallow deer today, the park was formalised by George Booth, 2nd Earl of Warrington, in the French style that was then fashionable. The first avenues were already installed by 1697, and the final, all-embracing landscape of radiating rides, *allées*, circular, triangular and oval plantations, canals, formal ponds and architectural eye-catchers (the whole bounded by brick wall) is

depicted in the series of fine bird's-eye paintings by John Harris the Younger that hangs in the Great Gallery; they date from about 1750. Very few such landscapes survived the change in eighteenth-century taste towards a more flowing, naturalistic composition, but at Dunham this informal style was practised in a new park to the east, leaving much of the old framework intact. The Trust has now repaired and replanted a number of these tree lines, so that from the south front of the house you can have the rare prospect of a triple row of lime trees either side of the forecourt, leading to a grand *patte d'oie* (goose foot) of six long avenues centred on a grass semi-circle.

An obelisk, dating from 1717, survives as a focal point for one of these. It is the only ornamental monument to remain, but as you explore the park, you come upon other handsome functional buildings, notably a two-tiered, brick deer barn. The garden also has its ancient features. Your first view of the house is across the moat belonging to the previous medieval and Elizabethan house. It appears as a broad, lake-like swathe of water, curving around the north and west walls. In one direction, the water runs from the garden as a narrow canal, while in the other, a channel leads past the cupola of the stables and coach house to a seventeenth-century saw-mill.

Just to the side of the house, a semi-circle of ground extends into the lake, and here, behind the trees, are the remains of a mount. The core may be Norman, but it was built up in the Elizabethan period to form a garden vantage point, a favourite feature, complete with circling terraces and a crowning pavilion; the garden then extended to the west of the house, where the service range now stands. The mound survives today as a mysterious hummock of grass under a grove of robinias. The remainder of the garden is, likewise, many-layered, thoroughly restored after years of gradual and almost terminal decline to convey the pristine flavour of a Victorian pleasure ground, but one founded on a late eighteenth-century layout of meandering lawns and shrubberies, and including some formal Edwardian touches and inspired contemporary planting.

You enter through a slice of woodland, brought into the garden in the last century and bordered by a stream. This area was totally overgrown in 1976, but clearance revealed some good trees, including two forms of sycamore, the rare *Acer pseudoplatanus* 'Corstorphinense', and 'Brilliantissimum' with eye-catching shrimp-pink leaves in spring. Moisture-loving perennials such as persicaria, shuttlecock fern and a mesmerising display of the blue Himalayan poppy, *Meconopsis* × *sheldonii*, in an intense turquoise form, appear in drifts above the water, and there is a good stand of the giant lily, *Cardiocrinum giganteum*.

**ABOVE** A sea of bluebells surges under the foliage of rheum and chestnut trees.

Since 2007, the plant display here has been embellished significantly by the additional 2.8ha (7 acres) that have been carved from the overgrown former pony paddock and turned into Britain's largest winter garden. Meandering paths take you past a meadow of blue-flowered bulbs including chionodoxas, scillas, crocus and the dwarf iris 'Harmony' and lead you on between carpets of other bulbs, such as daffodils, muscari, cyclamen and species tulips, all in myriad forms. There is a huge range of snowdrops, with 25,000 additional bulbs planted annually. These are joined by hellebores, pulmonarias and epimediums; trees and shrubs offering handsome winter barks, such as snakebark maples, willows, birches and dogwoods; winter flowers such as cherries and camellias; and winter fruits such as crab apples. There are scents from sarcococca, viburnums, daphnes and wintersweet, and variegated foliage from hollies and elaeagnus. The season begins in autumn with the tinting leaves of Japanese maples, amelanchiers and cercidiphyllum (which turns pink here) and the berries of rowans, and it extends well into spring with magnolias and rhododendrons.

The acid sandy soil and high water table make good azalea ground, and those in the woods here belong to a notable strain, being seedlings raised by an amateur Cheshire-born plantsman, Denny Pratt. His main purpose was to carry the colour and scent of the tribe into midsummer by crossing various Knap Hill azaleas with the late-flowering American species, *RR. viscosum*, *arborescens*, *prunifolium* and *bakeri*; seedlings were also produced from *R. atlanticum*, and from crossing *R. occidentale* with the common yellow azalea, *R. luteum*. So far, only a few have been named and widely propagated – 'Summer Fragrance' and 'Anneke' being the best known – but a June visit to Dunham is a revelation.

Hardy hydrangeas are also well represented here, with various forms of white-flowered *H. heteromalla* and *H. arborescens*, and the large, felted-leaved *H. aspera*, growing on the wood's fringe with the contrasting foliage of bamboos and grasses. Others, forms of *H. serrata* – more tolerant than the common lacecaps of the late frosts to which the garden is prone – grow in the dappled shrubbery along the boundary wall, with lilies, *Rhododendron yakushimanum* and a collection of skimmias.

You then emerge into spacious open lawn, studded with large specimen trees such as mature Lucombe, cork and red oaks; beside the house, a tall swamp cypress; and elsewhere, rarities such as tropical-looking (though bone hardy) *Magnolia tripetala*. Further plant riches are revealed as you break through the shrubbery, following a meandering grass path between birch and purple beech,

north to the canal. First you pass low beds of *Geranium macrorrhizum*, bergenia, tiarella, iris, astrantia and other ground-cover subjects – the pastel schemes finely tuned for textural contrast – and then, on the sunny banks by the canal itself (cleared and rebuilt by the Trust), there are lush waterside plantings; the panther lily, *Lilium pardalinum*, does especially well here, the orange Turk's cap flowers leaping out of the borders in high summer, and there is a memorable leaf partnership between two invasive colonisers, the purplish hearts of pink *Clerodendrum bungei* and the grey, feathery foliage of the Californian tree poppy, *Romneya coulteri.*

The main lawn, however, also has architectural attractions. Tucked into the shrubbery is an early nineteenth-century rustic arbour, made of robinia bark, and a fine eighteenth-century orangery. In the Edwardian era, the orangery was incorporated into elaborate formal gardens, set out when the house was restored. These had mostly fallen into disrepair during the Second World War and were removed afterwards, but traces do remain. The grove of purple beeches evolved from hedges that once enclosed the rose garden; this has now become a moss garden, and a new rose garden is being planned behind it. Other formal gardens can be found about the house.

A small parterre of 1905 lies between the north front and the lake, contained by hedges of golden yew and coloured with spring- and summer-bedding schemes on a yellow and blue theme. Permanent structure comes from spiky clumps of yucca and short, clipped evergreen domes – not of box, but, interestingly, of an unusual bushy oak, *Quercus phillyraeoides*. Iron railings give an open view across the water down the north avenue into the park, and if you penetrate it, you will find a long line of dogs' graves, beginning with that of a pug, Old Vertue, dated 1702; his portrait, by Knyff, hangs in the house.

Below the east front, there are blowsy borders, planted in dark rich shades to combat the strength of the red brick; they include peonies, dahlias, delphiniums and daylilies, with the grey-bloomed Dusty Miller vine as a backing. Within the house, you come upon a courtyard hung with climbing plants and set around a central fountain.

# Dyrham Park

DYRHAM, BATH, GLOUCESTERSHIRE

AREA 2.4ha (6 acres) within parkland • SOIL alkaline/sand, loam • ALTITUDE 137m (450ft)
AVERAGE RAINFALL 762mm (30in) • AVERAGE WINTER CLIMATE moderate to cold

Neptune, landlocked in Dyrham's deer park, now gestures down at the mansion like a madman. Armed with a trident, he once presided over a spectacular cascade of 224 steps and one of the grandest Dutch-style gardens of the late seventeenth century, extending from both sides of the house, complete with fountains and a canal, and an elaborate and extensive pattern of terraces and parterres, avenues and formal walks. But fashion changed, the cost of upkeep was too great, and the Bath to Gloucester road was improved behind his back. He was left, as it were, high and dry.

It is hard to regret the garden's passing, for the present setting is nothing short of stupendous. From the entrance, you plummet down the Cotswold escarpment and suddenly, between muscular folds of green hillside and splendid beeches, horse chestnuts and cedars, the handsome Baroque house is revealed in the valley. If the sun is drawing out the gold in the Bath stone and illuminating the distant mountains of Wales, so much the better.

The Tudor manor house was transformed into the present mansion by William Blathwayt, Secretary of State to William III, between 1692 and 1704. George London, the most celebrated contemporary designer of formal gardens, was consulted on the landscaping. The garden, though not wholly complete, was already impressing visitors by 1700. At that time, the main entrance was opposite the west front of the house, the carriageway leading from the west gate to the Italianate double stairway adjoining the terrace. The rectangular ponds on the west side were part of the original formal design, fed by water channelled under the stable block.

The long terrace above the church still exists, and the old limes are likely to be those shown in Kip's engraving of 1712. In the park, radiating avenues of elms were also spared, only to succumb, ironically, to Dutch elm disease. They have been replaced mainly with limes by the Trust. Little else remains of the formal garden, which had fallen into disrepair by 1779, after which it was extensively remodelled.

William Blathwayt IV engaged a Bath surveyor, Charles Harcourt-Masters, to 'mark out plantations' and 'dispose and plant trees', and Humphry Repton visited in 1800, contributing for several years and probably rebuilding the niched wall below the ponds. In turning the east garden into a deer park, Blathwayt made a connection with the past, for the name Dyrham is derived from the Saxon *deor hamm*, meaning 'deer enclosure'. The pale-coloured strain of fallow deer that graze the slopes is of great antiquity.

Today, the only detailed horticulture to be found on the east side of the house is pursued inside the Orangery. Built in 1701, this is one of the earliest greenhouses in the country to be given architectural importance, and was used to overwinter the pots of citrus fruits, bay trees and aloes that adorned the formal walks and parterres. Now restored, it reprises this role.

A ten-year restoration plan is now under way on the west side of the house to evoke the garden of the late eighteenth–early nineteenth century. The west terrace has been formalised with the addition of a box and gravel parterre, its pattern taken from one of the other lost parterres shown in Kip's engraving. It is fringed by beds of Dutch bulbs and pots of variegated holly topiaries. The borders in the church court below will gradually be restocked with period plants, the present cast including fine specimens of loquat (*Eriobotrya*) and *Magnolia delavayi*.

The planting that flanks the long axial approach drive is also being formalised with the clipping and shaping of the holm oaks and the insertion of box hedging and topiaries into the present herbaceous borders. Opposite the stables, a pair of *clairvoyées* are also being returned to the low wall overlooking the water gardens.

The garden was subjected to considerable change in the Victorian era, and some of this overlay is being retained, not least in the rockwork fernery uncovered at the head of the west approach drive and around the main pool, where mixed ornamental trees and shrubs are grouped in the company of old mulberries. Trees are one of Dyrham's chief glories, and include numerous North American species such as tulip trees, red oak and black walnut, reflecting the first William Blathwayt's position as administrator of the American Colonies. Many plants were sent from Virginia in 1694. Beyond the cobnut walk, there is also a traditional perry pear orchard, its meadow grasses infiltrated with daffodils, fritillaries and other wildflowers.

**LEFT** The view across the mill pond toward the West front of Dyrham Park.
**RIGHT** Tulips on the West Terrace typify the Dutch-style planting of this garden.

# Emmetts Garden

IDE HILL, SEVENOAKS, KENT

**AREA** 2.4ha (6 acres) • **SOIL** acid/greensand ridge over stone • **ALTITUDE** 198–220m (650–720ft) • **AVERAGE RAINFALL** 889mm (35in) • **AVERAGE WINTER CLIMATE** cold

Emmetts is one of Kent's highest gardens. After the 1987 storm, the views became panoramic: north to the North Downs, east towards Ide Hill village, and south and west over the great sweep of trees that lead towards Crowborough Ridge. Now the native trees have grown up again, though a fine view is preserved south to the Kentish Weald.

The garden is largely the creation of Frederic Lubbock, a banker who bought the property in 1893, but in its design and planting it owes much to the influence and advice of his friend William Robinson, the gardening writer, who lived not far away at Gravetye. Part of the rock garden was illustrated in Robinson's *Alpine Flowers for the Garden* (1903). The only touch of formality is the Italianate rose garden, in which purple 'Cardinal Hume', pink 'Escapade' and white 'Iceberg' roses, Hybrid Musk roses and catmint (*Nepeta*) are arranged around a central fountain pond. Following the discovery of photographic slides taken from before the First World War, swags for Climbing roses have recently been reintroduced, with *Rosa* 'Climbing Cécile Brünner' trained along them. The rock garden, with its cascade, pond and outcrops of Westmorland limestone, has also recently been invigorated with 95 tonnes of Kentish ragstone. This has created a montane scree for the cultivation of a diverse range of unusual alpines.

Otherwise, the garden follows a relaxed pattern of lawns, glades and meandering paths – an informal Edwardian design that evolved in response to a straightforward passion for plants displayed in a natural way, a mood that the Trust is actively fostering. The conditions are not perfect for a collection of trees and shrubs, the soil being light and fast-draining, but thanks to copious quantities of mulch, many Asian species flourish. Among the notable plants in the upper garden are *Eucryphia glutinosa*, showered in white blossom in August, *Magnolia denudata* and the heavily scented summer-flowering *M. × wieseneri*. These are accompanied by generous plantings of azaleas, including the white-flowered *Rhododendron quinquefolium*, while *Nyssa sylvatica*, *Enkianthus perulatus* and seed-raised *Berberis wilsoniae* give a panoply of berry and leaf colour in autumn.

Lower down the slope, across the former drive, the collection takes on the flavour of an arboretum, with individual trees and stands of shrubs displayed in grass. The tall Dawyck beech withstood the 1987 storm, and there are still good examples of *Cercidiphyllum japonicum*, *Davidia involucrata* var. *vilmoriniana* and *Stewartia pseudocamellia*, together with an enormous clump of *Pieris japonica* and a number of good rhododendrons, including *R. ferrugineum* and *R. smirnowii*. In spring, the grass here is patched yellow with daffodils and below the South Garden the path leads off enticingly into bluebell woods.

# Erddig

RHOSTYLLEN, WREXHAM

AREA 5.3ha (13 acres) • SOIL slightly acid/loam and clay • ALTITUDE 61m (200ft)
AVERAGE RAINFALL 889mm (35in) • AVERAGE WINTER CLIMATE moderate

'We call this the State Bedroom,' announced Philip Yorke III as he showed his television audience around Erddig, 'because it is always in such a state.' It is hard for me to maintain a proper perspective on this property, whose wooded park and minnow-filled brook was my childhood playground, and whose squire, frequently seen cycling around Wrexham on his penny-farthing, was the stuff of local legend. The bedroom was not the only part of Erddig to have fallen into disrepair. The garden was all but lost in a jungle of nettles, brambles, overgrown shrubs and seedling sycamores, with sheep as the only gardeners. After what has been described as 'a heroic holding operation', Philip Yorke eventually passed his beloved estate, tenaciously held by his family since 1733 and comprising nearly 809ha (2,000 acres), to the Trust in 1973.

There is no hint today of the monumental task of restoration that was faced in 1973. Spread out before the east front of the hall is a crisp pattern of straight paths and mown grass, avenues of pleached limes, groves of pyramid fruit trees, yews and variegated hollies, lines of Portugal laurels clipped to mimic orange trees in white Versailles tubs and a broad, smooth-edged canal. Remarkably, the bones of the design had been unaltered since the early eighteenth century, and thanks to the bird's-eye view drawn in 1740 by Thomas Badeslade, the Trust was given the opportunity to reconstruct fairly accurately this rare example of a formal garden in the Dutch style.

Fruit trees, marshalled into quincunxes and espaliered on walls, were then especially valued as part of the formal structure. Lists were made in 1718 detailing Erddig's wall fruits, and varieties still in existence have been reintroduced. Apples, now the most numerous wall fruit, were not, in fact, mentioned, suggesting they were grown only as free-standing trees. Today the collection includes some 180 varieties, including 'Nonpareil' and 'Fenouillet Rouge', supplemented by pears such as 'Bon-Chrétien d'Hiver' and 'Windsor', and plums 'Blue Perdrigon' and 'Red Magnum Bonum'.

All these were in cultivation before 1700. An annual apple festival is held here each October.

The borders are strewn with climbing and herbaceous plants, and beneath each fruit tree there are bulbs: in the orchard are strips of pheasant's eye narcissus (*Narcissus poeticus* var. *recurvus*), and in the borders, a number of old varieties of daffodil dating from before the First World War. 'Lord Kitchener', 'Will Scarlett', 'Saint Olaf', and 'Bonfire' are among the many unfamiliar names. The banks of the canal are also colonised by the wild Welsh Lent lily (*Narcissus pseudonarcissus*), followed in summer by thousands of common spotted orchids which were able to gain a foothold during the garden's long period of neglect. It is a fascinating collection.

Fruit trees were not merely decorative; their crops were an important part of the garden's utilitarian function. The pond, north of the canal, would also have been stocked with fish for the table,

ABOVE LEFT The Bluebell Bank in May at Emmetts Garden.
RIGHT A view across the Victorian parterre, with orange crown imperials.

and it seems likely that the strange yew niches beyond were designed for bee skeps and honey production. This same productive theme is evoked by the squadron of plump, egg-laying farmyard ducks waddling across the lawns, and the new border of culinary, medicinal and strewing herbs against the south-facing wall of the former vegetable garden.

Powerfully rooted in the early eighteenth century though they remain, Erddig's formal gardens continued to be embellished by the Yorkes, most notably in the late nineteenth century. The parterre is decorated with mossy, stalagmitic fountains, and the Trust's bedding schemes of cheerful annuals reinforce the Victorian flavour. The adjacent walled rose garden is being developed in the Gardenesque style; it houses, apart from Shrub roses, a large black mulberry (once a single stick in the undergrowth), pampas grass in the lawn, and a silver birch, whose trunk was at one time tapped for sweet sap to be used in wine-making.

The nineteenth-century mood is even stronger in the small Victorian Flower Garden, which was described in detail in the *Journal of Horticulture* of 1909. Here, pink 'Dorothy Perkins' roses and deep violet *Clematis* 'Jackmanii' are strung along swags of rope, around specimens of variegated *Acer negundo* against geometric plantings of Bush roses and annuals. Specimen trees, including a magnificent swamp cypress, date from the mid-1800s. *Taxodium distichum*, at the head of the fish pond, and the avenue of wellingtonias beyond the south wall of the garden also date from this period. Against the shadiest walls is a National Collection of ivy, that plant so popular with the Victorians.

The west front offers a quite different prospect – an abrupt drop into woods and undulating parkland. The landscape was moulded by William Emes, a contemporary of 'Capability' Brown who also worked at nearby Chirk Castle and Powis Castle in the dominant naturalistic style of the late eighteenth century, but the pastoral scene is now interrupted by the looming silhouettes of Hafod and Bersham collieries in the middle distance, binding Erddig firmly to its locality. Emes' most wonderful feature can be seen between trees to the north-west: an extraordinary circular weir, known as the Cup and Saucer, into which the waters of the Black Brook – no longer darkened by passing through coal seams – are flushed; at times of flood, it becomes a whirlpool in the meadow and, to an impressionable child, a vision that stamps itself forever on the mind.

**LEFT** A stone column with gargoyles decorates the garden at Erddig.

# Felbrigg Hall

## CROMER, NORFOLK

**AREA** 2.9ha (7¹/₄ acres) • **SOIL** alkaline/light loam • **ALTITUDE** 61m (200ft)
**AVERAGE RAINFALL** 635mm (25in) • **AVERAGE WINTER CLIMATE** cold

A short walk from the hall, across the donkey paddock, is one of the Trust's best walled kitchen gardens, 1.6ha (4 acres) in size and now returned to a high level of production, conjuring up the luscious atmosphere of a decorative potager in its country house heyday. The south-facing slope is divided into three compartments, with a handsome octagonal dovecote, probably dating from the eighteenth century, crowning the central axis. As they were in the past, the birds are a source of manure and meat, being used in the restaurant to make pigeon and rabbit pie. Borders of herbs fringe this northerly path, accompanied by espalier pears, ancient fig trees, cardoons and grapevines, including 'Madeleine Royale', 'Léon Millot' and the Strawberry Grape, grown on timber obelisks. The pyramid apple trees lined in front of the dovecote are 'Norfolk Royal Russet', one of the many varieties growing here associated with East Anglia; they are flanked by 'Norfolk Beefing'.

A range of produce from onions, carrots, courgettes and marrows to strawberries, asparagus, artichoke and sweet corn is cultivated in the large vegetable plots, intermingled with flowers for both decorative and practical effect, to distract and deter predatory insects and attract beneficial ones. The bright displays include seed-raised annuals such as nasturtiums, marigolds and cosmos and also dahlias and gladioli. Along the east-facing wall, the espaliered fruits, including the dessert pear 'Baronne de Mello', are joined by a ribbon border of dianthus, alliums, ixias and pink lavender. Morello cherries ripen on the north-facing wall, near to a fine old medlar tree.

The long double borders which cross the width of the central section of the garden are a magnificent sight in their rich summer livery that spans oranges, purples, reds and acid greens. Apricot 'African Queen' lilies and red bottlebrush are among the highlights, together with great bushes of grey-leaved, lilac-flowered *Buddleja crispa*. The adventurous and exotic planting in these and other of the walled garden's borders is indicative of the mild maritime influence – the sea is only 3.2km (2 miles) away. Tender *Dasylirion*, looking like a fibre-optic lamp, appears in the garden's gravel beds among sedums, euphorbias and kniphofia, and olive trees have been planted in the lawns of the garden's lowest compartment. The lean-to glasshouses are kept just frost-free to support spiky agaves, aloes, blue plumbago and citrus fruit.

Beyond the dovecote, a new orchard has been planted with fruit trees known to have been grown here in the nineteenth century. This area also holds a National Collection of colchicums, whose goblet flowers appear in early autumn. The uncommon *Colchicum tenorei* has long flourished along the walled garden's central cross-walk, and its presence and obvious liking for the compacted sandy soil prompted the Trust to build up the collection. This now comprises more than 60 varieties in all shades of lilac, mauve, carmine and white, single and double, plain and chequered. *Amaryllis belladonna*, another autumn-flowering bulb, is also long established, producing its pink funnels beneath the apricots and peaches on the central compartment's south-facing wall.

The Walled Garden has always been Felbrigg's main flower garden, but there is a small garden featuring yucca and lavender beside the hall and, on the rising ground below the Great Wood, a Victorian overlay of ornamental trees and shrubs around formal lawns. This pleasure ground was originally set out by William Broderick Thomas, who also landscaped for the future Edward VII at Sandringham, and has recently been renovated and replanted with camellias, rhododendrons, azara, drimys and other interesting plants. Many of the fine trees, including red oaks and wellingtonias, are North American. The centrepiece is the early eighteenth century Orangery. Given its glass roof in the nineteenth century when it became a conservatory, it is filled with old camellias, underplanted with the giant-fronded *Woodwardia* fern.

The hall's Jacobean south front looks onto open parkland receding towards Norwich. William Windham III, the great-great-grandson of the hall's builder, Thomas Windham, was landlord and patron to the young Humphry Repton from the mid-1770s, and it is likely that the Felbrigg landscape was the first sizeable project to which this great designer contributed. The woods and stands of oak, sweet chestnut, beech and sycamore are welcome breaks to the bleak horizontals of the Norfolk countryside, and give vital shelter to the hall and gardens from the bitter North Sea winds. The many trees felled for timber during the First World War were replaced in subsequent decades by Robert Windham Ketton-Cremer, who bequeathed the estate to the Trust; it was he who added the Coronation group of beeches and the Victory V rides to commemorate VE Day. In its turn, the Trust has done much replanting in the wake of the 1987 storm.

# Fountains Abbey and Studley Royal

FOUNTAINS, RIPON, NORTH YORKSHIRE

**AREA** 296ha (731 acres) • **SOIL** alkaline-neutral/limestone, boulder clay • **ALTITUDE** 80–100m (262–328ft) • **AVERAGE RAINFALL** 508mm (20in) • **AVERAGE WINTER CLIMATE** cold

This remarkable landscape garden, in an advanced state of restoration, has become one of the Trust's most popular properties. Nature's gift was a narrow, wooded gorge and the tumbling water of the River Skell. In the early eighteenth century, these features were seized upon and manipulated to create a sinuous garden of formal pools, canals and shady walks, adorned with classical temples, Gothic eye-catchers, grottoes and rustic bridges, and later, annexed as its climax, was the stupendous prospect of the great Cistercian abbey itself, its massive tower surprisingly intact and its ruined walls still standing high and pale against the hanging woods.

Excavated and planted over a period of some 65 years from 1716, the garden unfolds the early chapters in the story of Georgian landscaping, though none of the famous names of landscape gardening were involved here. The designer was its owner John Aislabie, who immersed himself in the project after his expulsion from Parliament for his role, as Chancellor of the Exchequer, in the South Sea Company scandal. After Aislabie's death in 1742, his son William completed the garden by acquiring the abbey. The nucleus of John Aislabie's design, and the oldest section, is the formal water garden, a serene composition of lawn-lapped moon- and crescent-shaped ponds, in which the golden Temple of Piety and statues of Bacchus, Neptune and Endymion are reflected as in a mirror. Beside them, the canal channels the river over a cascade between two fishing pavilions into the lake.

In this spot is most memorably captured the turn from French- and Continental-inspired gardening to the new classical English landscape. The symmetry and order of the water garden is set against the billowing curves of the wooded hillsides, where meandering paths lead you to discover a series of garden buildings and prospects down across the valley. On the west is the Banqueting House, at the head of a coffin-shaped lawn; on the east, the Octagon Tower, Temple of Fame and Anne Boleyn's Seat, from which you obtain that famous surprise view, across the Half Moon Pond and up the river, to Fountains Abbey.

The layers of trees and shrubs on the slopes are full of interest, with the beeches, oaks and limes capped with larch and Scots pine, and underplanted with predominantly native shrubs, with a generous complement of yews to furnish winter colour and permanent frames for views. The area is noted for its limestone flora, with fine displays of primroses, cowslips, common spotted orchid and field scabious.

Below the lake is the sharpest contrast to the formal water garden. Here, William Aislabie indulged in the new taste for the wildest landscapes. Instead of taming this stretch of gorge, he emphasised its plunging contours and exposed rocks by judicious tree planting and a zig-zag series of bridges to highlight the twists of the river. Originally he followed an oriental theme, with pagodas and pavilions, but this was later exchanged for a raw, rustic mood. It is one of the earliest examples of the Picturesque style in England.

A final surprise awaits you if you leave through the deer park at the eastern end of the estate. A sweeping avenue of limes carries your eye in one direction up towards St Mary's church, the Victorian masterpiece by William Burges. Looking the other way, you find, framed in the gateway, the distant towers of Ripon Minster. To have two noble medieval structures on his doorstep was an extraordinary stroke of good fortune for John Aislabie: for his landscape, they are borrowed eye-catchers that few other gardens can match.

**ABOVE** The River Skell, a natural landscape feature of the garden, provided the basis for much of its design.

# Glendurgan

**MAWNAN SMITH, FALMOUTH, CORNWALL**

**AREA** 10ha (25 acres) • **SOIL** acid/sandy loam • **ALTITUDE** 10–70m (33–230ft)
**AVERAGE RAINFALL** 1,016mm (40in) • **AVERAGE WINTER CLIMATE** mild

The woodland gardens of Cornwall's southern coast are a world apart. Glendurgan, wedged between folds of hillside, with grassy, stream-fed banks rolling down to the Helford estuary, has a site as snug as any to be found in this mild corner of Britain. Gales are the main enemy, and as soon as Alfred Fox, a Quaker businessman from Falmouth, bought the property in 1823, he set about erecting shelter belts of native deciduous trees, strengthened with Scots and maritime pines, silver fir, Norway spruce and holm oak. In the three valleys, the early emphasis was on fruit trees – this previous history being evoked in the recent re-creation of a small orchard. However, fruit production began to wane as the possibilities for growing the more flamboyant and tender trees and shrubs were exploited by successive members of this prominent Cornish gardening family and, latterly, by the Trust with the family's continued involvement. As shipping agents, the family were well placed to request seed and plants from abroad, and there was much exchange of material between their own gardens and those of friends.

Rhododendrons luxuriate in the warmth and humidity. *R. arboreum* and the Loderi hybrids create huge domes of scarlet, pink and white, supplemented by the blue of *R. augustinii*, the sulphur of 'Saffron Queen' and the fiery tints of Exbury azaleas. Additional lily fragrance comes from the white-flowered *maddenii* clan, including *R.* 'White Wings' and *R.* 'Fragrantissimum'.

In the Camellia Walk, there is a concentration of camellia blossom from numerous forms of *C. japonica*, including 'Debutante', 'Nobilissima' and 'Adolphe Audusson', complemented by 'Captain Rawes' and other of the more tender variants of the Chinese *C. reticulata*. Elsewhere, drama comes from a stand of white-tiered *Cornus kousa*, a glade of white magnolias and cherries, Chilean fire bushes (*Embothrium*), and a handkerchief tree (*Davidia involucrata*).

Yet in spite of the luxury of such scenes, the flavour of Cornwall is pervasive. There are the views of woods, estuary and fields; the rough paths that saunter gently down the slopes; the open sweeps of meadow that bring light and warmth into the garden, providing a simple backdrop to so many of the exotic displays; and there are the wildflowers. Primroses, violets and native

Lent lilies (*Narcissus pseudonarcissus*) spangle the meadows and woodland fringe in early spring; further on, there are bluebells, campions and naturalised columbines, and, in the damper sites, ragged robin, early purple orchids, and naturalised *Primula prolifera* (syn. *helodoxa*).

Halfway through the tour, having descended into the lower portion of the valley, you take a deeper draught of rural Cornwall by stepping out of the garden altogether. Crossing the old cattle rush, through which the animals were brought to the stream to drink, you find yourself in the hamlet of Durgan, consisting of some 20 cottages clustered around the cove. Refreshed by the sound of the lapping water and the tang of seaweed, you re-enter the garden by the kissing gate up the lane.

As the spring tide of colour ebbs away, a patchwork of greens is left in the valley. Many belong to evergreen plants: *Michelia doltsopa*, *Drimys winteri*, ferny-leaved *Lomatia ferruginea*, bamboos, self-sowing myrtles and *Cornus capitata*, with clotted cream bracts in early summer, are among the broad-leaved cast. Further contrasts of shape and texture come from conifers, including *Cunninghamia konishii* and *C. lanceolata*, *Pinus patula*, *P. bhutanica* and a massive

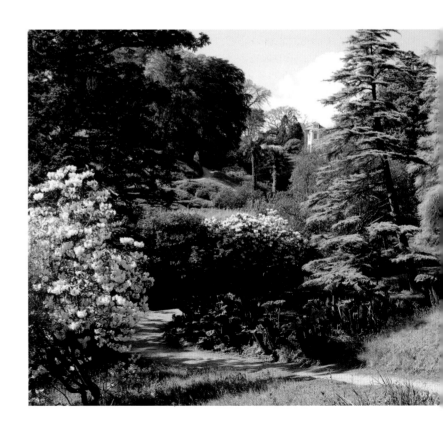

*Thuja plicata*. The collection has been boosted by a gift from the Royal Botanic Garden, Edinburgh, of tender conifer species seldom seen in British gardens, and by other wild-sourced plants. In spring, these are joined by the ephemeral greens of beech, sweet chestnut, oak and a host of other species, among which the two fine tulip trees planted by Fox and the weeping *Taxodium distichum* with its exposed knuckle-shaped roots lodge in my mind.

Following the line of pools and streams down the centre of the valley is some of the most startling greenery of all. On the shallow, well-drained banks near the house, the sight of gigantic, spine-tipped succulents, *Agave americana*, has everyone rubbing their eyes; the flower spikes rise over 6m (20ft). This unreal theme is continued by tall Chusan palms, and, in the deeper, damper ground, by Japanese bananas (*Musa basjoo*), giant-leaved *Gunnera manicata* and self-sowing tree ferns (*Dicksonia* and *Cyathea*). Hydrangeas, eucryphias, hoherias, streamside plantings of pink *Persicaria campanulata* and white *Zantedeschia aethiopica*, and an impressive specimen of *Rhododendron* 'Polar Bear' add summer flower.

Generally, this is a lush valley of woods and meadows with natural plantings and pastoral views, rather than expressions of self-conscious design. However, in the middle of the garden, on the west-facing slope, is an entirely unexpected leap into formal gardening: an asymmetrical cherry laurel maze. It was laid out by Alfred Fox in 1833. The entrance and exit routes are 1.2km (³/₄ mile) in length, and the hedges take two gardeners a full week to prune. The maze underwent a major restoration to mark the centenary of the National Trust in 1995, and the thatched summer-house was reinstated at the centre. The Christian symbolism of mazes may be contemplated on the Holy Bank above, where plants with Biblical associations are assembled, among them tree of heaven (*Ailanthus altissima*), *Colletia paradoxa* (syn. *C. cruciata*) and Judas tree (*Cercis siliquastrum*).

**LEFT** Glendurgan's paths follow the contours of the landscape between towering trees and lush foliage.
**RIGHT** The thatched gazebo in the centre of the laurel maze at Glendurgan.

# Goddards Garden

**YORK, NORTH YORKSHIRE**

AREA 1.2ha (3 acres) • SOIL sandy, silt loam • ALTITUDE 19m (62ft) • AVERAGE RAINFALL 483mm (19in) • AVERAGE WINTER CLIMATE cold

The tower of the old Terry's chocolate factory can still be glimpsed behind the stands of York racecourse, a convenient walking distance from Goddards, which is perched on the hill above. Noel and Kathleen Terry bought this site in the prosperous Dringhouses suburbs – then an open field at the edge of the village – in 1925, and commissioned the leading Yorkshire architect, Walter Brierley, to build their house. It is a homely sprawl of mellow brick and tile in the Arts and Crafts manner, with vernacular rooflines and leaded windows; from the road, you are led to it through a Tudor-style gatehouse and an avenue of pollarded horse chestnuts. Since its acquisition by the Trust in 1984, the house has been used as a regional office.

The series of shallow, formal, flagstone terraces beside the house, incorporating a circular brick basin which feeds rainwater from the roof down into a cruciform lily pond, is likewise a potent Arts and Crafts period piece. It was set out by the Sussex-based landscape architect George Dillistone, who contributed designs here from 1926 and on into the 1930s. Dillistone worked alongside Edwin Lutyens at Castle Drogo and it is possible he was introduced to the Terrys by their mutual friend Edward Hudson, the editor of *Country Life* magazine.

In the Terrys' time, these terraces contained myriad beds of roses and other flowers and a profusion of colours and scents even in the paving, which was studded with alpine plants. The Trust has grassed over and simplified much of this for ease of maintenance, although since 2006, when the decision was taken to open the garden, a programme of improvements has been under way. Today, the top terrace once again sports much the same planting schemes as those devised by Dillistone, who as a former nurseryman was knowledgeable about plants. The cast centres on catmint and the red *Penstemon* 'Newbury Gem', interplanted with bedding such as pink, purple and ivory tulips for spring and annual blue asters and pink lavatera for summer.

The middle terrace, edged in lavender, leads off to a pair of herbaceous borders. There are no records of their original content, but they are being refurbished more or less in the style of Gertrude Jekyll, the leading influence on border design at that period, with the present purple smoke bushes (*Cotinus*) retained as punctuation. Jekyll designed Walter Brierley's own garden, Bishopsbarns, in 1905.

There was clearly much interest in horticulture at Goddards, and at the bottom of the garden there is a substantial greenhouse by W. Richardson & Co. of Darlington, which has recently been restored. As you walk down the hillside, you also come to a bowling green and a grass tennis court, both contained within yew hedges, for this was also a relaxed family garden, intended for recreation. Indeed, Noel Terry liked a fairly wild and natural mood, especially around the formal garden's fringes. From the terraces it is not at all obvious how much garden there is below, and once you start following the winding paths and steps you soon become disorientated. The site is generously planted with trees, the many fine specimens including ginkgo, pine and robinia, and a sycamore that pre-dates the house. In the lower garden, the trees are underplanted with shrubbery beds of mixed evergreen and deciduous species such as mahonia, berberis, viburnum, escallonia and exochorda. The slightly acid soil, which promotes good growth in the conifers, also supports camellias. It is all rather overgrown and mysterious, and so makes an excellent habitat for birds from owls to treecreepers.

The heart of this lower section is the large rock garden, constructed with tonnes of weathered limestone presumed to have come from Malham Tarn, at the foot of the Yorkshire Dales. Rock gardens were in their heyday in the early twentieth century, and the naturalistic treatment of the rock at Goddards accords with that advocated by the most famous rock gardener of the time, the Yorkshire writer and plant hunter Reginald Farrer.

The layered outcrops and sections of pavement are a plausible presence here on the hillside, and over the years have become fused into the surrounding vegetation. They encase two pools, well colonised by rushes and other water plants, and are shaded by substantial junipers, yews and spruces, many of which were no doubt acquired as 'dwarf conifers'. The sudden view out from this tangled and introspective world into the adjoining racecourse is quite a surprise.

# Godolphin

HELSTON, CORNWALL

AREA 1.6ha (4 acres) • SOIL rich, sandy loam • ALTITUDE 65m (213ft) • AVERAGE RAINFALL 787–991mm (31–39in) • AVERAGE WINTER CLIMATE mild

An air of sleepy antiquity pervades this estate, of which the fields, woods and walls harbour the bones of many centuries of human activity, together with one of the very earliest gardens in England. At the summit of Godolphin Hill, with its panoramic views south to St Michael's Mount and north to St Ives Bay, the heathland, pasture and granite outcrops are crowned by a ceremonial stone enclosure thought to date from the Neolithic period; near the river below, the oaks and sycamores shade the legacy of mounds and depressions from the tin and copper mining which from medieval times onwards would bring wealth and status to the Godolphin family and fuel their rise from Cornish gentry to ennobled courtiers.

A winding lane, bordered by woods and mossy, fern-encrusted walls, leads to the house and accompanying farm buildings. The house – low, solid and soberly grand with its castellations and colonnaded loggia – was begun some time in the late fifteenth century and embellished over the following 150 years. It replaced the family's smaller, fortified medieval manor which stood close to the same site, its new garden enclosures overlapping with the old manor's precinct. This opens up an intriguing possibility, for the archaeology appears to suggest that Godolphin's Side Garden, with its compartmented design and raised perimeter walk, may well relate back to the medieval fortified manor which pre-dated the present house, with which it is strangely disconnected and out of alignment. This would provide a unique insight into the very deepest fourteenth-century recesses of English garden history. But any pre-Renaissance garden is a rare and remarkable survivor, and Godolphin's principal enclosures are thought to date from at least before 1520. Verification and exact dating here is invariably problematic, for there is a gaping absence of records, many of which were probably lost in the house fire of 1667.

The garden's survival stems largely from the fact that from the early eighteenth century this was no longer the family's permanent home, and although the grounds were periodically worked on, and the house subsequently tenanted and sold, the property became a quiet backwater, out of the eye of fashion. It was saved from modern development and rescued from disrepair by the Schofield

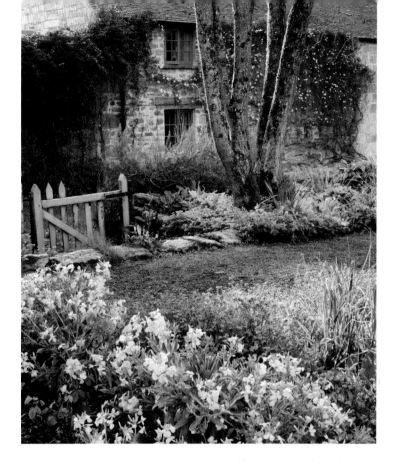

family, who owned it from 1937 to 2007, when it was bought by the National Trust, which already owned the wider Godolphin landscape.

From the road, there is a glimpse down the small straight drive, shaded by evergreen oak and sweet bay, to the entrance forecourt, set out as a turning circle between buttressed walls and with a curious stone column and water basin in the centre of the lawn. Through the colonnade is another simple walled lawn space, forming an inner green court within the wings of the house and the romantic ruins of the Great Hall, demolished in the early nineteenth century. But the visitor route is through the part-cobbled farmyard, and on past the piggery and the chickens scratching in their run.

Here, behind the stable block and below the house's first floor state apartment, is the high-walled privy (private) garden, later called the King's Garden to commemorate a visit in 1646 by the future Charles II on his escape to France via the Scilly Isles, of which Sir Francis Godolphin was Governor. Today, it presents a quartered design with four pads of lawn, edged in stones and set among straight gravel paths. While the walled framework is early sixteenth century, the raised terrace walks that would probably have

**ABOVE LEFT** The terraces in front of the Goddards House.
**ABOVE** Forget-me-nots and scented white stock by the path east of the house.

been here have long since disappeared, for in about 1800 the garden was filled in with soil and used for vegetable growing.

Gnarled and knobbly box bushes run down the central pathway, and they are joined by more recent additions including a run of old lavenders (among which ferns have naturalised, as they invariably do in Cornwall), *Magnolia × soulangeana*, and a border of herbs – which on sunny days infuse this sheltered space with warm aromas – and of other nectar-rich plants, for the stable wall has cavities for bee skeps.

On the other side of the entrance forecourt, you are led through the orchard, with its cider house dating from around 1700 and backdrop of old chestnut trees; this is now being replanted with fruit varieties associated with south-west England. The raised perimeter walk of the adjacent Side Garden, with its retaining earth walls faced with stone and rubble, gives views into this area. The walk is shaded by lines of wonderful veteran sycamores, which were introduced into Britain in the sixteenth century and widely planted at Godolphin. They are interspersed with wild holly in a medley of wildflowers, including primroses, polypody ferns and bluebells, the last of which also flood through the woods.

The estate map of 1786 shows the Side Garden and Garden Paddock, contained within hedges and raised walks and subdivided into nine square or rectangular compartments, each quite large and further subdivided by formal plantings and pathways. It has been

suggested that the surviving framework of the compartments in the Side Garden could represent the eastern side of a nine-compartment enclosure around the earlier house. The additional six compartments of the Garden Paddock were developed on a new site extending into former fields, probably after the house was rebuilt on a new alignment from the late fifteenth century. It was fashionable for early gardens, such as Lord Burghley's Great Garden at Theobolds in Hertfordshire, to have this nine-compartment design. Some of Godolphin's compartments were functional but others would no doubt have been decorative, perhaps incorporating pleached arbours, topiaries, knot gardens and heraldic or symbolic decoration, all conveying the high social status of the family.

The six newer compartments then disappeared back into the field in the nineteenth century – their outlines still visible in the mown strips cut into the garden paddock – while the remaining three compartments closest to the house appear to have survived both the fifteenth- and nineteenth-century phases of destruction. They could, in fact, date as far back as 1300, though they now have many later overlays of planting, including that carried out by the Schofields.

Throughout, their topography is varied by terraces and banks. The northern compartment comprises lawns contained by relaxed borders of shrubs, herbaceous plants and accompanying trees, including some large sentinel yews. The run of tall box hedging which forms one of its subdivisions may be very old indeed. The central compartment has fruit trees and, in its lower section, a kitchen garden interspersed with old Shrub roses, while the southern compartment, the most historically evocative, is taken up by the ancient depressions of two large rectangular fish ponds which would have produced a good supply of food for the household.

The task of repairing Godolphin and returning some of its lost features without disturbing the bewitching atmosphere of antiquity and quiet decay is the challenge faced by the Trust. The temptation to over-restore and over-tidy is being resisted, for much of the charm comes from the weed-bedecked cobblestones and crumbling, ivy-topped grey walls, which are home to an exceptional diversity of rare lichens. With the King's Garden and Side Garden listed as ancient monuments by English Heritage, even routine gardening requires careful deliberation. Meanwhile, continuing research and archaeology should provide a stronger factual basis for our conjectures about the ancient origins of this remarkable place.

**LEFT** Godolphin's compartmented design and raised walk are thought to be relics of a medieval layout.

# Greenway

**GALMPTON, BRIXHAM, DEVON**

---

**AREA** 12ha (30 acres) • **SOIL** neutral/shillet • **ALTITUDE** 30m (100ft)
**AVERAGE RAINFALL** 991mm (39in) • **AVERAGE WINTER CLIMATE** mild

Legend has it that the stone wall of the overgrown camellia glade which you meet amid the maze of woodland paths above the river at Greenway was built by Spanish prisoners of war from the Armada of 1588. Greenway was then owned by John Gilbert, half-brother of Sir Walter Raleigh, and a member of the seafaring family of Compton Castle. Such layers of history romanticise a property already charged with the heady atmosphere of a 'lost' garden, cut off from the modern world inside a large estate, on its own private wooded promontory over the Dart, and with its design overwhelmed by the luxuriance of a mild, humid climate.

'An ideal house, a dream house,' wrote the crime writer Agatha Christie, who bought Greenway as a holiday home in 1938 and featured it in two of her novels, *Dead Man's Folly* and *Five Little Pigs*. The Elton family, who owned Greenway until 1832, seem to be responsible for much of the framework of the present garden – the sweeping curves and picturesque views, decorative outbuildings and enclosed flower gardens. Although the style reflects that of Humphry Repton, the designer is not known. Following the Eltons came a series of plantsmen owners, including Agatha Christie's son-in-law Anthony Hicks, who described the garden as 'on the verge of going wild'. Today the impression is of a jungle of exotics and rarities rather than of carefully composed scenes.

Down the long, winding entrance drive, the hanging beech woods and fields of Devon Red cattle soon give way to the first exotics, set around grassy dips and knolls of ferns and wildflowers: Chusan palms, handkerchief trees (*Davidia involucrata*), cedars and large-leaved oaks alternating with eucryphias, variegated osmanthus, a large *Michelia doltsopa* (a tender magnolia-like tree with sweetly scented, cream flowers), and a host of rhododendrons and azaleas.

This eclecticism sets the tone for the enclosed gardens above the former stone barn and stable block. On one side of the drive a doorway leads into an old tennis court, overhung with *Rhododendron arboreum*, Judas tree, another handkerchief tree, and a pink-flowered *Magnolia campbellii*. On the other, a giant Chinese wisteria lures you into a large kitchen garden, its walls buried behind the most esoteric planting imaginable. The longer history of plantsmanship is signalled by the presence of the vinery on the north wall, where tropical stove plants would have been nurtured in Victorian times. Now fully restored, it houses passionflowers, ginger lilies and tender tree ferns, as well as grapevines.

The Victorian influence intensifies in the garden beyond, where a cast-iron Coalbrookdale fountain splashes onto a rockery backdrop of limestone and quartz, interplanted with giant-fronded *Woodwardia* and other ferns. It connects to another period piece, the Putting Green, a clock-golf course installed in the 1940s, fringed by white-flowered Judas tree (*Cercis siliquastrum*), smooth-barked *Cornus kousa*, and a bed of assorted dahlias, planted by Agatha Christie and not lifted since.

Next, the garden dissolves into woodland again, the paths leading you on a leisurely traverse of the steep riverbank at several parallel levels, each joined to the next by steps or serpentine passageways. It is easy to get lost. The upper Plantation takes you past pines and southern beeches (*Nothofagus*), yew-like *Podocarpus* and its relative *Dacrydium*, and old plantings of camellias, rhododendrons and red-lanterned *Crinodendron hookerianum*. From *Michelia yunnanensis* to *Azara uruguayensis*, it is full of delights and curiosities.

On the next level are tree magnolias and foxglove trees (*Paulownia*), a giant monkey puzzle and a huge Californian black oak (*Quercus kelloggii*). The far end of this path is the warmest part of the site, and a brick wall surviving from the Victorian era shelters a border of herbaceous exotics. At the opposite end of the path is a balancing piece of formality, in the form of a box-edged walk, planted with hydrangeas and scented white *Rhododendron maddenii*.

Spring-flowering, carmine-pink *Cyclamen repandum* has colonised here among the grass and primroses and around a modern sculpture, *Mother and Child* by local artist Bridget McCrumm. Nearby, bluebells surge in their thousands under the trees. This next path leads past coniferous *Cryptomeria*, *Cornus capitata*, *Magnolia virginiana* and white-flowered *Rehderodendron macrocarpum*, under a sunny slope of acacia and eucalyptus, and on to a pair of pools. In Victorian times, there was a more extensive water garden here, but most of it is now engulfed in vegetation.

Here and there along the circuit, between the tree trunks, you get glimpses of the River Dart, its yachts and river boats, wooded banks and settlements – Dittisham across the water, and Kingswear and Dartmouth 1.6km (1 mile) or so downstream. The paths now take you right to the river's edge, first to a late eighteenth-century Boat House, complete with plunge pool, and then to the Battery, with its castellations and canons. The picturesque route takes you home along a path edged in cherry laurel, past sweet chestnut, cork oak and, of course, ever more trees and shrubs to confound the most expert botanist.

**ABOVE** The Fernery at Greenway, with creeping saxifrage and bergenia.
**ABOVE RIGHT** Lavender lines a stone-flagged path leading to the walled Kitchen Garden at Greys Court.

# Greys Court

**ROTHERFIELD GREYS, HENLEY-ON-THAMES, OXFORDSHIRE**

**AREA** 1.2ha (3 acres) • **SOIL** limy • **ALTITUDE** 76m (250ft) • **AVERAGE RAINFALL** 686mm (27in) • **AVERAGE WINTER CLIMATE** moderate

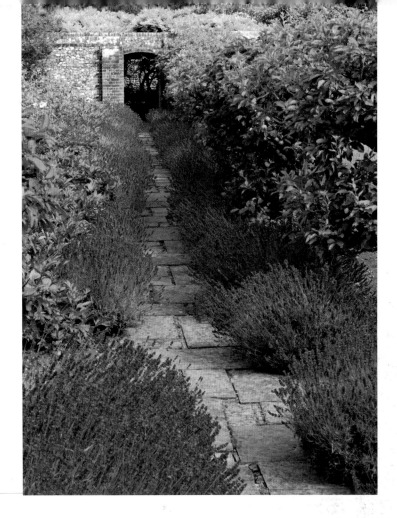

This garden has an almost mystical atmosphere. Cut off from the outside world by folds of Chiltern downland and hills capped with beechwoods, the gabled Elizabethan house and its accompanying medieval towers present their own reality. To this has been added the sensitive touch of Sir Felix and Lady Brunner, who bought the property in 1937. The result is a blend of ancient flint walls, dappled walks, fountains, scents and mellow colours which engulfs the senses. The house stands on the western edge of the fourteenth-century courtyard, surveying the Great Tower and its adjoining ruined walls across an expanse of lawn. Scots pines add their craggy shapes to the scene, and north of the house a venerable European larch rests its branches on the grass.

On both sides of the house the grass merges quietly with the park, assisted by the encircling ha-ha, but to the north the view is partly interrupted by a grove of strawberry trees, planted on the bank at the suggestion of the Brunners' friend Humphrey Waterfield, a painter and gardener. The Killarney strawberry tree, *Arbutus unedo*, carries bountiful crops of white pitcher-shaped flowers and red fruits simultaneously in late summer and autumn, while *A. × andrachnoides* contributes peeling branches of cinnamon and chestnut-red.

Slip through the gateway beneath the Great Tower, past the warm aromas of sun-loving Mediterranean cistuses and rosemaries growing in the rubble, and you find yourself surrounded by white flowers and grey foliage, in the first of a disorienting series of irregular-shaped enclosures. A new loggia in the White Garden, built in 2002, houses pots of citrus fruits, and by the entrance are two impressive Japanese bitter orange, *Poncirus trifoliata*, flaunting vicious spines. In spring, they bear fragrant white flowers. Later, there are heady scents from roses, honeysuckles and the pineapple-flavoured *Philadelphus microphyllus*.

The rosarian Hilda Murrell advised the Brunners on the planting of the Rose Garden, which is reached through the next gateway. Here, the lawn is shaded by a spreading foxglove tree, *Paulownia tomentosa*, and at midsummer the central beds are awash with old-fashioned roses. The surrounding borders are planted with herbaceous plants in colour schemes of pink and purple, yellow and orange.

The principle that if a plant is worth growing, it is worth having a decent show of it is followed happily at Greys Court. In the Wisteria Arbour, which connects the Rose Garden to the Kitchen Garden, there is a display of *Wisteria sinensis* such as you will never have seen. You duck right under it, weaving between the gnarled and part-rotten stems, under an enormous canopy of twisted branches and, in spring, dripping flowers. The gardeners refer to it as 'The Beast'. The Kitchen Garden is designed as a matrix of straight paths infilled with fruit trees, bushes and espaliers, as well as vegetables and unusual salad crops. Companion plantings of flowers and herbs among the beans and asparagus peas, gourds and pumpkins, make a lively display, and in front of the plums and greengages there is a long cut-flower border of cornflowers and other country favourites. A hedge of striped 'Rosa Mundi' (*R. gallica* 'Versicolor'), an avenue of 'Ballerina' crab apples, a sumptuous peony border, and a circle of fastigiate Irish junipers, with philadelphus, box, myrtle and lavender, arranged around a Roman-style fountain, complete the scene.

Equally striking is the tunnel of pink and white blossom in the adjacent Cherry Garden, through which a rustic path of stone and cobbles curves enticingly past another fountain, found on a farm in Switzerland and installed to mark the Brunners' 40th wedding anniversary. This grove, recently replanted, was another of Humphrey Waterfield's inspirations, and, like the other cherry highlights, comes into its own again in autumn when the leaves turn orange and russet. A soaring tulip tree (*Liriodendron tulipifera*) and ancient weeping ash over the wall enhance this scene, and provide part of the backdrop for the little knot garden, redesigned by the Trust, beside the Cromwellian stables; the building was reputedly commandeered by soldiers during the Civil War.

The garden has not been anchored in any single historical period, and modern additions have been welcomed. Furniture, fountains, ironwork and statuary have all been commissioned from contemporary local artists, and in 1980, inspired by the enthronement sermon of the Archbishop of Canterbury, in which Dr Robert Runcie drew an analogy between people searching for life's secret and being lost in a maze, Lady Brunner conceived the idea of a pavement maze at Greys Court. It was realised in brick and grass by Adrian Fisher, and, with its wealth of Christian symbolism and allegory, adds yet another contemplative layer to a timeless and tranquil garden.

**BELOW** Looking past a hedge of roses to the fourteenth-century Great Tower.
**RIGHT** The kitchen garden at Ham House is being restored to the 1671 plan and grows produce for the restaurant.

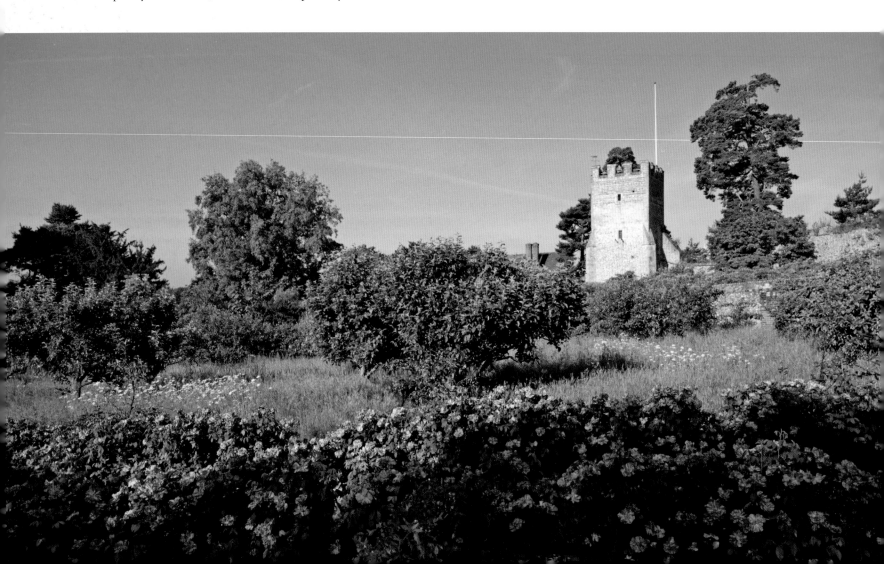

# Ham House and Garden

HAM, RICHMOND, LONDON

AREA 7.3ha (18 acres) • SOIL lime-free/sandy • ALTITUDE 15m (50ft)
AVERAGE RAINFALL 635mm (25in) • AVERAGE WINTER CLIMATE cold

'To see the House and Garden of the Duke of Lauderdale, which is indeed inferior to a few of the best Villas in Italy itself; the House furnished like a great Prince's; the Parterres, Flower Gardens, Orangeries, Groves, Avenues, Courts, Statues, Perspectives, Fountains, Aviaries, & all this at the banks of the Sweetest River in the World, must needs be surprising,' wrote the diarist John Evelyn, after walking to Ham on a summer's evening in 1678.

What strikes the visitor as most remarkable today is that so much of it is still here, little ruffled by centuries of change and the burgeoning of London. Its avenues of trees still stretch out towards Ham Common and the Thames – the most convenient means of getting to the City in the seventeenth century. The house itself is still almost exactly as it looked in the 1670s when it was enlarged: a tall, compact building of reddish-brown Jacobean brick dressed in white stone, and its rooms still with their original furnishings. Even better, the architectural bones of the formal seventeenth-century garden have also survived, making this one of the earliest and rarest garden layouts in the Trust's hands. The inspiration at the time came from the Baroque gardens of Europe, and Ham's style is a simple form of the typical Dutch garden, referred to by contemporaries as the New Mode. Sadly, the identity of the designer is unclear.

The clipped greens and statuary of the entrance forecourt set the mood. The topiary planted by the Trust comes as hefty drums of bay and, against the flanking walls, cones of yew and bedding squares of box. All these are kept sharp-edged and tight, the dark colours contrasting with the central oval of closely mown lawn, in which the large frame of a River God reclines. Thirty-eight busts, representing Charles I and II and Roman emperors and their wives, look over the scene from niches in the house and garden walls. Originally the court was completely enclosed, with a straight path leading to the front door, but alterations were carried out at the end of the eighteenth century and now the park is separated only by an ironwork screen and a ha-ha.

The adjacent East Garden, redesigned by the Trust after a plan of 1671, is the most intimate part of the composition. Fruit was integral to the formal Dutch garden, and the cherries may have been either trained *in situ* or grown in containers. Now the garden is purely ornamental, with the central diamond-pattern box parterre – filled with Dutch lavender and dwarf cotton lavender, clipped as silver knots within an embroidery – held in a *berceau*, or cradle, of hornbeam tunnels. It is a simple but striking treatment. Likewise, figs, vines and other espaliered fruits adorn the walls of the main enclosure, part of the green, expansive scene surveyed from the broad gravel terrace. In the foreground are the plats – eight large squares of close-mown grass, separated by paths – which were remade out of the existing lawn in 1975. Beyond, an avenue of limes carries the eye past the garden gates, deep into Ham Common.

Occupying the middle ground is the Wilderness, a fashionable contemporary adjunct to the formal garden offering a taste of mystery and solitude. The Trust has reimposed its geometric pattern with hedges of hornbeam, speared by field maples, and the grass paths once again radiate, as in the 1671 plan, in a *patte d'oie* (or, more recognisably, a Union Flag design) from a central circle. Each compartment is planted as a thicket of deciduous and evergreen trees and shrubs – with scented plants next to the grass paths – and lead statues have been commissioned as centrepieces, as illustrated in the painting attributed to Henry Danckerts which hangs in the house. The narrow borders around the garden are planted in seventeenth-century style, with rows of plants in front of wall-trained fruit trees. The Vine Border, directly below the South Terrace, has recently been replanted with old-fashioned pinks (*Dianthus*) and columbines.

In 2003 work began on the furthest compartment, in front of the Orangery, reached through an avenue of evergreen oak, *Quercus ilex*. The 1671 plan shows this as the kitchen garden, divided into 32 plots, and as the restoration advances, these are being filled with an assortment of fruits, vegetables, herbs, roses and flowers for cutting, displayed within box hedges. Peaches, plums, apricots and cherries are trained as espaliers and fans on the walls. The Orangery itself, built in 1674 and one of the oldest to survive in Britain, is draped in eleven wisterias and overlooks a terrace furnished with olive trees and citrus fruits in wooden planters.

**LEFT** The East Garden, with its box-hedged compartments filled with santolina and lavender, after a design of 1671.
**ABOVE** The south-facing terrace below the house is coloured by the Vine Border.

# Hanbury Hall

DROITWICH, WORCESTERSHIRE

AREA 8ha (20 acres) • SOIL neutral/clay • ALTITUDE 66m (216ft) • AVERAGE RAINFALL 635mm (25in) • AVERAGE WINTER CLIMATE moderate

Before 1993, you would have found this decorative William and Mary squire's house, built in red brick, with hipped roof, cupola and pavilions, somewhat stranded in well-treed but flat parkland. Now, one of the rarest and most curious forms of English garden has sprung up beside it – a flower parterre, topiary fruit garden and formal Wilderness in the style of 1700.

The restoration, financed by two generous private legacies and a heritage award from the EU, is based on the scheme installed by the celebrated lawyer Thomas Vernon to accompany his remodelled mansion. The designer appears to have been the leading garden advisor of the day, George London, since the plans are endorsed 'Mr London's Draughts'. This is exciting, for London's elaborate, labour-intensive gardens were immediate victims of the abrupt swing in eighteenth-century taste in favour of naturalistic landscapes, and not one has survived to the present day. At Hanbury, this destruction happened in the 1770s. No one knows if Lancelot 'Capability' Brown himself was the vandal responsible, but since his portrait was hanging in the house at the time of the 1790 sale, it seems likely.

In the Victorian era, formality was back in fashion and the small forecourt beside the south front of the house was remade, even using copies of the original ironwork gates, which had been sold in 1790 to the owners of nearby Mere Hall. Had its creator, another Thomas Vernon, not died at the age of 27, he might well have set to work re-creating a parterre on the lawn to the west. As it is, this was left to the National Trust. Other than a dip in the lawn not a trace remained, so the starting point was the existing plans and illustrations, especially the bird's-eye drawing of 1732 by James Dougharty. The exact layout was then established by archaeology. There are some peculiarities: the garden is not properly aligned with the house; the sunken parterre is not a true square; and the twin pavilions at the northern end are not at right angles to the garden.

Equally odd, to modern British eyes, is the arrangement of plants. In the Sunken Parterre, you look down on four giant grids of green and gold-tipped box, each with a large central topiary, and punctuated with further cones of box and corner-posts of golden-variegated hollies, topped with golden balls. Inserted into this pattern is a colourful array of annuals and perennials, drawn from lists used by the royal gardener Henry Wise, with whom London ran the celebrated Brompton Nursery, and from information found in *The Retir'd Gardener*, the French work translated by London and Wise in 1706. Each plant is set out in strictly regimented rows, separated by bare earth: French, African and English marigolds, London pride, pasqueflower, snapdragons, carnations, armeria, *Aster amellus* and of course Brompton stocks, with no attempt at a unified scheme of colour or form. This highly formalised composition reveals the mastery over nature that was the essence of the prevailing French- and Dutch-inspired fashion. A ribbon border of bulbs, running along the yew hedges above the parterre, contributes spring colour.

On axis with the Sunken Parterre is a decorative fruit garden, featuring 'Black Worcester' pears and 'Ribston Pippin', 'Golden Pippin' and 'Ashmead's Kernel' apples in the grass, framed by box-edged lavender beds and topiary bay trees. A re-created pair of trellis timber 'green houses' flank the iron railings of a *clairvoyée*, through which you have a view down over a mirror pond into the park beyond.

There is no relaxation of formality in the adjacent Wilderness, where Damask, Gallica and wild roses, philadelphus, hazel, hibiscus, phillyrea, rhamnus, ruscus and Italian cypress are marshalled into lines and rigorously pruned. Their arbitrary arrangement within the goose-foot pattern, however, gave the desired taste of wild disorder to the eighteenth-century visitor. Behind, great blocks of clipped beech enclose a circular pool – a survivor from the London garden.

More recently reinstated are the Bowling Green, with another new pair of garden pavilions and the Grove. This combines order and disorder within an oval pattern of box and upright English juniper, its compartments comprising a mix of rowan and service tree, guelder rose and the elm *Ulmus* 'Dodoens'.

The pots of lemons in the formal gardens come from a handsome brick Orangery west of the Bowling Green, probably built some 25 years after Thomas Vernon's death in 1721. An assortment of oranges, lemons, pomegranates, agaves and oleanders are displayed outside in summer, while clipped cones of evergreen *Phillyrea angustifolia* stand all year round between the high windows.

Tucked into the adjacent spinney is a mushroom house, now back in production. Like the nearby apple and pear orchard, this was a Victorian addition to the eighteenth-century walled kitchen garden, which is reached along a primrose walk, a straight ride between yew and holly. Other formal elements to survive are an oak avenue and a cedar walk, the latter dating from London's garden, and leading to an exceptionally fine eighteenth-century ice-house.

# Hardwick Hall

**DOE LEA, CHESTERFIELD, DERBYSHIRE**

AREA 7ha (17<sup>1</sup>/2 acres) • SOIL alkaline/light sandy loam • ALTITUDE 178m (584ft)
AVERAGE RAINFALL 660mm (26in) • AVERAGE WINTER CLIMATE cold

'A woman of masculine understanding and conduct, proud, furious, selfish and unfeeling. She was a builder, a buyer and seller of estates, a moneylender, a farmer and a merchant of coals and timber; when disengaged from those employments, she intrigued alternately with Elizabeth [Tudor] and Mary [Stuart], always to the prejudice and terror of her husband.' So wrote Edmund Lodge in 1790, describing Bess (Elizabeth) of Hardwick, Countess of Shrewsbury. It was she who, in the 1590s, built this awe-inspiring house; the initials ES, carved above the high, square towers and topped by a coronet, proclaim her name and status across the estate.

The Old Hall, now a ruin, was once her childhood home and she had it extensively rebuilt in about 1585; but on the death of her fourth husband, Lord Shrewsbury, Bess had control of her fabulous wealth and embarked on a second, grander residence a short distance away. There have been gardens around the New Hall since its completion, and the courts we see today, with their decorative gateways and garden houses, finial-capped walls and banqueting house, were set out at that time. However, the smart hedges and colourful plantings within them date from the last two centuries.

Colour is concentrated in the surrounding borders, which the Trust redesigned in the mid-1980s, basing the planting on a Jekyllian

sequence of lively harmonies. Variegated aralias, flowering grasses and cimicifugas furnish creamy highlights, while crocosmias, penstemons, argyranthemums, dahlias, heuchera and cotinus progress through the hottest shades, and sedums, verbenas, asters and buddleja through the warm reds and purples. There is a generous complement of half-hardy perennials which alone are worth a trip to Hardwick in late summer.

Along the other side of the south wall is a border of cooler, pastel colours. Clematis, vines and roses cloak the walls, accompanied by hardy perennials such as euphorbias, asters and campanulas and half-hardy plants such as salvias, osteospermums and gazanias for later in the season. This border is part of the South Court, which covers an area of 3ha (7<sup>1</sup>/2 acres) and was laid out in its present pattern of four quarters, divided by *allées* of hornbeam and yew, by Lady Louisa Egerton, daughter of the 7th Duke of Devonshire, in 1861. The Devonshires are direct descendants of Bess, and the fact that Hardwick has changed so little over the centuries is due in large part to its being owned by a family whose principal seat was elsewhere, at Chatsworth. At one time, this entire court was given over to fruit and, probably, vegetable production. Today two of the quarters are orchards replanted by the Trust, and in the third, *Magnolia* × *soulangeana* and other specimen trees grow in the grass.

The fourth quarter contains one of the largest herb gardens in Britain, accompanied by a nuttery. Installed by the Trust in the mid-1970s, this has recently been redesigned to incorporate a box 'snake' and taller, pyramidal plantings in the centre. Wigwams of golden and green hops echo the gilded posts that were a favoured ornament in Elizabethan gardens. The great array of culinary and medicinal plants on show here would all have been familiar to gardeners of the time, and in constant demand for the house.

The scale and crispness of this court can be appreciated fully from the upper landing of the house, where you can see it set against a broad backdrop of Turkey and pedunculate oaks, limes, sycamores, estate buildings and farmland. From the adjacent long gallery, there is a fine view over the East Court, with its lawn, roses and central pond, across the ha-ha, and down the lime avenue, planted in the 1920s. The limes curve to embrace the field opposite the house, giving the effect of an upturned wine glass with an 800m (<sup>1</sup>/2 mile) stem.

Among the many fine tapestries in the house is a series of 32 octagonal panels embroidered with botanical subjects, with accompanying aphorisms – a further reminder of the delight the Elizabethans took in flowers and another happy link between house and garden. Many carry Bess's monogram. The initials ES are likely to haunt you long after you have departed this extraordinary place.

# Hidcote Manor

HIDCOTE BARTRIM, CHIPPING CAMPDEN, GLOUCESTERSHIRE

AREA 4ha (10 acres) • SOIL alkaline • ALTITUDE 183m (600ft) • AVERAGE RAINFALL 635mm (25in) • AVERAGE WINTER CLIMATE cold

An encounter with England's most influential twentieth-century garden begins softly. The high, twisting lanes of the Cotswold countryside lead into a courtyard only slightly more distinguished than those accompanying the other large houses that pepper the hilltops. It takes an eagle-eyed plantsman to notice that the sober plantings against the golden walls are a little out of the ordinary – *Schizophragma hydrangeoides*, *Magnolia delavayi*, *Schisandra rubriflora* and *Mahonia lomariifolia* are among the cast.

In a recent change of the visitor route, you now enter the garden through the house, emerging through the door into the tiny front garden, decorated with variegated shrubs and bedding plants. Immediately, your eye is carried across the farm lane down an avenue of lime trees; at its head is a statue of Hercules, cleverly illuminated by the gap left in the tree line for the afternoon sun to penetrate. This juxtaposing of grandeur with Cotswolds vernacular is typical Hidcote.

Then, walking beyond the corner of the house and the old cedar of Lebanon shading the lawn, you turn to find another exciting vista is upon you. This one, far more varied and colourful, runs down the heart of the whole garden, through half a dozen different spaces. Hidcote is now revealed as a patchwork of passages, open spaces and flower-filled enclosures, a network of private gardens each gaining impact from the garden before it, with changes in scale, design, colour and atmosphere at each turn.

Within the walled garden by the house there is a tiny White Garden, surveyed by a thatched cottage, animated by topiary doves, filled with 'Gruss an Aachen' roses in a wash of dianthus, phlox and other plants, and contained by yew hedges dripping in early summer with blood-red flame flower. There is also a garden of Japanese maples, a corridor of acid-loving plants such as meconopsis and rhododendrons growing in imported Somerset peat, and, either side of grass walkways, a series of large mixed borders stuffed with the pink, purple, white, blue and magenta colours of tulips, geraniums, peonies, campanulas, roses, deutzias, salvias and dahlias.

Slightly giddy from all this intensive plantsmanship, you step out into the Circle, an enclosure so intimate in size that there is scarcely room to pass the other visitors, but with the refresher of a

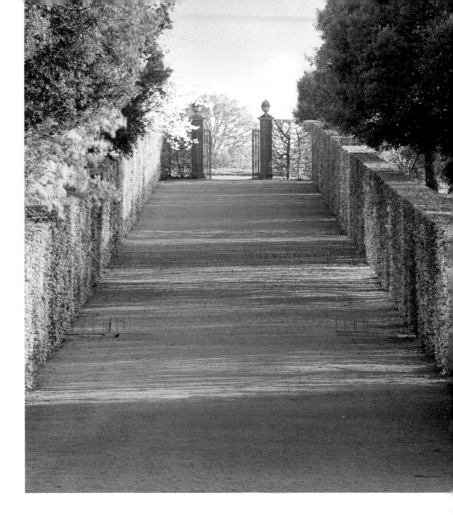

roundel of lawn, surrounded by lilacs and other cool-coloured shrubs, and beyond, the crisp symmetry of the grass vista between the Red Borders. Turn right, and in a great *coup de théâtre* the world expands; the Theatre Lawn is revealed. It is vast, incomparably bigger than you would expect in such a garden. Rather – with its immaculate sward, crisp surround of dark yew, and elevated stage containing a solitary beech tree – it seems to have strayed from an early eighteenth-century landscape park.

Turn left from the Circle, and you find yourself in a succession of green gardens: a brick parterre; a dark garden filled with a huge, circular stone basin; and then a small, empty circle of lawn. Rough, meandering paths lead on into the Stream Garden, a large, loose, shady area of ditches and spinneys. Here, the sticky banks and gulleys are furnished with fat clumps of leafy perennials, including comfreys, darmera, *Rodgersia pinnata* 'Superba' –

LEFT View across red valerian and golden hop to the south front of the New Hall at Hardwick.
ABOVE View down the Long Walk, designed to lead the eye into the landscape.

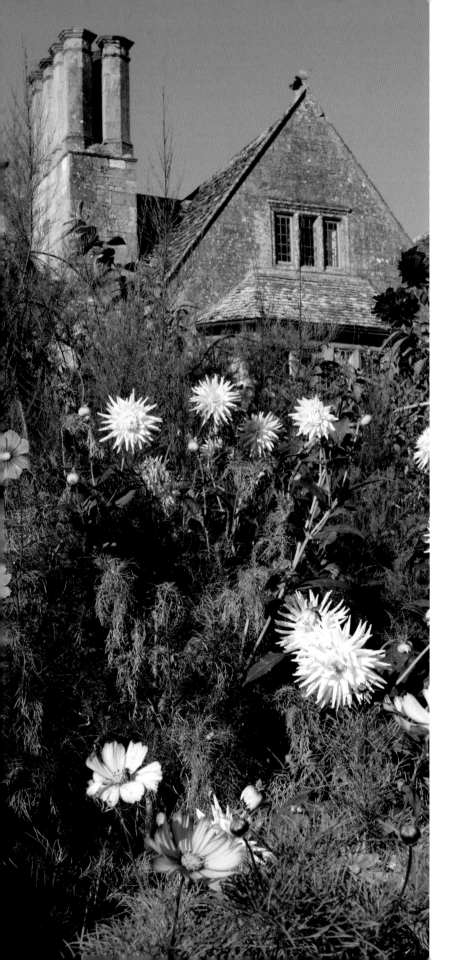

splendidly partnered with blue-leaved hostas – and colonies of *Lysichiton americanus*, which illuminate the garden in spring with yellow, sour-smelling flares. These grow among a choice collection of trees and shrubs, including magnolias, hydrangeas, daphnes and *Osmanthus yunnanensis*.

Now, another *coup de théâtre*. From the wooded wilderness, you step directly into the grand, open sweep of the Long Walk. Really, it needs to be viewed from the gazebo above to savour the full drama of the plunging and ascending hornbeam hedges, but from this intermediate point the climb to the empty horizon is thrilling enough. And so the garden goes on, varied and enticing, through 4ha (10 acres) of compartments. Hidcote's linear patterns recall earlier, Continental styles of gardening. The Theatre Lawn, Fuchsia Garden and Bathing Pool Garden are part of this, as are the pillars of yew in the Pillar Garden, the umbrellas of Portugal laurel in the Pine Garden, the avenue of Irish yews in the Old Rose Walk, and, famously, the stilt hedges of hornbeam, or *palissades à l'Italienne*, which flank the last section of the main east-west axis. The abundance of evergreen oaks also add to the Continental flavour.

It was an American-born Englishman, brought up in France, who had the vision to pull these disparate threads together. When Lawrence Johnston and his mother, Mrs Winthrop, came to live at Hidcote in 1907, the present garden was exposed farmland. It does not appear that Johnston ever had a master plan; rather, land for the garden was snatched piecemeal from the farm over a number of years. The design draws on many contemporary themes, but he moulded and fused them together with triumphant originality. The sequence of terraces, lawns and flower gardens seen in larger country houses he reduced to a chain of intimate rooms; Gertrude Jekyll's art of arranging plants with one eye on nature and the other on associations of texture, form and colour he carried to new levels of romantic informality, with shrubs, climbers, self-sowing perennials and bulbs spilling into one another in carefree style. He owed a large debt to his close friend Norah Lindsay, a gifted gardener who designed and planted with great panache.

Plants at Hidcote are assembled principally by colour, texture and flowering season. Mrs Winthrop's Garden blends acid green euphorbias, glaucous-leaved thalictrum, blue salvias and copper cordyline, while in high summer the Red Borders swelter with dahlias, verbenas, red salvias and Floribunda roses, supplemented by the sombre leaves of purple berberis, heuchera, plum and sloe.

Vita Sackville-West believed Johnston would want to be remembered principally as a botanist and plant-hunter, and at heart

Hidcote is, of course, a plantsman's garden. The plant collection is huge; at every turn there are choice and rare subjects, and the garden offers the maximum diversity of planting sites. Johnston participated in two notable plant-hunting expeditions: to China with George Forrest, and to South Africa with 'Cherry' Ingram. To the former, we owe *Mahonia lomariifolia* and the pot jasmine, *Jasminum polyanthum*. Johnston's sharp eye for a superior garden variant is evident in the number of excellent plants bearing his or Hidcote's name, including a lavender, hypericum, verbena, campanula, penstemon and rose.

At present, Hidcote is undergoing a great renaissance, in the wake of a major historic survey carried out in 2000 which revealed just how much of its original character had been lost – for when it was taken on by the Trust in 1948, as the first property accepted on the merits of its garden alone, there was limited expertise within the Trust, no garden records and a serious shortage of funds. Vita Sackville-West's 1949 description of the garden as a 'jungle of beauty' captures the spirit of Johnston's Hidcote. Its high content of tender and exotic plants, over-wintered both in temporary glasshouses and a heated Plant House, gave 'a general impression of dripping luxuriance'. There were even humming-birds, macaws and flamingos. The planting was very loose, almost wild. 'Plants grow in a jumble … spilling abundance.' And the plant content extended into comprehensive collections of alpines and other rarities.

Already Mrs Winthrop's Garden has taken on this more relaxed and mingled style, and reflects more of a Mediterranean flavour. The Bulb Slope and Rock Bank, previously planted up by the Trust in labour-saving shrubs, have been cleaned and restocked, with the help of the rediscovered notebooks of both Johnston and Jack Percival, who worked here as a gardener in the 1920s and '30s. Johnston intended the effect of walking up this western flank of the garden to be like climbing up the maritime Alps through bulb and boulder fields, across scree and past glacial meltwater pools. His more formalised Alpine Terrace below the pleached hornbeam hedges has also been reinstated; it has a glass roof in winter to counter excess rain, allowing the survival of plants such as aeoniums, aloes and Chilean puya.

Perhaps the most dramatic change has been beside the lily pool to the north of the house, where Johnston's large Plant House has been reintroduced. A copy of its predecessor and with much the same exotic plant content, it has glass panels which are removed in summer. In winter, its lemons, plumbagos and tender jasmines are kept just frost-free.

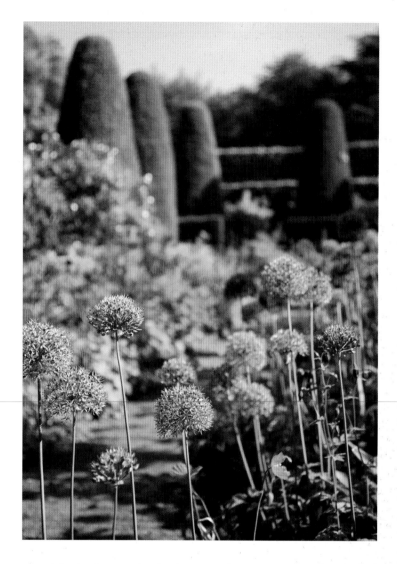

The kitchen garden has recently been revived, with vegetables, flowers for cutting and new apple and pear espaliers grafted from the original trees. Johnston's yew-enclosed clay tennis court has also been reinstated, complete with thatched pavilion; he employed a tennis professional through the summer because his friends were not of a sufficient standard to give him a proper game.

**LEFT** Dahlias in September in the Old Garden, with the manor house beyond.
**ABOVE** Alliums and poppies in May in the Pillar Garden at Hidcote Manor.

# Hinton Ampner

**BRAMDEAN, ALRESFORD, HAMPSHIRE**

**AREA** 5.3ha (13 acres) • **SOIL** alkaline/clay, chalk • **ALTITUDE** 122m (400ft)
**AVERAGE RAINFALL** 838mm (33in) • **AVERAGE WINTER CLIMATE** moderate

Ralph Dutton, the 8th and last Lord Sherborne, inherited this estate in 1935 at the age of 37, and devoted the following 50 years to improving and embellishing it. A deeply cultured man, a connoisseur of art and architecture, author of *The English Garden*, and with the wealth and leisure to indulge his tastes, he produced as elegant a composition of house, park and garden as the last century can show.

The Georgian house stands on a ridge of chalk above well-treed farmland. You pass through a series of gentle transitions as you climb to it, curving through parkland, and then, across a cattle grid, through ornamental shrubberies speared by conifers and specimen trees. There is a pocket of deep acid greensand here on the northern fringe, which allows rhododendrons, azaleas, camellias,

blue hydrangeas, *Magnolia* × *soulangeana* and various Japanese maples to accompany the more chalk-tolerant species like *Magnolia wilsonii* and *Parrotia*, but the colour scheme is kept soft, as it is throughout the grounds, with the richer tints of yellow and orange confined to highlights.

As the house looms between the trees, the drive straightens and the grounds become more formal. On one side is the walled kitchen garden belonging to the original house, demolished in 1793. In recent years, this has been brought back into the Trust's management, having previously been leased out, and after much restoration it is now producing a range of fruit and vegetables. Ralph Dutton extended its path-line to turn the area on the other side of the drive, backed by a Norman church, into a formal cherry orchard. Its trees – pink- and white-blossomed, and in a meadowy carpet of early bulbs, daffodils and then cow parsley – stand inside four box-edged enclosures, making an unusual and very effective combination of the natural and the ordered. This pattern of simply designed, rectangular compartments and strong long axes connecting them provides the framework for the many flower-filled scenes to the south, in classic mid-twentieth-century style. A lily pond, partnered by a bed of 'Iceberg' roses and magenta *Verbena rigida* (syn. *V. venosa*), aligns with the east front of the house, while the main, sunny façade looks onto a sweeping grass terrace, inherited by Dutton and retained as the necessary quiet counterbalance to the surrounding colours.

Before the Second World War, Dutton created further terraces below, using the lines and proportions of the Georgian façade to set the parameters of the central space and carrying the cross-path east and west to form another long axis, running one way through an avenue of Irish yews and the other between ornamental shrubberies; both views conclude in a classical ornament, one backed by trees and the other by open park. It is a beautiful passage of design, further enhanced by a flight of steps providing a graceful change of level *en route*. Later, he cleverly connected the lime avenue, dating from the eighteenth century and cutting across the park in alignment with the original house, by extending and connecting it, via a straight walk, to this axis, and erecting a temple at the intersection.

As well as valuable lessons for the design student, there is much to absorb the plant-lover. Shrubs are the principal source of colour. Evergreens, including *Magnolia grandiflora*, pittosporums and bay grow against the house's south wall, and, below the stone terrace, they are joined by lower-growing subjects, including lavender, caryopteris, perovskia, escallonia and seams of

Headbourne Hybrid agapanthus, all appreciative of the hot, dry conditions. Crisply partnered for foliage contrast, larger shrubs also flank the many grass walks fringing the terraces, especially those to the east, around the tennis court lawn. The smoke bush, *Cotinus coggygria*, is prominent in its purple and green-leaved cultivars, together with lilacs, various viburnums (especially evergreen *V. davidii* and *V. rhytidophyllum*, and the deciduous wayfaring tree, *V. lantana*), scented philadelphus, berberis, cotoneasters, buddleias, weeping silver pear and many different Shrub roses.

At one point, the ground suddenly plunges into the basin of a chalk pit – giving the garden a strong sense of locality – and you find yourself looking up at steep banks clad in yew, rampaging Rambler roses and paulownias. They are joined, in the damper pockets, by foliage plants such as spotted lungwort, hostas, rheum and giant hogweed, and in the drier parts by euphorbias and Corsican hellebore. It is a peaceful and atmospheric place in which to linger, especially in June.

Around the house, the shrubs also give way here and there to other plants. Delicately blended bedding plants fill the small, yew-hedged room, east of the main lawn terrace, while to the south you descend to a lawn appointed with topiary figures, where dahlias traditionally follow a spring show of bulbs, to the accompaniment of a border of pastel perennials and silvery foliage. I remember striking partnerships here between Regale lilies and blue shrubby euphorbia, pink helianthemum and the trailing *Convolvulus althaeoides* (hardy here), and, best of all, magenta *Allium cernuum* and *Artemisia schmidtiana* 'Nana', the former's magenta heads sprouting through the rug of grey leaves. But schemes like this are being tended creatively, with new plants and combinations of plants allowed to play variations on the themes, and they do not remain static.

An opening in the hedge, directly opposite the house, gives an interlude in the garden tour, bringing you out above the ha-ha and to a grass bastion. Ahead, the park rolls away into the Hampshire countryside, past the stands and belts of trees, rigorously thinned by Dutton to ensure the development of good, spreading specimens. Trees were his favourite plants, and the large specimens of beech, lime, oak and pine shading the garden's drives and neat lawns contribute to the sense of history, spaciousness and tranquillity he so valued, as well as supplying the much-needed shelter against the wind.

**ABOVE** Thirty clipped Irish yews line the Long Walk.
**LEFT** A bank of pastel colours, including silver-leaved ballota and helianthemum.

# Killerton

**BROADCLYST, EXETER, DEVON**

AREA 8ha (21 acres) • SOIL acid/sandy loam • ALTITUDE 50–107m (164–351ft)
AVERAGE RAINFALL 914mm (36in) • AVERAGE WINTER CLIMATE mild

It takes little effort to imagine the excitement of gardening in those decades of the nineteenth and early twentieth century when exotic and untried woody plants, collected in far-flung corners of the world, were flooding into Britain. Killerton was one of the first gardens to indulge, and for a period of over 130 years the enthusiasm only briefly waned. Today it offers an arboretum of the highest calibre, with a dramatic and distinctive skyline of trees, and a springtime spectacle that few gardens can equal.

The garden lies on the slopes of Killerton Clump, a volcanic outcrop that rises several hundred feet above the flood plain of the River Exe. The soil is free-draining, deep, fertile, acidic and a rich, Devon red; coupled with the southerly aspect and comparatively mild climate, it provides excellent growing conditions. The foundations for the collection were laid in the 1770s, when Sir Thomas Dyke Acland decided to create a landscape park to accompany his new house; the present flat-topped, pink-washed building was originally intended as a temporary residence, but a grander mansion was never built.

Acland chose as his gardener and land steward John Veitch, who soon proved an exceptional landscaper. With Acland's help, he also started a nursery at nearby Budlake. It was to become the most celebrated of its day, and in 1840, under the direction of his son James, was the first to dispatch plant-hunters into the wild. The association between the Acland and Veitch families held until 1939, and, apart from a 30-year period following Sir Thomas's death in 1871, Killerton received batches of new plants with regularity. Old specimens of *Thuja plicata* and *Sequoiadendron giganteum* in the garden are almost certainly from seed brought back from the west coast of America by Veitch's collector, William Lobb, in the 1850s. A great many other trees and shrubs are either original plantings or direct descendants from seed collected in South America, China, Japan and the Himalayas during the nineteenth and early twentieth centuries.

From the house, the view up the hillside is of mown grass, specimen trees and flowing shrub beds, capped by an exotic woodland of mixed conifers and broad-leaved trees. Fine specimens of the erect Japanese walnut, *Juglans ailantifolia* var. *cordiformis*, and the wide-spreading *Zelkova serrata* are some of the highlights among a cast that includes *Nothofagus obliqua*, Indian horse chestnut, blue Atlas and incense cedars, golden Monterey cypress, wellingtonias and redwoods. Early in the year, the banks are peppered with daffodils, the flowers of magnolias and rhododendrons, and the blossom of Japanese cherries.

The hillside paths reveal countless treasures: a stand of cork oak, with thick, rugged bark; the evergreen, acid-loving *Quercus acuta*; a magnificent *Stewartia pseudocamellia*, with patterned trunk and fiery autumn colour; *Ehretia dicksonii*, with fragrant flowers in June, and *Taiwania cryptomerioides*, a rare and tender conifer, both from seed gathered in China by Ernest Wilson from 1899 to 1905; *Cornus kousa*, producing a cascade of white flowers in June; and *Cryptomeria japonica* and its variant 'Lobbii', grown from Thomas Lobb's Javanese seed.

This is only scratching the surface. Drifts of scented azaleas and further hummocks of *Rhododendron arboreum*, in red, pink and white, colour the glades between trees. Early in the year, crocuses and *Cyclamen coum* create pools of lilac and carmine; later come *Cyclamen repandum*, primroses, violets and bluebells; later still, campions and Queen Anne's lace; and finally, in the autumn, *Cyclamen hederifolium*. At every turn, there are fresh surprises and framed vistas.

In the early part of the twentieth century, two significant features were added to the garden, enabling the vast plant collection to expand still further. In about 1900, the great garden writer William Robinson was asked to advise on the garden, which over the previous 30 years had fallen into a sorry state. His legacy is the Great Terrace, west of the house. Originally planted with roses, which did not succeed, the generously proportioned beds here now contain an assortment of low-growing Mediterranean shrubs and other plants in soft, pastel tones, their shapes contrasting with stands of yuccas and the heavy verticals of Coade stone vases. Over the terrace wall, there are broad views of the gently undulating park. The herbaceous border that runs alongside the parterre was originally planted by John Coutts, who became head gardener as this part of the garden was being completed. The present Jekyllian colour schemes of pastel tints, blending into a hotter core of reds and oranges, is more recent. It has a long season, beginning with crown imperials in spring, reaching its climax at midsummer with peonies, irises and Shrub roses, and continuing into autumn with buddlejas, dahlias and other late perennials.

The second significant feature installed by Coutts is the rock garden, sited beyond the thatched summer-house, known as the Bear's Hut (it once housed a Canadian black bear). This precipitous composition is a superb period piece, busily intricate in rockwork, and capped by a stand of Chusan palm, *Trachycarpus fortunei*. It has recently been replanted with Asian plants introduced in the Edwardian era. A cool and private part of the garden, the silence is broken only by the stream that trickles softly into the rock pool, edged in ferns, primulas and astilbes. Following exposure to all this colour and variety, there is refreshment to be had in the green shadows around the Victorian chapel, where you can walk among oaks, chestnuts and conifers, and search for the lime-yellow flowers on the two great tulip trees planted in 1808 by John Veitch.

**LEFT** Osteospermum 'Whirligig', an exotic typical of those brought back by plant hunters.
**BELOW** William Robinson's Great Terrace, looking towards the exotic woodland.

# Kingston Lacy

**WIMBORNE MINSTER, DORSET**

**AREA** 13ha (32 acres) • **SOIL** alkaline, some acid/varied • **ALTITUDE** 61m (200ft)
**AVERAGE RAINFALL** 813mm (32in) • **AVERAGE WINTER CLIMATE** moderate

The high-chimneyed Italianate mansion, remodelled in the 1830s by Sir Charles Barry for William John Bankes, stands pale and elegant in the midst of an open park. Oaks, beeches and other venerable trees, survivors of the gale of January 1990, are dispersed, singly and in clumps, over the level terrain. Animating the scene is a herd of what seems, from a distance, to be bison; at closer range, they reveal themselves as horned, red North Devon cattle.

This relaxed pastoral scene was set in the late eighteenth century as the original linear landscape laid out by Sir Roger Pratt, the builder of the house, was dismantled. But, as in so many of the great country seats, the pendulum of fashion continued to swing, and as you walk around the house, you find the strict formality reimposed on the immediate surroundings in Victorian and Edwardian times in the form of terrace gardens, avenues of trees and axial vistas. Rose and herbaceous borders, and in spring big

splashes of red 'Oxford' tulips, lead you around the house's south front to the impressive sunken parterre, studded with topiary 'skittles' and balls of golden yew accompanied by brightly clashing carpets of spring hyacinths and summer begonias.

Kingston Lacy's gardens had their heyday in the early twentieth century under Henrietta Bankes and her head gardener Mr Hill, though near the house much of the panache comes from the architectural ornaments enthusiastically assembled by William John Bankes on his travels. Veronese lions, well-heads and vases – some endearingly supported by tortoises, which were kept here as pets – decorate the terrace, while, in line with the door, a soaring pink obelisk, brought from a temple beside the Nile, casts a crisp shadow across the broad expanse of lawn that recedes to the ha-ha and parkland.

The gardens were in a sorry state when the Trust took possession of the property in 1982, but fortunately the restoration has been aided by good records. The large, box-edged fernery beside the main lawn, which had become buried under seedling sycamores, was one of the first features to be tackled. It is now a bewitching part of the garden, a strange and shady world of meandering gravel paths, horizontally trained yews, stone walls and raised beds, in which some 40 varieties of ferns, so appealing to the Victorians for their eccentricities and Gothic habits, hold court. They are joined by cyclamen, lily of the valley, and a National Collection of *Anemone nemorosa*.

Snowdrops are to be found here, too, as they are in much of the garden. They are a particularly memorable sight along Lady's Walk and the Lime Walk, where they are complemented by the glowing red twigs of the limes; there is also a warm glow from the base of the trees, where, unusually, the epicormic growth has been allowed to remain. This avenue, extended by Walter Ralph Bankes in the 1870s, is in fact a vestige of the seventeenth-century formal layout. Beyond the fernery, a long border of blue and white plants, including irises, phlox and crambe, has been recently re-created. Opposite is the patterned sunken garden, enclosed by yew hedging and formally bedded out following the original late nineteenth-century design by William Goldring of Kew. Pampas grass and rodgersia occupy the central bed, and further on you come to an island bed of *Osmunda* fern set into the lawn.

On breezy days, you will hear the distinctive hiss of the cut-leaved beech, *Fagus sylvatica* 'Asplenifolia', as you enter the Blind Walk, so-called because it is hidden from view by evergreens. Here the Victorian taste for coloured leaves is fully indulged, the thickets

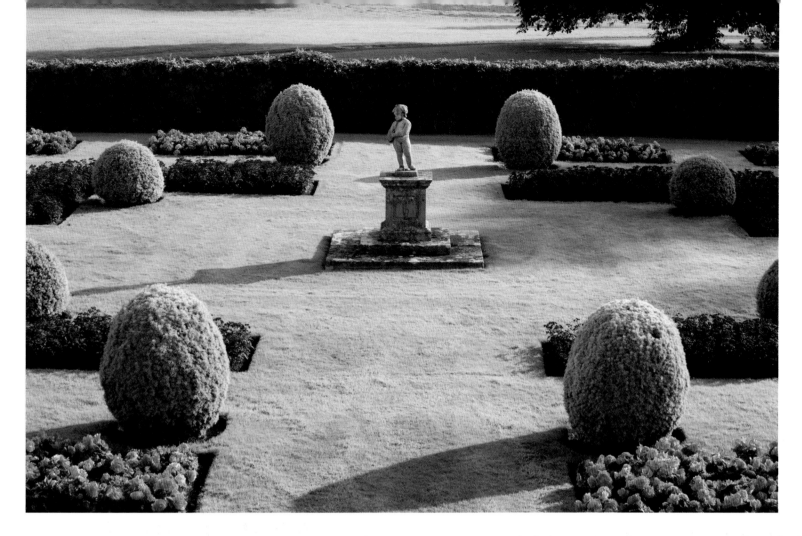

of purple and gold shrubs and small trees, underplanted with pulmonarias, leading to a monument erected to celebrate Queen Victoria's Golden Jubilee. Maples, plums, privets, berberis and elders add to the indigestion. The shrubbery extends into the nearby Cricket Walk (so-called because it once led to the family cricket pitch) in the form of cistus and hydrangeas, accompanied in spring by massed daffodils.

Along the wooded Lady's Walk, you come to the newly restored Japanese Garden, spanning 2ha (5 acres) and with an enclosed tea garden as its centrepiece. Inspired by the Japan-British Exhibition of 1910, this is an interpretation rather than an authentic re-creation of a Japanese garden, with a thatched entrance gate leading into a miniature landscaped valley appointed with dry stream, rocks, cut-leaved maples and traditional ornaments including a tea hut and waiting arbour. It is set within extensive plantings of cherries, maples, azaleas and cloud-pruned box.

The path leads across the road to the 2.4 ha (6 acre) kitchen garden, which is currently under restoration. In the nineteenth century, 20 gardeners were employed here, and the standard of cultivation was so high that members of Queen Victoria's own gardening staff came for training. There is a good range of glass and forcing houses, including a fine vinery awaiting repair.

There is a further assembly of ornamental trees and shrubs in Nursery Wood, part of the loop walk that takes you out along the camellia grove and lime avenue and back through the Cedar Walk to the house. A pocket of acid soil allows a colourful run of lime-hating azaleas and rhododendrons here, which would not thrive on the chalk and clay elsewhere in the garden. The trees include Hungarian oak, black walnut, ginkgo, tulip tree, and some striking young *Prunus serrula*, with polished chestnut trunks. The Bankes family were meticulous in recording tree planting, and at one time all the trees in the Cedar Walk carried commemorative plaques. Sadly, the cedar planted by King Edward VII fell in a recent gale; that planted in 1907 by the Kaiser remains.

**ABOVE** The 'Dutch', or parterre, garden designed in 1899 by C. E. Ponting.
**LEFT** The Japanese garden, inspired by the 1910 Japan-British Exhibition.

# Knightshayes Court

**BOLHAM, TIVERTON, DEVON**

**AREA** 101ha (250 acres) • **SOIL** acid-neutral/heavy • **ALTITUDE** 122–152m (400–500ft)
**AVERAGE RAINFALL** 914mm (36in) • **AVERAGE WINTER CLIMATE** moderate

This garden, developed by Sir John and Lady Heathcoat Amory – the former champion golfer Joyce Wethered – is one of the best-displayed plant collections in the country, comprising formal gardens, conservatory, alpine beds, naturalised bulbs and hectare upon hectare of exotic woodland and glade, stocked with the choicest trees, shrubs and perennials. Neither had any experience of gardening when they began married life here in 1937, but Sir John became a dedicated collector, Lady Heathcoat Amory a gifted plant arranger, and they worked with a small staff of gardeners, turning for outside help to some of the best contemporary designers and landscapers – Lanning Roper and Sir Eric Savill – and plantsmen, including Graham Stuart Thomas, Norman Haddon and Miss Nellie Britton, who ran a well-known alpine nursery near Tiverton.

The setting is potently Victorian. The red sandstone house, standing high on the eastern flank of the Exe Valley with open views across the Devon countryside towards Tiverton, was designed by William Burges and built between 1869 and 1874. The long, curving entrance drive through the park takes you past its western flank, uphill between Burges's stable block with its fairytale tower and the walled kitchen garden, and onwards to the car park. Favourite Victorian trees, including Scots pine, cedar, wellingtonia and purple beech join the parkland oaks (English and Turkey), and beyond the walled garden is a suitably sombre plantation of Douglas firs, offering a hushed, cool walk through the box and bracken understorey.

In front of the house, the scene is livelier. The terraces here were set out by the garden designer and writer Edward Kemp in the 1870s, but they are no longer the scene of swashbuckling bedding schemes. Instead, you look down upon clean patterns of lawn, clipped yew, paving and stone ornament, fringed by pastel schemes of rosemary, cistus, lavender, iris, agapanthus and other sun-lovers.

Restraint and profusion: these two themes interplay throughout the garden, the contrast heightened here by the tension between the crisp, formal groundplan and the curves and spill of the flowers and foliage. It is felt still more intensely in the yew-hedged compartments, up the short flight of steps to the east. Here, you come to a small paved garden, patterned with low silver and ice-blue perennials, a lead cistern and flanking pair of standard wisterias; and formal terraces of alpine (in a lowland setting, far more harmonious a feature than an eruption of rock), including scented daphnes, dianthus, dwarf iris, zauschneria and bulbs.

These are placed in contrast with an empty lawn, around which topiary hounds chase a topiary fox – a much celebrated touch of whimsy added by Sir Ian Heathcoat Amory, a keen huntsman, in the 1920s; and a larger space (formerly the bowling green) framed by Victorian battlemented hedges and backlit by *Acer pseudoplatanus* 'Brilliantissimum', where a circular pool, the solitary statue of a bather, stone benches and a weeping silver pear are the only ingredients: a charming piece of modernist composition, simple and complete.

Another few steps and you are inside Knightshayes' most famous planting, the Garden in the Wood. This area was gradually annexed from about 1950 and now encompasses some 10ha (25 acres) of ornamental walks and glades, under the canopy of the thinned and high-pruned nineteenth-century oaks, beeches, limes and conifers. It begins with a straight grass walk, bordered by Shrub roses and rhododendrons (not a partnership often encountered in gardens), underplanted with geraniums, pulmonarias and electric blue omphalodes. As the walk breaks into curves and glades, you

come upon traditional woodland raised beds colonised by mosses, ferns, wood anemones, violets and much else. Larger grass glades open up, speared by the trunks of the tall pines and native trees. At the edges are herbaceous schemes – perhaps shrubby euphorbias, their lime-yellow cylinders of flower matched with purple-leaved violet and Bowles's golden grass, or, later in summer, a flush of yellow, apricot and orange crocosmias. Sword-leaved phormiums and silver astelia punctuate views, and in one spot, a purple thundercloud looms, created by massed *Rhododendron augustinii* hybrids.

**ABOVE** Looking down the Pool Garden towards distant fields.

Gravel paths meander through a grove of larches and lead into an area of distinctive character where waves of creamy-white and pink erythroniums break against outcrops of bronze *Polystichum* ferns; later, white Excelsior foxgloves and white gentian filter between the conifers. Naturally, spring and early summer see the main flowering of the wood – the former a magical time when the chalices of tree magnolias are lighting a largely leafless canopy, and hellebores are blooming in thick carpets under their shrubby cousins – but hypericums, hydrangeas, clethras, tricyrtis, clerodendrums and Japanese anemones keep the colour flowing into high summer and autumn, when the large colonies of cyclamen, growing on the dry banks and around the boles of trees, are performing their pink and white butterfly dance.

Mahonias are a favourite tribe, and ferns are ubiquitous – delicate maidenhair ferns beside the discs of *Cyclamen repandum*, and the creeping, rust-coloured *Blechnum penna-marina* picking up the suede undersides of *Rhododendron falconeri*, among the many memorable associations. Knightshayes cannot support the more tender trees and shrubs encountered on the Cornish peninsula, but the soil is rich and the climate is still warm and wet enough for some of the early-flowering and more exotic-looking trees and shrubs denied to many inland gardens. There is a concentration of them on the grass slope below the wood. These 1.6ha (4 acres) also support a collection of southern beeches (*Nothofagus*), as well as cherries, magnolias and ever more hardy rhododendrons; crimson-red rhododendrons blooming in front of white-trunked birches create a striking picture. Elsewhere, an area of native woodland plants has recently been developed.

Momentously, in 2003 the Victorian Walled Kitchen Garden also opened to the public for the first time. Just over 0.8ha (2 acres) in size, with stepped, tile-capped stone walls and decorative conical-roofed corner turrets, this was designed by William Burges very much as a showcase garden and, enhanced by its backdrop of trees, is one of the most handsome in the Trust's hands. But having been grassed over in the 1960s, it has required much work to bring it back to a high standard of presentation and production. It slopes from north to south, with, ingeniously, a little slatted gate at the lowest point to allow the frost to drain away. The long, buttressed upper wall shelters double borders of exotic plants appreciative of the warm micro-climate, including giant *Dahlia imperialis*, *Rosa bracteata*, *Tetrapanax papyrifer*, *Leptospermum myrtifolium* and *Fitzroya cupressoides*. There are also herbaceous and cut-flower borders, and beds for culinary and medicinal herbs.

Vegetables and fruit, however, take centre stage. Unusual and heritage varieties abound in the large permanent and rotational plots, among them 'Purple Dragon' carrot, 'Fat Lazy Blond' lettuce, walking stick cabbage, oca (*Oxalis tuberosa*), skirret, and Taunton Deane cottager's kale, a variety that doesn't produce seed and crops all year. Gages, damsons, cherries and plums grow on the north-facing wall behind the rhubarb varieties, and elsewhere there is an array of soft fruit, pears and Devon and Cornish apples. Pumpkins and squash grow in hot beds, there are mulberry trees in little roundels, and there is even a vineyard plot – the red 'Regent' and white 'Orion' grape varieties being blended to make rosé. The walled garden is a major addition to a tour of the grounds, and for the visitor completes the experience of a country house garden in the round, seen in its heyday. Its produce can be tasted in the restaurant opposite, a fine example of 'plot to plate'.

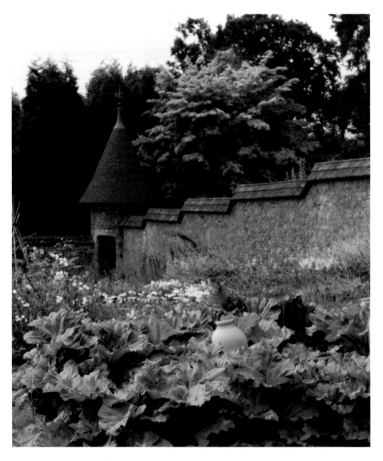

**ABOVE** Forcing rhubarb in the kitchen garden at Knightshayes.

# Lanhydrock

**BODMIN, CORNWALL**

**AREA** 12ha (30 acres) • **SOIL** acid/good loam • **ALTITUDE** 122m (400ft)
**AVERAGE RAINFALL** 1,524mm (60in) • **AVERAGE WINTER CLIMATE** moderate

Hanging beechwoods, plunging entrance drives and tree-studded parkland rolling down to the River Fowey provide a dynamic setting for this low, labyrinthine house of silver-grey granite, with its accompanying church and ornate, obelisk-capped gatehouse. The buildings, part seventeenth-century and part late Victorian, are tucked close into the wooded ridge and face east, down the valley and away from the prevailing wind. For although this is Cornwall, the house stands at 122m (400ft), 11km (7 miles) from the sea and with the south-western edge of windswept Bodmin Moor only 4km (2¹/₂ miles) away.

This chillier climate and shadier aspect distinguishes Lanhydrock from the balmy coastal gardens, depriving it of the more tender and earliest-flowering exotics. But the spring display is every bit as spectacular and, as the season advances, colour surges through the woods. Thickets of camellias and enormous specimens of *Rhododendron* Smithii Group ('Cornish Red') become beacons in the landscape, while above, various forms and hybrids of *Magnolia campbellii*, the first in a long succession of tree magnolias, hold their pink and white chalices to the sky. By late April, countless other shrubs are in bloom, together with waves of daffodils and bluebells.

Most of the other great Cornish woodland gardens are made on slopes below their houses, but here the main garden is above, and the flower-framed views down across the rooftops, gatehouse and accompanying lines of Irish yew trees are one of the property's most memorable features. The yews are part of a very different style of garden set out around the house for the 1st Baron Robartes in the 1850s. It was thought that its design emanated from the architect George Gilbert Scott, who was engaged to work on the house, but pen and wash drawings recently uncovered in the archive show the inspiration behind this formal Italianate garden to have come from George Truefitt, a London architect and founder member of the Architectural Association. His design was then condensed and reworked by Richard Cound, Gilbert Scott's Liskeard-based associate, with the planting scheme probably devised by the family in collaboration with their head gardener. The design was further simplified in the 1920s and '30s.

It is a crisp and satisfying composition of lawns, yews, urns, roses and bedding schemes, enclosed and partitioned by the low battlement walls. Floribunda roses – pink 'Octavia Hill', white 'Margaret Merril', yellow 'Bright Smile', the well-scented, rosy-violet 'Escapade' and 'Songs of Praise' – give a long display of colour opposite the east front, while in the parterre, the schemes are usually based on tulips, pansies and forget-me-nots for spring, with begonias later. Fine trees fringe these formal lawns, including cork oak, chestnuts, a towering Monterey pine, and two copper beeches planted by the prime ministers William Gladstone and Lord Rosebery. Behind the Croquet Lawn stands a remarkable field maple, its limbs caked in lichens, mosses and polypody ferns, which flourish in the clean, moist air. It was not until after 1930, when the 7th Viscount Clifden inherited, that the more flamboyant species of trees and shrubs – for decades, the sensation of other Cornish gardens – began to be sampled at Lanhydrock.

As you walk towards the Higher Garden, you get an inkling of the displays to come. In spring the shrubby *Magnolia loebneri* and its hybrids 'Leonard Messel' and the exquisitely scented 'Merrill' will be in bloom and beyond, the first of the show-stopping trees: among them forms of *M. × veitchii* and *M. dawsoniana*. Rhododendrons, including the crimson-flecked, creamy 'Dr Stocker', pink 'Mrs C.B. van Nes' and *R. arboreum* var. *roseum*, add to the scene. Later, there will be scented Occidentale azaleas, *Magnolia tripetala*, and, in high summer, 'Rostrevor' eucryphias.

**ABOVE** Summer bedding of begonias in the box parterre.

The winding paths lead through ever richer banks of blossom, on and on, past a stream up to the Holy Well and thatched gardener's cottage. Everywhere, the magnolias billow and the rhododendrons and camellias surge. *Magnolia sargentiana* var. *robusta*, *M. sprengeri* var. *diva* and hybrids of *M. cylindrica* make spectacular trees, while the shrubby *M. × soulangeana* and its many selections are ubiquitous; at one point, lines of *M. × soulangeana* 'Lennei' form a tunnel of blossom. In late spring, *M. sieboldii* and its relatives, with pendant flowers, enter the stage, followed by *M. ashei*, fragrant *M. thompsoniana*, and *M. hypoleuca* and *M. × wieseneri* (syn. *M. × watsonii*), both carrying the pervasive scent of ripe melons.

Hardy Hybrids make up a large proportion of Lanhydrock's rhododendron collection and they are here in all colours. Massed lacecap and mophead hydrangeas reproduce for summer some of this springtime spectacle, but now attention shifts to the great circle of clipped yew below the woodland banks. Here, beside a barn, is a distinctively designed circular garden of herbaceous plants, the southern half of which was set out by Lady Clifden before 1914. The Trust completed the hedge and added matching perimeter flower-beds in 1971. The foliage of *Yucca recurvifolia*, yellow tree peony, *Melianthus major*, fascicularias, rodgersias, hostas and ligularias set a lush, exotic theme, against which the flowers of agapanthus, penstemons, *Canna iridiflora*, *Cautleya* 'Robusta', and other perennials appreciative of the long, warm, moist summers are displayed.

In April, the Higher Garden's Top Walk is bordered by a notable colony of white pheasant's eye narcissi, the bulbs having naturalised luxuriantly since their introduction in the mid-1970s. A new summer-house has been installed here and a gate leads into the wilder Woodland Garden, where ferns and bluebells invade the steep banks, beneath oak and beech. The finest views of the house and park are now revealed, complemented by the dazzling blood-reds of the rhododendrons 'Tally Ho', 'Matador' and Smithii Group ('Cornish Red'), and the elephantine leaves of *R. maccabeanum*, *R. grande* and other giants.

**ABOVE** The East Front and forecourt with yew hedging and topiary.
**RIGHT** Looking towards Lutyens' Lindisfarne Castle on Holy Island from the Walled Garden.

# Lindisfarne Castle

**HOLY ISLAND, BERWICK-UPON-TWEED, NORTHUMBERLAND**

**AREA** 0.05ha (¹/₈ acre) • **SOIL** alkaline/free-draining loam • **ALTITUDE** 5m (16¹/₂ ft) **AVERAGE RAINFALL** 813–1,194mm (32–47in) • **AVERAGE WINTER CLIMATE** cold

The island fortress of Lindisfarne, standing on a steep crag and cut off from the mainland at high tide, is a potent eye-catcher amid the raw beauty of the Northumberland coast. Built in the 1570s to guard against incursion from the Scots, it was in a sorry state when discovered by Edward Hudson, the founder of *Country Life* magazine, in 1901.

To convert it into a comfortable holiday home, and add a cheerful and productive garden, it was natural that Hudson should turn to his famous friends, the architect Edwin Lutyens and the garden designer Gertrude Jekyll, who was changing the face of English gardens with her advocacy of cottage-garden exuberance and painterly plant combinations in place of the stiff artifice of Victorian bedding. The pair had recently worked together on his Berkshire home, The Deanery in Sonning. By the time Miss Jekyll ventured to Lindisfarne, in May 1906, she was in her sixties, extremely short-sighted, and seldom away from home. She was rowed across to the island, accompanied by Lutyens, who was somewhat encumbered by a recuperating raven, given to him by his dentist, which he was carrying in a Gladstone bag. It provided much entertainment. There were also musical evenings in the castle, with Jekyll singing to the guitar.

Initial ideas for planting close to the castle were abandoned, and efforts were concentrated some distance away on flat ground, consisting of a small plot, enclosed by low grey walls. Lutyens drew up a simple formal pattern of flower-beds and stone paths, which defied the irregular geometry, and Jekyll set about devising a planting scheme. Her first plan was for a vegetable garden, jollied up by sweet peas and other annuals, but this was revised to concentrate on flowers, both annual and perennial, some of which would have been intended for cutting.

The early research and archaeology for the restoration of the garden was carried out by Michael Tooley of Durham University, his wife Rosanna, and volunteer students. Since then, the present scheme by Jekyll expert Richard Bisgrove has been planted, although extensive research has gone into the restoration, which is as faithful as possible to the spirit of the garden.

Banks of sweet peas raise curtains either side of the main axis, framing the view to the castle as well as screening off the vegetables and early flowering roses in the side borders. These last include the dark red Shrub rose 'Hugh Dickson', and the Climbers 'Madame Abel Chatenay' in pink and 'Madame Alfred Carrière' in white. Pink *Clematis montana*, purple *Clematis* × 'Jackmanii' (filtering into silver-leaved *Hippophaë rhamnoides*), lavenders and sweet-scented mignonette are among the supporting cast.

The principal south-facing border blends the more vibrant reds of hollyhock, bergamot and fuchsia with the yellows and whites of helianthus, santolina and Japanese anemones. Carmine

*Gladiolus byzantinus* sprouts from Jekyll's own 'Munstead Red' sedum in the central bed, and in the surrounding beds blues are introduced into the mix, courtesy of *Scabiosa caucasica*, *Centaurea cyanus* and delphiniums. Jekyll used the spent stems of the delphiniums as a support for creamy *Clematis flammula* – one of her trademark touches of genius.

**BELOW** Extensive research has gone into the restoration of Jekyll's original planting scheme in the Walled Garden.
**RIGHT** The Dutch Garden's central fountain is surrounded by a symmetrical parterre of summer bedding at Lyme Park.

# Lyme Park

DISLEY, STOCKPORT, CHESHIRE

AREA 6.5ha (16 acres) • SOIL acid/clay • ALTITUDE 152m (500ft)
AVERAGE RAINFALL 1,016mm (40in) • AVERAGE WINTER CLIMATE cold

The contrasts between the formal elegance of Lyme Park and its gardens, and the wild landscape in which they sit, gives spice to this property. On the edge of the Peak District, the hall surveys wooded slopes and rolling moorland, grazed by ancient herds of red deer. The climate is harsh, with high rainfall, a cool, late spring and a short summer – conditions that have prompted complaints from gardeners at Lyme Park since the late seventeenth century, when the first garden records appear.

The Elizabethan house was given its Italianate grandeur by Giacomo Leoni in the early eighteenth century. The gardens had their heyday in the late nineteenth century, and their present planting and patterns are reminders of that sumptuous era of country-house living. But by 1947, when Lyme Park was transferred to the Trust, the property had declined as a result of high taxation and shortage of staff. Until 1994 Stockport Metropolitan Council was responsible for its upkeep, but funds were not available for the restoration of the hall until the early 1970s and attention was turned to the garden after that.

The starting point was the most spectacular feature, the huge sunken Dutch Garden to the west of the hall, created in the early eighteenth century. In 1973, a violent summer storm caused a torrent of water to flow into the lake above, to which the ancient sluice system proved unequal. The south-east corner of the wall could not support the pressure from the floodwaters, and cracked; the result was a cascade of mud, water and stones across the parterre. Today, however, you look down once more on the pristine scheme as installed by the 1st Lord Newton. Surrounding the central fountain, the intricate pattern of beds, edged in ivy, are filled with seasonal schemes with a strong period flavour. Daffodils and tulips are the mainstay of the spring display, and impatiens, cineraria, marigolds and calceolaria in their thousands are highlights of the summer show, while among the heavy evergreen and variegated shrubberies that clothe the banks come further bursts of colour from rhododendrons, osmanthus, philadelphus and viburnums.

The smaller sunken garden to the north is set out with trees and shrubs mainly given by or commemorating the Hon. Vicary Gibbs, a renowned gardener and friend of the 2nd Lord Newton. *Malus* × *purpurea* 'Aldenhamensis', 'Gibbs' Golden Gage' and *Ligustrum* 'Vicaryi' are among the plants carrying Gibbs's name or that of his garden in Hertfordshire.

In the nineteenth century, no fashionable country house was complete without its conservatory. Lyme's grand Orangery was designed by Lewis Wyatt in about 1815, but the interior, with its central fountain and floors in Minton patterned tiles, was remodelled some 50 years later by Alfred Derbyshire, who also added the glazed cupola. Once warmed by the excess heat from the laundry and brewhouse behind, the Orangery is no longer heated, but the fig tree and two great camellias survive from Victorian times, and, together with choisya, pittosporum, *Cestrum elegans*, ferns and scented *Lilium regale*, continue to project the exotic mood.

Terrace beds in front of the Orangery, in summer often displaying the half-hardy, white-throated *Penstemon* 'Rubicundus' raised at Lyme in 1906, a recently reinstated early nineteenth-century geometric garden, and the Rose Garden to the east, planted with standard 'Sander's White Rambler' and Floribunda roses, are further expressions of formality. Beyond, the garden's lines are more flowing: the eye follows first the sweep up to the Lantern Tower, erected as a folly in the eighteenth century and framed by woods, and then turns to trace the curving path between hedged herbaceous borders.

From Hamper's Bridge, you follow the stream through still more meandering and naturalistic plantings. The area known to the gardeners as 'Killtime' is sufficiently moist and sheltered to suit rhododendrons and azaleas, accompanied by ferns and other pondside plants. Swiss Arolla pine, Bhutan pine and small-leaved lime are among the many good trees. Behind the lake, you walk through rhododendron shrubberies until you are in line once more with the centre of Leoni's south façade. The Lime Avenue to the south, is, together with the lake, one of the four remaining vestiges of the seventeenth-century garden. It was planted by Richard Legh, whose family was associated with Lyme for nearly 600 years.

**ABOVE** The formal Rose Garden and Orangery look to the parkland to the east of the house.
**RIGHT** Guarding the path to the entrance of Lytes Cary Manor are the twelve 'Apostles'.

# Lytes Cary Manor

CHARLTON MACKRELL, SOMERTON, SOMERSET

AREA 2ha (5 acres) • SOIL alkaline/clay • ALTITUDE 61m (200ft) • AVERAGE RAINFALL 762mm (30in) • AVERAGE WINTER CLIMATE cold

In 1907, the medieval and Tudor manor of Lytes Cary, home of the Lyte family for five centuries from 1286, found its champion in Sir Walter Jenner, son of Sir William Jenner, the eminent physician. As well as restoring and sympathetically enlarging the decaying house, Jenner set out a series of simply furnished, grassed and paved formal enclosures, aptly described by Christopher Hussey as 'a necklace of garden rooms strung on green corridors'. Like the house, Jenner's garden is broad and low-slung, crouching for shelter in its flat, exposed farmland. The yards of yew are important buffers, in addition to giving the garden its patterns and secrets.

Although the bones of the gardens are largely unaltered since Sir Walter's day, a programme of renovation and improvements was begun by the Trust in 1963. This included the replanning and enrichment of the main flower border, which runs along a corridor opposite a buttressed yew hedge. The planting is mixed and follows a deliberate colour sequence, in the Jekyllian manner, warming from the blues and yellows of potentilla, caryopteris, *Hibiscus* 'Blue Bird', achillea, polemonium and *Aster × frikartii*, into the purples and rich crimsons of smoke bush, berberis, self-sowing *Atriplex hortensis* and mats of purple sage. Floribunda roses, including 'Magenta', 'Lavender Lassie', 'Rosemary Rose' and 'Yellow Holstein', together with annuals and dahlias, help to ensure a good succession of flowers, and the wall behind is hung with a range of climbers, including clematis. Beyond is a white garden with 'Iceberg' roses, hebe, philadelphus, tobacco flowers and silver foliage.

Other parts of the garden have their bursts of colour too. The ornamental orchard, planted with crossing avenues and symmetrical pairs of medlars, quinces, crab apples, walnuts and corners of weeping ash, is spangled with daffodils, camassias, cowslips, fritillaries and other wildflowers in spring and early summer. Between the Irish yews on the raised walk above, a stream of *Hypericum calycinum* contributes yellow flowers later in the year.

The house itself is clad in evergreen magnolia, the Climber rose 'Paul's Lemon Pillar' and yellow Banksian roses, with its south façade, around a handsome oriel window, lapped with myrtle, *Teucrium fruticans*, *Lilium candidum*, *Gladiolus byzantinus*, rosemary and a wealth of other Mediterranean herbs. These are some of the plants that appear in the 1578 translation by Henry Lyte of Dodoen's Flemish text, the *Cruedeboek* (1569), a copy of which – *A Niewe Herball or Historie of Plants* – is on display in the Great Hall.

Recently, the floral display in this area has expanded into what was formerly the tenants' private garden. Here, you are led into a sunken lawn, flanked by beds of richly tinted perennials and Shrub roses, and on into a small parterre. This is presided over by a weeping silver pear and enlivened by box-edged borders of sweet peas and other flowers for cutting, herbs, white flowers, and – following on from tulips and alliums – a bed of summer exotics such as castor oil plants, dahlias and deep red lilies.

However, the predominant colours of Lytes Cary are the greens of trees, lawns, yew hedges and countryside, and the mellow tints of the golden stone walls and dovecote (in reality, a disguised water-tower). From the raised walk above the orchard, from which there are wide views towards Yeovilton and Camel Hill, you descend through a long grass alley into a series of restrained enclosures: a pool garden; an oval of evergreen and variegated shrubs, reached through a hornbeam tunnel; a grass arena quietly washed with box-edged beds of lavender; and a wide sweep of open croquet lawn. They are reminders that the simplest treatments make for some of the most satisfying garden pictures.

**ABOVE** The Pond Garden is surrounded by yew hedging interspersed with statuary.
**ABOVE RIGHT** The hot colour scheme in the East Court garden at Montacute House was first devised by Phyllis Reiss of nearby Tintinhull.

# Montacute House

MONTACUTE, SOMERSET

AREA 4.9ha (12 acres) • SOIL alkaline/sandy silt loam, some clay • ALTITUDE 76m (250ft)
AVERAGE RAINFALL 762mm (30in) • AVERAGE WINTER CLIMATE moderate

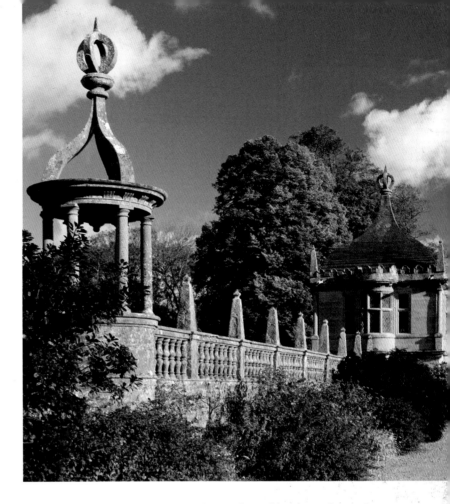

The Elizabethan mansion, ascending through three tiers of massive leaded windows, surmounted by soaring chimneys and high curved gables, dominates its site. Montacute was built of the same golden stone as nearby Tintinhull House for Sir Edward Phelips, at the turn of the seventeenth century. Its west front, which was added in 1785, was in fact a Tudor construction taken from another house, and is an edifice ornate with pillars and balustrades, statues, pinnacles and other carved details. Because the drive dips and rises, it looks deceptively close. In fact, it is 0.4km (¼ mile) from the wrought-iron gates to the door.

Such scale and ornament, designed to impress, is reflected also in the garden, where decorative walls and pavilions, lawns, trees and processions of trim Irish yews (96 in all) make for a stately setting of green and gold courts, terraces and gravel walks. While the framework is largely original the internal design was altered in the eighteenth century, and what you see today is the work of Ellen Helyar, who married into the Phelips family in 1845, and, with her able gardener, Mr Pridham (whom she brought with her from her family home, Coker Court), re-created and reinterpreted the Elizabethan style of gardening here. It is one of the many historic reconstructions prompted by the awakened Victorian interest in the architecture and gardening of the past.

The southern approach walk takes you past cauldrons of golden yew, variegated holly, and curious feathery evergreen tumps – in fact, giant redwoods transformed into multi-stemmed shrubs after their trunks were felled in the last war – and onward to the North Court, the grandest of the green enclosures. This is the site of the original Elizabethan garden, its shape and probably its raised walks dating from that period. Like many contemporary gardens, it once featured a mount, but this seems to have vanished by 1825 and is now replaced by a substantial balustraded lily pool, in a setting of neat lawns, broad gravel walks, seats and ornaments.

Ellen Phelips had this as an elaborately patterned flower parterre, but today's is a simpler scheme, framed by the Irish yews and a high, contoured yew hedge, and with the flowers confined to those of *Yucca recurvifolia* growing by the entrance to the lower court and, below the terrace, a pair of borders filled with old-fashioned species and Hybrid Musk roses, including the incense-scented Climbing Musk, *Rosa* 'Princesse de Nassau' (syn. *R. moschata* 'Autumnalis') – all quietly underplanted with the bluish-leaved *Hosta fortunei* var. *hyacinthina*. The Orangery, with its fern-covered fountain of stone and tufa, is currently closed for repair.

The main flower garden is now within the East Court, presided over by the house's most decorative front and framed by balustraded, obelisk-capped walls and a romantic pair of pavilions. This was the former Tudor entrance court, and at that time you would have arrived through an outer court and through a gatehouse, and had a better prospect of the high façade, which is rather overpowering at close range. Golden euphorbias and achilleas, orange and red roses and dahlias, and numerous other hot-coloured perennials, in a scheme first devised by Phyllis Reiss of Tintinhull, now contribute to the summer kaleidoscope in this part of the garden. Claret-leaved vine and smoke bush and an assortment of crimson and deep purple clematis cloak the walls behind. Acanthus and macleaya add some structural foliage, and evergreen magnolias, crambe, peonies, yuccas and the highly scented Rugosa rose 'Blanc Double de Coubert' give some contrasting notes of cream and white. Flower gardens do not come more richly appointed.

Next to the car park – formerly the kitchen garden – a spacious lawn, shaded by blue and green cedars and a fine pair of sweet chestnuts, leads to an arcaded garden house and a hedged semi-circle of lawn (added in the twentieth century), adorned with stone columns, yew topiaries and mirror beds of spiky yucca. Weeping silver lime and cut-leaved beech grow nearby, with evergreen oaks, pines, koelreuteria and Judas tree, underplanted with a succession of bulbs, to be found in a small adjunct of rough meadow.

Although the garden is formally severed from the village and park by its walls, hedges and railings, the raised walks allow you to survey the rolling countryside and the lines and scattered clumps of the nineteenth-century parkland oaks. This adds to the sense of space. From various parts of the garden, you also have a prospect of the wooded conical hill above the village and church – the *mons acutus*, which gives Montacute its name – and the folly tower erected on it in 1760.

**BELOW** The quarter-mile drive provides a grand approach to the West Front.
**BELOW RIGHT** The rose garden at Mottisfont Abbey was laid out to conserve old and rare rose varieties.

# Mottisfont Abbey

MOTTISFONT, ROMSEY, HAMPSHIRE

AREA 12ha (30 acres) • SOIL alkaline/thin loam over gravel • ALTITUDE 34m (110ft)
AVERAGE RAINFALL 737mm (29in) • AVERAGE WINTER CLIMATE moderate

Push open the white door of Mottisfont's walled garden in midsummer and you plunge into a sea of roses. Not the gaudy roses of today, but the pink and crimson roses of yesterday, eulogised by the classical poets, painted by the Dutch masters, assiduously collected by the Empress Josephine and hybridised by the nurserymen of nineteenth-century France: rounded, petal-packed, drenched in fragrance and giving, in the main, one bountiful, mid-June to early July performance. There is nothing to equal them.

The paths lead you along their ranks, past the Apothecary's Rose and Red Rose of Lancaster, *R. gallica* var. *officinalis*, and its pink-striped sport 'Rosa Mundi'; the Jacobite Rose, 'Alba Maxima', the White Rose of York, 'Alba Semi-plena' and the soft pink 'Great Maiden's Blush', known since the fifteenth century; past damask roses, cabbage roses, moss roses and on to those carrying the inheritance of the autumn damask and, more importantly, of the China roses, conferring the much-desired ability to flower late or continuously: the short Portlands, the Bourbons, the Hybrid Perpetuals, the China roses themselves and their early Tea rose hybrids.

The collection was assembled over many years by the eminent rosarian and Gardens Adviser to the Trust, Graham Stuart Thomas, and brought here in 1972, when the garden became available. The formal design, echoing the original kitchen garden layout, is founded on four open plots of grass, framed by borders and an outer box-edged walk – a clever piece of geometry, in fact, since none of the walls was parallel or is the same length. The centrepiece is a circular lily pool, flanked by pillars of Irish yew and with a low dome of the pink rose 'Raubritter' spilling into it, providing the enhancing note of asymmetry. It is to this that the sweep of yellow gravel carries the eye as you enter the garden.

The borders either side of the path, also planned by Graham Stuart Thomas and almost entirely herbaceous, are a lesson in planting design, demonstrating the virtue of a restricted palette, of orchestrating the colours in clear bands, of providing vertical shapes to complement the mounds, of repeating key subjects and of much else. They are among the most perfectly schemed borders I have come upon. In 1982, ten years after this garden was planned, the adjacent enclosure to the north became available, allowing a home for a further collection of old roses, acquired by Graham Stuart Thomas from the German National Rose Garden at Sangerhausen.

However, the rose gardens are by no means Mottisfont's only attraction. The abbey itself, a grand and romantic medieval house remodelled in the Tudor and Georgian periods, lies low amid undulating parkland, sweeping lawns and gigantic plane, cedar, sweet chestnut and beech trees. The prize specimen is a twin-trunked London plane (in reality, two trees melded together), over 40m (130ft) high, with a 12m (40ft) girth and with a canopy covering a 0.13ha ($^1/_3$ acre); it is possibly the largest tree in the country. But there are also fine old mulberry and crab apple trees; good specimens of hornbeam, walnut, tulip tree and the more upright bean tree, *Catalpa speciosa*; and a short-trunked oak, probably as old as the medieval abbey itself.

The topsoil here is dry and gravelly, but underneath there is water. A tributary of the River Test, famous for its trout, flows just to the east of the house. The adjacent spring, or font, probably gives the abbey its name – mottis being derived from the Saxon *moot*, meaning 'meeting-place'. The clear water rises into the deep pool at a rate of at least 909 litres (200 gallons) a minute, and is carried off by a stream, bordered by blue hostas and yellow *Primula florindae*. Recently, a richly coloured and scented winter garden has been created nearby, incorporating rivulets of foliage plants which appear to wind through banks of willow and dogwood and spill into the stream.

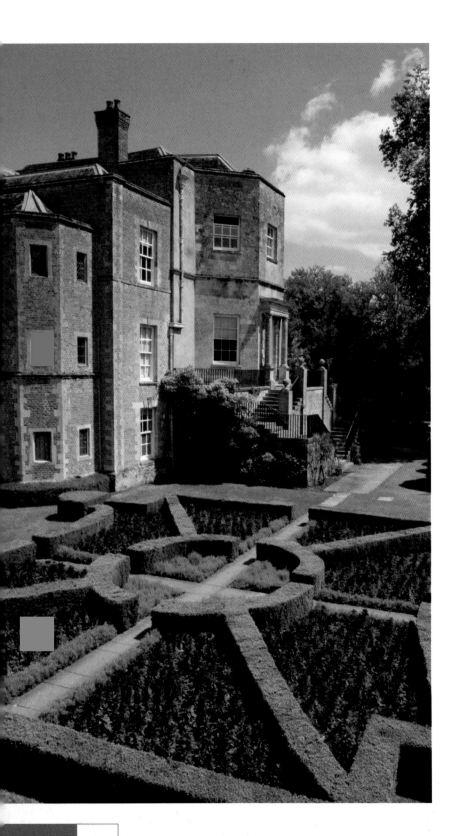

Two noted designers have contributed effective formal details to this part of the garden, both commissioned by Mr and Mrs Gilbert Russell, who bought the property in 1934. Geoffrey Jellicoe introduced grass terraces, one bordered by a contrasting run of lavender, speared by clipped Irish yews; an octagon of English yew; and a connecting walk of pleached limes, underplanted with chionodoxa. It is a crisp and simple linear treatment, in his own words, 'muted to leave the existing ethos of place undisturbed'. A couple of years later, in 1938, Norah Lindsay set out a small parterre on the south side of the house, edged in lavender and box, and filled seasonally with bedding plants in a pattern of blue and cream for spring, and yellow and mauve for summer.

Later, Russell Page was asked to recommend shrubs for the garden. Some of these, with later additions, are grouped along the house walls – among them, *Schizophragma integrifolia* growing on the north-east corner, and, on the sheltered, sunny wall behind the parterre, quite tender plants such as *Acca sellowiana* syn. *Feijoa sellowiana*, *Hoheria lyallii*, *Ceanothus thyrsiflorus* and the climbing Tea rose 'Lady Hillingdon' picking up the apricot tints in the brick. Others, primarily for a late summer display, are massed in beds flanking the eighteenth-century Gothick summer-house; hypericums, fuchsias, hebes, potentillas and the paperbark maple, *Acer griseum*, are among those demonstrating their tolerance of the chalk.

Elsewhere, there is a collection of *Magnolia × soulangeana* varieties, underplanted with crocus and daffodils; recently, the Trust has been enriching the area beyond the river with more bulbs and autumn-coloured shrubs, including Shrub roses and viburnums, to enhance the existing display from the red-stemmed dogwood. But none of these interrupts the peace of the garden, induced by the grass, the trees and the sound of bubbling water.

**LEFT** The parterre to the south of the Abbey.
**RIGHT** Cabbage trees and purple berberis hedges contribute to the exotic mood at Mount Stewart.

# Mount Stewart

**NEWTOWNARDS, CO. DOWN**

**AREA** 39ha (97 acres) • **SOIL** acid/brown earth overlying beach deposits
**ALTITUDE** 0–24m (0–80ft) • **AVERAGE RAINFALL** 889mm (35in) • **AVERAGE WINTER CLIMATE** almost frost-free

This is an extraordinary place, a flight of fancy on the grandest scale. It is a garden founded on rare and exotic plants, strange and mythical beasts, poetry and symbolism, and only the most sullen of visitors will be able to resist the dreamlike state it induces the moment you plunge into its 39ha (97 acres) of lush woodland. Yet when its creator, Edith, Marchioness of Londonderry, first visited her husband's family home, some years before he inherited in 1915, she thought 'the house and surroundings were the dampest, darkest and saddest place I had ever stayed in'. From 1921, the transformation began.

The hillside's south-facing aspect, its all-important sheltering woods, the influence of the adjacent salt-water lough, and above all its close proximity to the Irish Sea and the Gulf Stream create mild, humid, almost subtropical conditions. These, with the help of her gardening mentors, Sir John Ross of Rostrevor, Co. Down, and Sir Herbert Maxwell of Monreith, Scotland, she exploited to the full, joining them to an idiosyncratic design and a theatre of imagery, evoking family history and Irish legend.

The house opens exotically onto a view of New Zealand cabbage palms and 30m (100ft) high Tasmanian gum trees, *Eucalyptus globulus*, punctuating stone terraces, a grand sunken Italian parterre and, terminating the vista, a Spanish water parterre and tiled garden house. The quantity of architectural and horticultural detail is mind-boggling, and it takes a moment to adjust to it. The cast of plants on the upper terrace alone will provoke a good many gasps: fat clumps of spiky fascicularia, *Puya alpestris* and *Beschorneria yuccoides*, planted in 1922; soaring white and yellow Banksian roses and *Rosa gigantea*; scarlet lobster's claw, *Clianthus puniceus*, above a hummock of China blue Chatham Island forget-me-not, *Myosotidium hortensia*. Edgings of purple berberis and white heather frame the herbaceous plants on the parterre below, and in the Spanish Garden, Leyland cypresses are clipped to make an open hedge of tight arches.

Already there are references and allusions in the design – among them coronets and a picture of George and the Dragon made in cobbles on the terrace. On the adjacent Dodo Terrace, the imagery is at its most playful. Here, cement statues of the Ark and various living, extinct or mythical creatures, including a stegosaurus dinosaur, hedgehog, mermaid, frog and monkey, as well as four dodos, relate to the First World War and Lady Londonderry's Ark Club; members, drawn from the family, politics, the armed forces and other branches of the war effort, were given the Order of the Rainbow (the sign of hope) and an animal name. Close by is the Mairi Garden, named after Lady Londonderry's daughter, Lady

Mairi Bury, overlooked by a summer-house and dovecote, and designed in the shape of a Tudor rose, with a blue and white colour scheme. Everywhere there are choice tender and luxuriant plants, grouped for harmony of flower colour and contrast of shape and foliage: among them you will find *Melianthus major*, *Lapageria rosea*, *Camellia japonica* 'Akashigata' (syn. *C. japonica* 'Lady Clare'), *Fuchsia excorticata*, *Pittosporum eugenioides*, *Olearia phlogopappa*, *Stipa arundinacea* (syn. *Apera arundinacea*), agapanthus and crinums.

To the west of the house, further rooms are revealed. The large Sunk Garden, divided from the terrace by great domes of clipped sweet bay (like those on the north Front Court, imported fully grown from Belgium) and based on a design sent by post by Gertrude Jekyll, is enclosed on three sides by a stone pergola, hung with vines, yellow and apricot roses (including another superb *R. gigantea*), and blue and violet clematis, ceanothus and solanum. Tender varieties join them, such as *Lardizabala biternata*, *Dendromecon rigida* and *Mutisia oligodon*, and borders of the azalea 'Coccineum Speciosum', flame red but peppered with orange- and yellow-bloomed branches that have arisen from the rootstocks, fuel the colour scheme. In summer, the herbaceous beds below flaunt electric-blue delphiniums and hoops of imperial purple *Clematis* 'Jackmanii'. Beyond is the famous garden of Irish symbolism, a

hedged enclosure in the shape of a shamrock, containing a topiary Irish harp, and, coloured in seasonal annuals, the Red Hand of Ulster.

This lush wooded backdrop, a patchwork of greens and an assortment of silhouettes from oaks and limes, pines and wellingtonias, cypresses and eucalyptus, is highlighted in spring with flashes of colour from rhododendrons. I recall my first foray into this wood on a balmy afternoon in early May, walking through cool glades of emerald ferns and blue Himalayan poppies and, with each breath, tasting the scents of tender, white-flowered rhododendrons. At every turn, there is a plant to amaze or confound you: *Luma apiculata* (syn. *Myrtus luma*), *Rhododendron sinogrande*, *Gevuina avellana*, nothofagus, eucalyptus, magnolias, candelabra primulas, *Dryopteris affinis* (syn. *D. pseudomonas*), tree ferns and giant lilies (*Cardiocrinum*).

There is more in the Memorial Glade, planted by Lady Mairi Bury after her mother's death in 1959: scarlet embothriums, yellow azaleas, orange-cupped narcissi, white lilacs, purple hydrangeas and *Prunus sargentii*. Among the towering conifers beyond, huge specimens of *Rhododendron arboreum* and *R. macabeanum* light up the drive with spring colour; later, the beacons are handkerchief tree, hydrangeas and white-flowered eucryphias, including the tender *E. cordifolia*.

As you return to the green woods and open lawns to the north of the house, you might easily assume that this dream sequence was now reaching its end – but you would be mistaken. A short walk up the hillside, and you find yourself looking across a 2ha (5 acre) lake, excavated by the 3rd Marquess of Londonderry in the 1840s, fringed by water plants, a new cast of ornamental trees and shrubs, including some superb red rhododendrons such as half-hardy *R. elliottii* and *R. facetum* (syn. *R. eriogynum*), and, in the distance, the towers and walls of yet another formal garden. The larger part of the garden tour is yet to come.

The towers and walls belong to Tir Nan Og (Gaelic for 'The Land of the Ever Young'), the family burial ground built by Lord and Lady Londonderry in the 1920s. According to a legend with pagan origins, a great white stag bears your soul to the west, and on the east side of the lake you will glimpse it between the trunks of trees, standing in a glade. The burial ground hillside is the sunniest and best-drained part of the garden, and an extensive range of Southern Hemisphere plants has been established here: among them, leptospermums, acacias, corokias, sophoras, callistemons, cassinias, hakeas, watsonias and kniphofias. This esoteric character is taken to extremes on Tir Nan Og's south wall, where the company includes such rarities as *Metrosideros umbellatus* (syn. *M. lucidus*), *Kennedia rubicunda*, *Vallea stipularis* and *Picconia excelsa*. Below are fine stands of echiums.

The eastern return route is through the Jubilee Avenue, planted in 1936 to mark the Silver Jubilee of King George V and Queen Mary. The patriotic theme of red, white and blue is achieved with embothriums, fuchsia, photinia and *Rosa moyesii*; cherries, philadelphus, rhododendrons and white hydrangeas; ceanothus, solanum, blue hydrangeas and *Eucalyptus globulus*. A streamside garden of primulas and complementary plants follows, decorated with ornaments brought back from Japan by Lord and Lady

Londonderry. And then, once again, it is headlong into rhododendrons, 6ha (15 acres) of hybrids and species leading you down to the house. In addition to the many with richly coloured flowers, there are choice forms grown for their scents, including tender *RR. burmanicum*, *maddenii* and *johnstoneanum*; for their elephantine foliage, such as *sinogrande*, *magnificum*, *rex* subsp. *arizelum* and *falconeri*; and for their fine bark, such as chocolate-hued *genestierianum*. This is a garden no one can afford to miss.

**ABOVE** The Italian Garden was created by Edith, Lady Londonderry, in the 1920s.
**ABOVE LEFT** This fountain is one of many whimsical eyecatchers dotted through the garden.

# Nymans

HANDCROSS, HAYWARDS HEATH, WEST SUSSEX

AREA 12ha (30 acres) • SOIL acid/sandy loam • ALTITUDE 152m (500ft)
AVERAGE RAINFALL 762mm (30in) • AVERAGE WINTER CLIMATE moderate

The high, wooded ridges of the Sussex Weald, with their acid, sandy topsoil and excellent frost drainage, offer perfect conditions for many of the trees and shrubs from the world's temperate forests. From the 1860s, the opportunities were seized by stockbroker Ludwig Messel and his talented head gardener James Comber, and subsequently by Messel's son Leonard, with the cast of rare and wild-collected woody plants accompanied by herbaceous and rose gardens, flowing lawns and superb views, and with every habitat fully exploited.

The collection spills over almost all the garden, but each area has its own mood. Below the lime avenue of the entrance drive the parkland plunges into a woodland bowl, lit up in early autumn by the tinting leaves of North American liquidambar, nyssa, taxodium and red oak. Nearby, the skyline of the garden's northern boundary is speared by the rocket shapes of giant and dawn redwoods, arranged in a horseshoe shape at the edge of a wide paddock in the company of golden conifers, big clumps of pampas grass, and specimens of the superb August-flowering, evergreen shrub *Eucryphia × nymansensis* 'Nymansay'. Raised by James Comber (its name being a corruption of 'Nymans A seedling'), it is one of around 40 plants named after the garden.

Meandering paths lead from this pinetum into a dappled plantation of large trees, rising from grass and shrubberies of camellia and rhododendron. Here there are fine specimens of *Styrax japonicus* 'Fargesii', *Nothofagus menziesii* from New Zealand, and the tree magnolias *M. × veitchii* and melon-scented *M. hypoleuca*. A young, seed-raised collection of the Chinese handkerchief tree, *Davidia involucrata* var. *vilmoriniana*, grows between box topiaries, creatively shaped by Alistair Buchanan of the Messel family, and a new bamboo jungle bisected by a boardwalk. Many trees in the garden are from wild-sourced seed, with *Meliosma veitchiorum*, *Aesculus wilsonii* and *Thuja koraiensis* being among those collected by Ernest Wilson on his plant-hunting expeditions to China in the first decade of the twentieth century.

Magnolias are a Nymans speciality, and their pink and white waterlilies and goblets are major contributors to the long spring season in many parts of the garden, often accompanied by carpets of narcissi, fritillaries and other bulbs. Excellent hybrids, derived from the shrubby species, have been raised here, the best-known being the lilac-pink *M. × loebneri* 'Leonard Messel', which grows beside its parents, *M. kobus* and *M. stellata* 'Rosea'. Tree magnolias were also planted with abandon. There are impressive plants of *M. campbellii*, its hybrid 'Charles Raffill', and *M. sargentiana* var. *robusta* in the nearby Wall Garden – all producing their blooms on bare branches in spring, often followed by impressive fruits – in addition to cultivars of *M. × soulangeana* and *M. liliiflora*, and the summer-flowering *M. sieboldii*. *Styrax hemsleyanus* and *S. obassia*, *Cornus kousa* (also striking when bearing its red fruit and crimson autumn leaves, as well as when covered in white bracts in June) and August-flowering eucryphias are also here as fine specimens.

On the night of 16 October 1987 drama came to Nymans, with winds of 160kph (100mph) ripping through the garden, taking down much of the shelter belt and more than 80 per cent of its specimen trees. That there is no sign of damage or absence of mature tree cover today is evidence of how over-stocked the garden was, and how quickly new plantings establish here – but the loss of so many heritage plants was a tragedy.

Fortunately, there was much that could be salvaged. The detailed records held in the Trust's Woody Plant Catalogue – a continuously updated listing of the trees growing in the more important collections – gave the name and origin of the fallen species. Propagation material was taken from the rarest specimens and those with the most valuable genetic pedigrees and dispatched to nurseries. The resulting plants, together with those supplied by other tree collections and botanic gardens, and the spoils of more recent plant-collecting expeditions, formed the basis for a replanting programme, with the result that there is now a richer range of plants at Nymans than at any time in its history.

One notable collection that been expanding here recently centres around the plants associated with Harold Comber, James's son. Born in the old head gardener's cottage, and with his botanical education part-funded by the Messel family, Comber carried out two plant-hunting expeditions in Chile in the mid-1920s. Sheltered by the warm south-facing wall of the Wall Garden, a spectrum of Chilean plants is now displayed, ranging from shrubby *Luma apiculata*, *Cryptocarya alba*, *Desfontainia spinosa* and pungently scented *Escallonia illinita* to herbaceous *Lobelia tupa* and even species of spiky *Puya*. Comber also collected in Tasmania, and a

'Tasmanian Walk' is going to be developed within the Wild Garden across the road – an area of some 3.2ha (8 acres), which also features collections of oaks and other woody species, notably *Quercus kelloggii*, *Pyrus pashia*, *Stewartia ovata* var. *grandiflora* and *Castonopsis sclerophylla*, arranged in loose groups among rough grass.

In the Top Garden, the trees and shrubs are spliced by double borders of predominantly June-flowering perennials, with loose drifts of daylilies, geraniums and other stalwarts interspersed with smaller clumps of contrasting shapes such as *Sanguisorba officinalis* 'Arnhem' and *Phlomis tuberosa* 'Amazone', as well as the Nymans form of *Philadelphus delavayi*, which has plum-coloured calyces around its highly scented white flowers. Elsewhere, new groupings of woodland perennials including varieties of *Disporum* and *Arisaema* have also been added.

Behind banks of fuchsias and salvias, you come to a formal garden of Shrub and Climbing roses, recently renovated and extended by the Trust to include longer-flowering English varieties. Roses were the enthusiasm of Maud Messel, who began collecting them in the 1920s during their lull in fashion; many were given to her by the rosarians Ellen Willmott and Edward Bunyard, others she found in France, and the collection became an important repository of old varieties. Organic methods of pest and disease control are practised on them, with sprays of milk to control mildew and garlic solution against blackspot disease.

Down the main axis of the Wall Garden is the much-photographed pair of high-summer Edwardian borders, steeply tiered, kaleidoscopically coloured, and fuelled with a large proportion of annuals (watered sparingly so they become stocky and self-sufficient) to ensure a long and continuous performance. They run either side of an Italian marble fountain, flanked by intricate yew topiaries, and in their structure and impact have changed little since they were installed by Ludwig Messel, taking advice on the design of this garden from the influential garden writer William Robinson.

The house looms over the wall to the east. It was built in 1928 in the style of a late-medieval manor house by Colonel and Mrs Leonard Messel as a replacement for his father's Victorian villa but, in the winter of 1947, it caught fire. The standpipes were frozen and before the flames could be brought under control the building was gutted, with the loss of almost all its contents, including a notable library of botanical books. So the 1987 storm was not Nymans' first disaster. The event was turned to advantage, however, for although its rear section was rebuilt, the remainder was left as a ruin, roofless, jagged-walled, and with its high mullioned windows glassless and gaping. Thus the garden gained a wonderfully romantic centrepiece. It stands, clothed in roses, honeysuckle, clematis, wisteria and (of course) evergreen magnolia, with some suitably quaint Old English accompaniments – fat topiary hens brooding on the gravel, a circular dovecote and a flock

**ABOVE** The ruins of the house, destroyed by fire in 1947, seen across the cedar lawn, with drifts of anemones in the foreground.

of white doves. Making use of the warm micro-climate beside them, bananas and other luxuriant foliage plants set an exotic mood, joined by flowers such as eucomis and ginger lilies, and a fine specimen of ferny-leaved *Lyonothamnus floribundus* subsp. *aspleniifolius*. The side gardens, featuring lavenders and pink 'Mevrouw Nathalie Nypels' roses, are a more restrained period piece.

There are further late nineteenth- and early twentieth-century touches on and beside the lawns that lead off to the south and east: a living basket, woven with winter jasmine and filled with red hydrangeas, and a sunken garden, where a Byzantine urn stands in a pattern of spring and summer bedding, backed by an Italian loggia. The shrubberies around the lawns have recently been refreshed with the clearance of old Hardy Hybrid rhododendrons and the planting of other shrubs, notably a collection of Ghent azaleas and hybrids of scented, June-flowering *Rhododendron viscosum*.

Although planting at Nymans continues to be adventurous and experimental, without historical constraints, the Trust is frequently guided in such work by the comprehensive plant survey compiled by Ludwig Messel's daughter Muriel in 1918, shortly before her untimely death in the flu pandemic.

The Kurume azaleas that Ernest Wilson selected in 1918 from a nursery on the southern Japanese island of Kyushu – Wilson's Fifty, as they are known – certainly used to be cultivated here, and those that are still available have been returned to a bank beside the Croquet Lawn. Other Japanese touches in this part of the garden include a long wisteria pergola and stone lanterns acquired from the Japan-British Exhibition of 1910.

Along the perimeter of the garden, colourful camellias, azaleas, rhododendrons and hydrangeas give way to landscaped ground of hillock and dell. The acid sand is well suited to heathers, and Ludwig Messel made a collection here – possibly the first heath garden in the country. The display includes many Sussex-bred varieties of our native *Calluna vulgaris*, such as 'Crowborough Beacon' and 'Scaynes Hill', and they grow in the company of low conifers, berberis, birches and some of the plant-hunters' dwarf rhododendrons such as *RR. anthopogon* subsp. *hypenanthum*, *calostrotum*, *saluenense* and *cerasinum*. Beyond, the ground falls and rises to give a fine view of the South Downs.

**LEFT** The long herbaceous borders at Nymans are spectacular in late summer.
**RIGHT** Circular beds form part of the Pleasure Grounds at 18th-century Osterley Park.

# Osterley Park

**ISLEWORTH, MIDDLESEX**

**AREA** 145ha (357 acres) • **SOIL** varied, gravel and clay • **ALTITUDE** 30m (100ft)
**AVERAGE RAINFALL** 610mm (24in) • **AVERAGE WINTER CLIMATE** moderate

'It is a pleasant drive between sweet little villages and villas to this park,' wrote one visitor in the autumn of 1786. How things have changed. Osterley has been engulfed in London's western conurbation, Heathrow is only 8km (5 miles) away, and the M4 has amputated the northern section of the park. But there are still 57ha (142 acres) of oasis remaining, and it is a surprise and relief suddenly to exchange the roads, housing and light industry for a landscape of meadows, trees and lakes. The house itself, designed and refined by Robert Adam through the 1760s and '70s, is the park's principal ornament, standing in the centre of the flat parkland, and as you follow the circuit walk it provides a series of eye-catchers between the trees. From the east, there are views also of the stable block, the legacy of Sir Thomas Gresham, Chancellor of the Exchequer to Elizabeth I, who built the first great house here in the mid-sixteenth century.

The flowing landscape park, which is also quite likely to have been moulded by Adam, changed radically during the nineteenth century, in response to the taste for heavier and more varied scenery. By the 1980s the grounds were short-staffed and in serious decline, and it was then that a major project was initiated to restore its eighteenth-century character, which is now potently re-established.

On the west side of the house, you look out onto a large area of park, girdled with iron railings. The Great Meadow within is grazed by impressive and benign Charolais cattle, and kissing gates allow you to wander across. It has never been ploughed or fertilised, and supports a wide range of wildflowers. As well as the many scattered trees inside it, including black walnut and Turkey oak, there are plantations comprising mixed trees such as horse and sweet chestnut, oak and hornbeam, all underplanted with hazel or ringed with hawthorn, reminiscent of eighteenth-century clumps.

The trees in the adjacent pleasure ground gradually blend into a pinetum, with closely mown lawn lapping about them. The Temple of Pan, with its Rococo plasterwork, pre-dates Adam, but it was he who designed the handsomely decorated semi-circular Garden House, where the 45 tubs of orange and lemon trees listed in the comprehensive 1782 inventory would have spent the winters. In front of it, Mrs Sarah Child had her flower garden, which has now been put back with gusto. The design is based on a pattern of paisley beds in which the plants are arranged in theatrical tiers and flowering 'cones', some around wooden tripods. The flavour is lively and romantic, with billowing stands of verbascums and sweet peas, Canterbury bells and cornflowers, salvias and sweet rocket, and self-seeding poppies, nigella and feverfew, following a wash of spring bulbs. It is a delightful re-creation of a now rare gardening style.

There are more flower displays in the Tudor walled garden, which includes annual and perennial cutting beds, a Long Border and heirloom vegetables. Colour is also found in the American Garden, a popular feature in eighteenth-century gardens, when plants from the New World were coming into cultivation for the first time. Mrs Child's collection has been evoked here in the form of a broad border of trees, shrubs and perennials she is known to have grown. They include liquidambar, calycanthus, chionanthus, echinacea, mertensia and Shrub roses such as white *Rosa carolina* and pink *R. virginiana*.

Beyond the pinetum and meadow, the lazy wilderness walk takes you through glades of Hungarian and other oaks, fringed with foxgloves, campion and massed snowdrops, daffodils and bluebells, to the lower lake and boathouse. Beginning as a narrow river, the channel swells as it curves past the ice-house and the fine cork oak, cedars and other specimen trees south of the house, to conclude in a wide pool, elegantly rafted with waterlilies.

Beyond the drive, the second lake leads off to the north-east corner of the park. The main eighteenth-century attraction here was the menagerie of exotic birds on the east bank, reached by a rope-drawn ferry. Now it is native species that prevail, the park being peaceful enough for grebes, jays, owls and many other birds that have been driven from the rest of London. There is even a heronry on the lake's island, a stone's throw from the rumbling motorway.

# Oxburgh Hall

OXBOROUGH, KING'S LYNN, NORFOLK

AREA 7.5ha (18½ acres) • SOIL alkaline-neutral/sandy, clay • ALTITUDE 30m (100ft)
AVERAGE RAINFALL 635mm (25in) • AVERAGE WINTER CLIMATE cold

This moated hall rises from flat ground into a broad Norfolk sky. Built and fortified for Sir Edmund Bedingfeld in about 1482, it was romanticised and remodelled for the 6th and 7th baronets in the mid-nineteenth century. The landscape has also been tamed, for the surrounding fields were marshland until drained and dyked in the late eighteenth century. Woods and belts of trees give some intimacy and shelter from the worst of the wind, and the warm red brickwork is cheery even on a grey day.

The garden's *pièce de résistance* lies beneath the hall's east front, an elaborately scrolled and patterned *parterre de compartiment* laid out by Sir Henry Paston Bedingfeld, 6th Baronet, and his wife Margaret, in about 1845. The design was taken from a garden they saw in Paris, and is very similar to one illustrated in *La Théorie et la pratique du jardinage*, published anonymously in 1709 by the French engraver and writer on the arts Antoine-Joseph Dezallier d'Argenville. Originally, the colour in such parterres was provided not by flowers but by gravels and other materials. Here, crushed chalk, black stone and painted cement were used, but in addition to massed annuals. It is remarkable that such a labour-intensive feature managed to survive for so many years, although it was in urgent need of attention by the time it came into the Trust's hands.

To reduce the amount of bedding required, blue rue and 'Hidcote' lavender have been added to some of the shapes, but each spring, the gardeners still plant out quantities of 'Paul Crampel' pelargonium, marigolds and ageratum – the violet-blue and yellow in the pattern being reversed each year to ring a subtle change in appearance. Crushed stone, tightly cropped grass, yew globes and dwarf box edging complete the scheme, and the whole design is set off by lawn. Such a ground-hugging scheme preserves the sense of openness and isolation, for the hall stands alone in the smooth, empty plane of water, grass and gravel drives. The trees serve as a frame beyond the lawn, the tall oaks and beeches being joined by the favourite Victorian cedars and wellingtonias. Beside the Gothic chapel, a path leads into the recently restored Victorian Wilderness. The lime avenue here is sheeted with bluebells in late spring, and the meandering paths on either side are bordered with snowdrops and daffodils.

Across the lawn from the parterre, a clipped yew hedge screens the long herbaceous border, where aconitum, lupins, delphiniums and irises rise behind a run of catmint, and the old wall is cloaked with clematis, roses and soft shrubs. The large Victorian kitchen garden behind, enclosed by castellated walls and turreted towers, is in the process of regeneration by the Trust, with produce such as pumpkins and asparagus, herbs and edible flowers now returned to the beds. The orchard has also been planted with traditional Norfolk apple and pear varieties, and the grass underneath them is managed as wildflower and bulb meadow. Sun-loving flowering and foliage shrubs bask against the potting shed wall, on the site of the old peach and vinery houses. The scheme includes cistuses, romneya, potentilla, trumpet vine (*Campsis radicans*), woolly *Buddleja crispa*, ceanothus and the large-leaved vine *Vitis coignetiae*.

From the space and formal order of these areas, you can follow the stream beyond the border of spring bulbs and summer shrubs and walk across the wooden drawbridge that leads into My Lady's Wood. Now you are in the peaceful shadows of oak, beech and sycamore, among thickets of snowberry and carpets of snowdrops, winter aconites, violets and other wildflowers. The circular walk leads you to a thatched summer-house, recently rebuilt as part of the wood's restoration. A second circular walk has also been completed in woodland re-acquired by the Trust, south of the hall.

# Packwood House

**LAPWORTH, SOLIHULL, WARWICKSHIRE**

**AREA** 3.2ha (8 acres) • **SOIL** alkaline/heavy soil • **ALTITUDE** 121m (396ft)
**AVERAGE RAINFALL** 686mm (27in) • **AVERAGE WINTER CLIMATE** cold

On rising ground to the south of this house is one of the great topiary gardens of Britain. Mystery surrounds its origins and theme, though by tradition it is a representation of the Sermon on the Mount, with The Master on the summit of the mound, the twelve Apostles and four Evangelists on the cross-walk below, and the lawn filled with the assembled Multitude. The 1723 plan may indicate some of these yews, but the Multitude does not appear to have been planted until the mid-nineteenth century. Whatever the true history, the topiaries are today an impressive sight. Leaning or bulging, cylindrical or conical, each is a character in the throng. Some now stand 15m (50ft) high, others are considerably less, either because they have a more taxing site or because they are replacements for earlier casualties (poor drainage and badgers being among the hazards). The cutting is done with the aid of a lorry-mounted hoist, and takes over three months to complete.

In the remainder of the garden, the flavour is more domestic, set by the house, bristling with gables and tall chimneys, and by the formal pattern of walls, gazebos, gateways and flights of steps that accompanies it. It is a handsome assembly of mellow orange brickwork, rich in design detail. The development of the garden's rectangular enclosures was probably begun after the Restoration by John Fetherston, whose father remodelled the existing timber-framed house. The raised terrace between the South Garden and the Yew Garden, affording a fine view of the lake and park, and the north-east gazebo, are attributed to him. They are both clearly depicted in a drawing of about 1756, as is the wall with its 30 recesses for bee skeps. The present appearance of this main South Garden, however, reflects the sensitive hand of Graham Baron Ash, who devoted much of his early life to the rescue and embellishment of a neglected Packwood, bought for him by his father, a wealthy industrialist and racehorse owner, in 1905. It was he who rebuilt the missing gazebos, installed the Sunk Garden in the lawn and set out the double borders on the raised terrace.

Flowers are the third prominent element at Packwood, adding delicacy and complementary colours to the composition of greens and orange brick. They are arranged with a remarkable lightness of touch, capturing that romantic, mingled and deliciously carefree quality that you see in Victorian watercolours of cottage gardens. The style, adapted from that recommended by J.C. Loudon in his *Encyclopaedia of Gardening* of 1822, was perfected by E.D. Lindup, one of the Trust's first head gardeners, and has been developed by his successors. Perennials, climbing plants, and a host of spring and summer annuals and biennials contribute to the mix, with the structure, rhythm and harmony achieved by the continual repetition of the contents within each border. There are very few architectural plants, bold eye-catchers, or big clumps; everything here merges and intertwines.

Each border also has its colour scheme. Those in the East Court are in misty pinks and purples to give a heightened sense of depth in this smaller space, while over the wall in the main South Garden is the Yellow Border, its daisy-flowered heleniums and helianthus, golden hop and lemon potentilla tempered by a wash of catmint, nigella and corncockle. The new double borders, which flank the newly reinstated central axis path opposite the front door, are subtly liveried in plums, browns and silver-greys to echo the tints of the house – the cast including *Stipa gigantea* grasses, sanguisorba, cirsium, atriplex, artemisia, cardoons and *Yucca recurvifolia*. On the raised Terrace Walk, the daylilies,

**FAR LEFT** The mid-Victorian parterre at Oxburgh was inspired by a Parisian garden, much enjoyed by Sir Henry Paston Bedingfeld and his wife.
**ABOVE** Daturas and verbascums flower along the raised Terrace Walk.

rudbeckias, red astrantias and the scarlet oriental poppy 'Beauty of Livermere' deliver hotter tones, complemented by the fresh, luxuriant foliage of *Euphorbia mellifera* and *Helianthus salicifolius* and the black of succulent aeoniums. The colour schemes are not always gentle. The rose beds, for example, which are set into bays of box and yew by the east wall, are shameless in their bands of brilliant red and yellow.

In 2007, the Sunk Garden, which had been flamboyantly bedded out in Baron Ash's time, was redeveloped as an exotic garden. The focus is now on more permanent planting, with the opportunity being taken to trial plants that are of borderline hardiness in the Midlands, for the beds are well-drained and sheltered. Succulent echeverias and Californian zauschnerias are among the company, growing with other more reliable perennials with characterful appearance such as euphorbias, kniphofias, eryngiums and *Parahebe perfoliata*. Crushed red brick has been used as a top dressing to blend with the surrounding walls.

A series of fine wrought-iron gates offers glimpses into the park and connects the various courts. The two quietest courts are to the west and north of the house. The former, Fountain Court, is named after the strange plunge bath built in 1680, while the north court contains a well, shaded by a young collection of lime trees; there is a good show of snowdrops here in late winter.

Fruit and vegetable growing has also resumed in recent years. A new orchard has appeared between the Yew Garden and the lake, planted with pre-1920 trees associated with the region, such as 'Worcester Pearmain' apple, 'Warwickshire Drooper' plum and 'Black Worcester' pear. The ground beneath the trees is managed as wildflower meadow, with this theme also extending into the areas beyond – the diversity enriched by daffodils and experimental plantings of perennials such as blue *Iris sibirica* and orange *Hieracium aurantiacum*. Conversion to different mowing regimes has seen the return of numerous species, including orchids.

Across the road, the restoration of the walled kitchen garden is now under way, the vegetable and cut-flower beds set into a traditional quartered design around a circular dipping pond. Altogether, Packwood has been evolving into a very absorbing garden, rich in plantsmanship.

**RIGHT**. The avenue of giant yews, popularly known as 'The Sermon on the Mount'.

P

# Peckover House

**WISBECH, CAMBRIDGESHIRE**

AREA 0.8ha (2 acres) • SOIL neutral/rich alluvial loam • ALTITUDE 30m (100ft)
AVERAGE RAINFALL 381mm (15in) • AVERAGE WINTER CLIMATE cold

A thrilling example of the Victorian gardenesque style, this spacious town garden is one of the Trust's lesser-known jewels. The first impression is of Georgian elegance – a square, russet-brick house, standing in a handsome residential row on the north bank of the River Nene. Behind it, you might expect a sober composition of grass, evergreens and gravel walks, and these are indeed the ingredients of the garden's eastern section – but the lines of paths, croquet lawn and shrubberies surprise you by twisting and turning the moment they leave the house. The hollies, laurels, box and yew are joined by Victorian favourites such as spotted aucuba, golden privet and ferns; there is a wrought-iron seat with a fern design; and as you walk onto the adjacent lawn, you suddenly come upon exotic specimens of monkey puzzle, California redwood and Chusan palm, a rustic summer-house, a circle cut in the grass to make space for an ever-changing spring and summer bedding display, and a border where perennials, including thrift, saxifrages and purple sand cherry, play parts in a permanent bedding scheme.

In 1999, the Trust re-created Alexa's Rose Garden from archival photographs. Named after the Hon. Alexandrina Peckover, who gave the estate to the Trust in 1943, the rose arches now support old-fashioned highly scented roses that were popular in the Victorian and Edwardian eras, including 'Phyllis Bide', 'Aimée Vibert', 'Madame Grégoire Staechelin', 'Honorine de Brabant' and 'Céline Forrestier'.

The scenes now unfolding show both the best and 'worst' aspects of the gardenesque style, the term first proposed in 1832 by the author J.C. Loudon, to mean planting designed to display the character of each plant and the art of the gardener. There are crisp juxtapositions of shape, foliage and flowers – cypress next to bergenia and ivy; palm with variegated holly, yew and *Viburnum davidii* – and space is provided for each plant to grow and parade itself well. But there is also the frantic eclecticism that the style soon came to embody: a large and diverse plant collection, assembled in a startling variety and quantity of geometric and abstract beds, with no theme to unite them. Here, mercifully, walls and hedges do provide some visual barriers. However, it is all conducted with such panache, and tended with such minute attention to detail, that critical faculties are readily suspended.

Little is known of the garden's history, and the Trust has taken its cue for expanding this gardenesque theme from the layout, mature planting and garden buildings inherited from the Hon. Alexandrina Peckover, the last of the house's Quaker owners. It is a surprise to discover that the garden is not confined to a strip directly behind the house, but runs westwards along the backs of half a dozen other properties in the row. Behind the first dividing brick wall is a small enclosure, where a green and white pavilion overlooks an oval lawn and thyme-fringed waterlily pond. Beds of hydrangeas, peonies and lilies (excellent companions for a hearty soil), edged in sedum and liriope, complete the outer oval.

Through a gap in the hedge, a pair of double borders is revealed, segmented by short hedges and mixed in content. *Dianthus* 'Mrs Sinkins' runs either side of the gravel path, and iron supports holding Climbing roses and clematis punctuate the groups of shrubs and perennials, which include white 'Iceberg' roses, hydrangeas, guelder rose, asters, euphorbias, Japanese anemones and agapanthus.

The brick-based glasshouse in which the vista terminates is called the Orangery. Supported by other exotic pot plants, its centrepiece comprises three orange trees in glazed tubs; these are thought to be over 300 years old, and still bear heavy crops of fruit. The neighbouring glasshouse, adjoining cold frames and compost heaps (open to inspection), is used for propagation.

Vibrant beds of roses and tender perennials give you a thirst for the refreshing greens of the westernmost enclosure, where a quince and other fruit trees grow on the lawn. Rambler roses hang from the hollies, and silhouetted against a curving hedge of golden privet, a bed of fiery reds and purples is a final, potent sample of what Sir John Betjeman called Victorian 'ghastly good taste.'

**LEFT** Two topiary peacocks guard a gravel path bordered with pinks.
**ABOVE** The Orangery is used to display a wide range of flowering pot plants and three orange trees; in front is a metal arch for climbing roses.

# Penrhyn Castle

**BANGOR, GWYNEDD**

**AREA** 19ha (48 acres) • **SOIL** neutral/sandy and stony • **ALTITUDE** 46m (150ft)
**AVERAGE RAINFALL** 1,092mm (43in) • **AVERAGE WINTER CLIMATE** mild

'Got up to look at the glorious view of the splendid range of hills lit up by the sun, which has not entirely risen … After breakfast I went out with Col. and Ly. L. Pennant, our children, & almost all the company & planted 2 trees in Albert's and my name … The view on the sea with Pen Man Mear [Penmaenmawr] rising above it is very beautiful,' wrote Queen Victoria in her journal in October 1859. The tree the Queen planted, a wellingtonia, is still standing and, with the many other exotic conifers and specimen trees added during the nineteenth century, continues to inject the sloping pleasure grounds with the flavour of that period. The views, south towards Snowdonia, east along the coastline and north across the Menai Strait to Anglesey and Puffin Island, remain spectacular. And, above and within the Walled Garden, there is the bonus of a treasure trove of rare plants.

The scene is, of course, dominated by the great mass of the castle built for G.H. Dawkins Pennant between 1822 and 1838, and considered the outstanding example of the short-lived Norman Revival. Its scale drops the jaw the moment it comes into view on the crest of the hill; picturesque Austrian pines and croaking jackdaws add to the ambiance. Dawkins Pennant accompanied his building with extensive tree planting, and the collection was steadily augmented over the years. From 1880, it was entrusted to the distinguished Scottish forester and botanist Angus Duncan Webster (son of Prince Albert's head forester at Balmoral), who, over a period of thirteen years, added many new and untried species.

The walks lead past this wealth of trees – redwoods, Douglas firs, bishop and Scots pines, evergreen and deciduous oaks, Caucasian and grand firs, sycamore, beeches, limes, ashes and self-sown strawberry trees (*Arbutus unedo*); tucked under the castle walls are some impressive Japanese maples. Quantities of bulbs and wildflowers accompany the trees on the slopes, and as you explore the glades you will come upon other features – the Gothic chapel to the former house, left as a romantic ruin; a heather slope; and a rhododendron walk – *R. arboreum*, *R. yunnanense*, *R. irroratum* and *R. decorum* are some of the highlights.

Descending this west side of the hill, through the plantations of evergreen broad-leaved shrubs, you sense you are moving into a warmer temperate zone. In the Walled Garden, you have arrived – for, with the benign influence of the Gulf Stream, the climate at Penrhyn is exceptionally mild and, given shelter from the wind, a very rarified vegetation can be staged.

Among the many surprises on the sunny walls are *Mutisia decurrens*, *Sophora japonica*, *Lomatia ferruginea*, *Lapageria*, *Decumaria*, *Camellia reticulata* and the pot jasmine (*Jasminum polyanthum*) – all shrubs and climbers from the world's softer climates. The very tender *Cordyline indivisa* is also here, together with *Pittosporum eugenioides* and huge-leaved *Magnolia tripetala*. But this is no lush subtropical scene; the exotics are displayed in ordered fashion within a formal, period framework. Box-edged beds, lily ponds, fountains and loggia adorn the upper terrace, the whole composition remodelled from the original Victorian parterre by Lady Penrhyn in the 1930s. Formerly, the parterre would also have been a showpiece of complex exotic bedding, its planting supervised for many years by the noted head gardener, Walter Speed

– one of the inaugural recipients of the Royal Horticultural Society's highest award, the Victoria Medal of Honour, in 1897; extensive fruit and vegetable gardens then complemented the flower garden, and Penrhyn had the reputation of being one of the best properties in the country for the training of young gardeners.

Below the upper terrace, the impressive collection of taller shrubs and trees is displayed on sloping lawns, divided into rectangles by the grid of gravel paths. Among the cast are *Drimys winteri*, *Davidia involucrata* (handkerchief tree), *Crinodendron hookerianum*, *Magnolia tripetala* and *Sciadopitys verticillata* (Japanese umbrella pine) along with a notable sequence of late summer eucryphias.

An ironwork pergola runs along the lowest terrace. This was reinstalled by the Trust and again plays host, according to precedent, to the dripping red flowers of *Fuchsia* 'Riccartonii' and the purple stars of *Clematis* 'Jackmanii Superba'. Accompanying it is one of the oldest specimens in Britain of *Metasequoia glyptostroboides* (dawn redwood), the Chinese conifer known only in fossilised form until rediscovered in the wild in 1941.

Dramatic contrast to this safe and steady formal layout is now revealed, for the garden drops abruptly into damp meadows and the scale changes. Rising from the grass are stupendous clumps of giant rhubarb, gunnera and tree ferns, New Zealand flax and bamboo, backed by holm oaks, eucalyptus and purple maples. The area was once a more intricate stream garden, again created by Lady Penrhyn in the 1930s, but the present scheme is perhaps more fitting – as a link with, and reminder of, the gigantic and slightly forbidding architectural spectacle on the hill above.

**ABOVE** A view of the ironwork pergola entwined with fuschia and clematis.

# Petworth House

PETWORTH, WEST SUSSEX

AREA 12ha (30 acres) within parkland • SOIL acid/sandy loam and clay • ALTITUDE 33–130m (108–426ft) • AVERAGE RAINFALL 813mm (32in) • AVERAGE WINTER CLIMATE moderate

By 1751, the reputation of Lancelot 'Capability' Brown was established, and for the next 35 years he would be the dominant force in English landscape gardening. The park at Petworth is arguably his finest remaining landscape, the scene surveyed by the magnificent, 98m (320ft) long, west façade of the house, created for the 6th 'Proud' Duke of Somerset in about 1690. The duke also created an important formal garden, almost certainly designed by the Royal Gardener George London. The park is a typical open and uncomplicated composition of grass, water and well-spaced specimens and clumps of trees, predominantly sycamore, oak and beech, concealing the bounds, outlining the contours and standing sentinel on the ridges. A herd of fallow deer roams among them.

At the heart of the landscape is the serpentine lake, fashioned by Brown from an existing series of small fish ponds. Willow, birch and poplar fringe the water and cover the lake's islands, accompanied by some fine stands of swamp cypress; the Trust has recently replanted the clump of trees Brown planned at the head of the water. The boathouse was added by the 3rd Earl of Egremont, who is also responsible for the urns and sculptures that punctuate the park. J.M.W. Turner spent much time at Petworth during the time of the 3rd Earl, and his studio is often open for tours.

The Pleasure Grounds to the north of the house were devastated by the 1987 storm, and although the Trust has replaced the central original core of dense woodland as it was 180 years earlier, it will be many years before the new plantings restore the patterns of wood and glade. Yet there is much to see. Brown suggested the Doric temple and Ionic rotunda as eye-catchers, and enclosed the whole with a ha-ha. He also enriched the planting, drawing on many ornamental species of tree and shrub introduced from America and southern Europe during the previous century. Further phases of adventurous planting took place in the late eighteenth, nineteenth and early twentieth centuries, and the tradition continues today under the guidance of the present Lady Egremont and the National Trust.

The greensand seams and the diversity of dry, damp, sunny and shady habitats allow a remarkable rate of tree growth, and a far wider range of plants than would grow in the exposed ground of the park. You walk from plantations of Shrub roses and crataegus, crabs, rowans and wild pear to banks of massed azaleas and rhododendrons, and marshy stands of willows and dogwoods.

Elsewhere, cornus, arbutus, aesculus, hydrangeas and Japanese maples provide highlights between laurel and aucuba, Hungarian and American oaks, tulip trees and the twisted trunks of Spanish chestnuts. In early spring, the Pleasure Ground is flooded with Lent lilies and primroses; later, there are bluebells, fritillaries and camassias, and an increasing population of common spotted and twayblade orchids: in short, colour and variety to complement the sublime expanses of landscape.

ABOVE The Rotunda, built in 1766, with native daffodils, known as Lent lilies, in the grass. RIGHT Azaleas in the quarry dell in spring at Plas Newydd.

# Plas Newydd

LLANFAIRPWLL, ANGLESEY

AREA 16ha (40 acres) • SOIL varied • ALTITUDE 0–46m (0–150ft) • AVERAGE RAINFALL 1,118mm (44in) • AVERAGE WINTER CLIMATE mild

With yachts coursing the tidal water below its sloping lawns, the mountains of Snowdonia rising behind the Vaynol woods on the far shore, and, to the east, Robert Stephenson's Britannia railway bridge cutting across the curve of the Strait, Plas Newydd has as fine a setting as any coastal property in Britain. There is the further boon of a mild climate, announced immediately by the massive screens of the half-hardy New Zealand evergreen *Griselinia littoralis*, which flank your descent to the house. The summers here tend to be cool and sunny, the winters wet and windy and, given the sheltering woods, the site proves ideal for many woody plants from the warmer temperate regions of the world. The planting, however, is not in competition. The drifts of trees and shrubs are bold and harmonious, framing the views and providing expanses of green and islands of colour to echo the sinuous shapes of the landscape.

The bones of this layout were set out by the leading landscape designer of the late eighteenth century, Humphry Repton, engaged by Henry, Earl of Uxbridge, as work on the house was nearing completion. His proposals are contained in one of his famous Red Books, dated 1798–9. But much has happened since Repton's day. Lord Uxbridge's son, the 1st Marquess of Anglesey – the celebrated Waterloo commander – undertook a great deal of tree planting after 1815. Between the First and Second World Wars, the 6th Marquess added a range of conifers, specimen deciduous trees and ornamental shrubs, in particular rhododendrons and camellias, and the present Marquess continued to augment the collection through the 1950s and '60s. Since the transfer of ownership to the Trust, this momentum has been maintained, with several major new features established. Within the historic framework, the garden thus reflects twentieth-century taste.

West of the house is the area known as the West Indies, a long and broad sweep of lawn fringed and broken by trees and shrubberies. In May, the shadows are lit with pastel-coloured azaleas and in summer with hydrangeas, whose blooms, indicating the increasing acidity, change from pink near the house to purple and intense sky blue and gentian as the garden flows deeper on to the greensand. *Magnolia* × *veitchii* 'Isca', *M. wilsonii* and *Prunus* 'Tai-

Haku' add further early highlights, with eucryphias and hoherias giving showy white flowers in July and August. The hybrid *Hoheria* 'Glory of Amlwch' is a speciality and seems to perform better here than in any other Trust garden – appropriately, since it originated on Anglesey. Unfortunately, another noted feature, the hedges of *Viburnum plicatum* f. *tomentosum* 'Lanarth', have suffered from the spread of honey fungus in the grounds.

A small quarry dell, snaked with stone paths and stairways, adds to the adventure. Camellias, pink 'Donation' prominent among them, are massed here, with cherries, pieris and hedges of scented *Osmanthus delavayi* giving an April boost of colour. In the

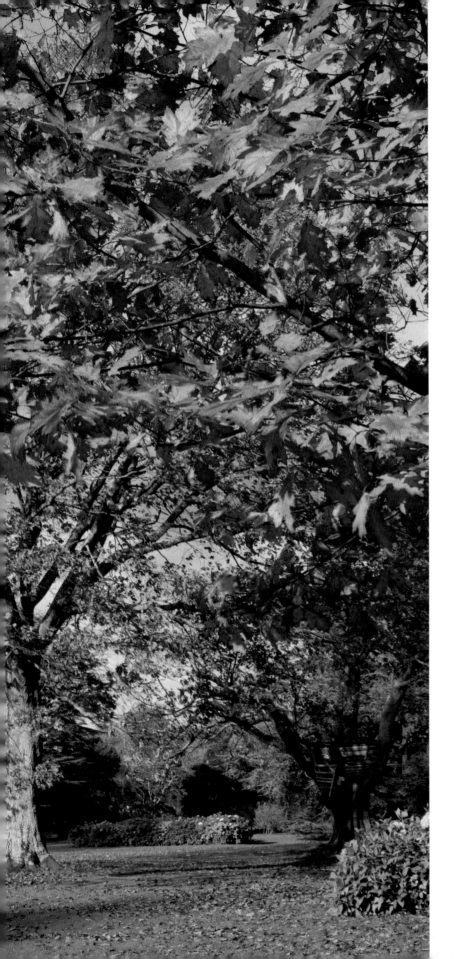

summer sunshine, the dell offers a cool and shady respite from the glare on sea and lawn. The garden's rarest tree, the tender Asian evergreen *Schima wallichii* var. *khasiana*, is found at this end of the garden; it produces its white flowers in autumn.

Following the line of the Long Walk, a double avenue of yew and *Chamaecyparis pisifera* 'Squarrosa' introduced as a windbreak in the 1930s, you arrive in the arboretum known as 'Australasia'. Planted in 1981 to replace the exhausted wartime orchard, this features a collection of eucalyptus and nothofagus grown among wildflowers and meadow grasses, with a fringe of Australasian shrubs. These are fast-growing trees and the Southern Hemisphere mood is well established.

The most recent improvements have centred on the formal terraces east of the house. On the upper level, a trellis garden house with bubbling tufa fountain has been erected, marking the site of the former Edwardian conservatory. On the levels below, the Italianate flavour set by the 6th Marquess has been reinforced with the introduction of pools and water features, additional hedging and clipped evergreens. In high summer, there is a fine show of agapanthus on the middle terrace, with hot borders opposite including crocosmias, heleniums, *Dahlia* 'Bishop of Llandaff' and marigolds.

Almost a mile's walk along the line of the Strait brings you to a quite different garden, a wild and exotic rhododendron wood. The 6th Marquess began introducing choice species and hybrids here in the 1930s, including *R. fortunei, R. thomsonii, R. praevernum, R.* 'Shilsonii', *R.* Nobleanum Group, *R.* 'Loderi King George' and *R. montroseanum*, which self-sows freely. The collection has been steadily augmented by the present Lord Anglesey, who received 'thinnings' from Bodnant as a wedding gift from the 2nd Lord Aberconway; for three seasons, beginning in 1948, lorry-loads of rhododendrons arrived, accompanied by two gardeners to plant them. Many of Bodnant's famous scarlet *R. griersonianum* hybrids were among them. Large-leaved species, such as *R. falconeri, R. macabeanum* and *R. sinogrande*, perform particularly well here at Plas Newydd, and the climate is also mild enough for scented conservatory varieties such as 'Lady Alice Fitzwilliam', 'Princess Alice' and 'Fragrantissimum'. Open only until the end of May, this isolated corner of the Plas Newydd gardens is a bonus for springtime visitors and should not be missed.

**LEFT** Autumn colour in the garden at Plas Newydd.
**RIGHT** A view of the Lavender Walk at the eastern end of the Rose Garden at Polesden Lacey.

# Polesden Lacey

GREAT BOOKHAM, DORKING, SURREY

AREA 12ha (30 acres) • SOIL alkaline/some clay and flint • ALTITUDE 91–143m (300–470ft)
AVERAGE RAINFALL 762mm (30in) • AVERAGE WINTER CLIMATE cold

From 1906, this was the home of the Hon. Mrs Ronald Greville, one of the most celebrated hostesses in the Marlborough House circle of Edward VII, and the mansion and gardens offer a delicious insight into the life of Edwardian high society. The present house, a yellow-washed and green-shuttered villa, was built in the 1820s, but enlarged and refurbished for the Grevilles in the French Neo-classical style by Mewes and Davis, the architects of the Ritz Hotel. Captain Greville died in 1908, and his plans for an equally grand scheme of parterres for the garden were never implemented. Instead, his wife enriched the planting within the inherited framework of avenues, formal walks, lawns and kitchen garden.

The setting is magnificent. The house stands just below the southernmost ridge of the North Downs, and the trees on the lower lawns frame sweeping views over the valley and across to the wooded crest of Ranmore Common. One of the garden's principal features is the panoramic Long Walk that stretches for 0.4km (¼ mile) eastward above the valley. This was begun in 1761, but considerably enlarged by the playwright Richard Brinsley Sheridan, who bought the property in 1797; it is the only remnant of his garden.

The chalk and sunny aspect make for a hot, dry hillside. Wildflowers do well among the hungry meadow grasses, and the open, mown lawns are stained purple by creeping thyme. But the site is well furnished with trees, and seams of richer, acid loam allow the chalk-tolerant beeches, oaks, maples and pines to be supplemented by sweet chestnut, wellingtonia, Douglas fir and other more fastidious species. The plantations were badly hit by the great storm of 1987, and to a lesser extent that of 1990, but new plantings are now maturing. Ornamental gardening is concentrated

across the lawn to the west, except in the immediate vicinity of the house, which is hung with wisteria, yellow Banksian rose and other climbers and wall shrubs, and fringed with box-edged borders of spring and summer bedding.

Here, in the nineteenth-century walled kitchen garden, is Mrs Greville's rose garden. Set out in a simple cross pattern, with long, box-edged, wooden pergolas, adjoining seams of 'Munstead' and deeper 'Hidcote' lavenders, walls draped in clematis and a water tower festooned in an old Chinese wisteria, it is a mass of pink, white and crimson during the summer months. A little earlier in the year, the same colours occur in the first of the yew enclosures beyond, containing double borders of peonies. The other compartments present collections of lavenders – and of bearded iris, a selection of early hybrids, some of which have been invigorated through laboratory propagation of virus-free tissue.

As in the house, there is fine classical ornament at every turn. A Venetian well-head stands at the junction of the rose garden paths, a discus thrower disports in the lavender garden, and the theme is pursued elsewhere in the form of a Roman bath as well as further well-heads, urns and statues, all adding luxury to the compositions.

To the west, the path leads past herbaceous borders to a winter garden, shaded by three large Persian ironwood trees. Beyond, a thatched bridge leads over the sunken estate road to the Edwardian kitchen garden, now grassed over and patterned with limes and cherries. To the south runs the main herbaceous border, 137m (450ft) long and divided into four sections. The pastel colours rise into yellow climaxes of achilleas, daylilies and kniphofia, and spiky yuccas and blue-grey *Crambe maritima* contribute emphatic foliage to the corners. Agapanthus do particularly well in the hot, dry ground here, supreme among them a magnificent midnight blue form of the pendulous *A. inapertus*. Below, colour comes from the shrubs and trees on and adjacent to the bank of Westmorland limestone that plunges into the Sunken Garden. Berberis, lilacs, hydrangeas and perovskia give a succession of flowers, beautifully complemented by pear trees with silver foliage (*Pyrus nivalis*), whitebeam, smoke bush, large-leaved *Viburnum rhytidophyllum* and a massive Pfitzer juniper.

Mrs Greville died in 1942 and lies buried outside the Walled Garden, in an enclosure presided over by eighteenth-century French statues of the Four Seasons.

**LEFT** Evening light in the Rose Garden, with a view towards the well-head.
**RIGHT** *Clematis armandii* is the backdrop to a show of tulips.

# Powis Castle

**WELSHPOOL, POWYS**

AREA 10ha (25 acres) • SOIL acid woodland area, otherwise neutral to alkaline/clay
ALTITUDE 0–137m (0–450ft) • AVERAGE RAINFALL 813mm (32in) • AVERAGE WINTER
CLIMATE cold

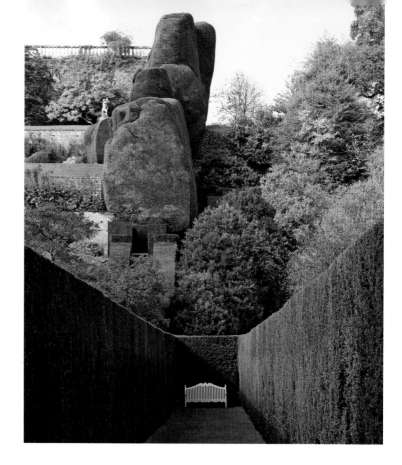

It will annoy visitors following behind you, but I recommend slowing the car as you come to the ornamental wrought-iron gates between the park and the garden, on your way up the hill. Behind the railings, and from a platform of smooth grass, appointed with finely clipped topiaries, your eye is swept up over a canopy of mixed trees to a steep ridge in the middle distance. Mellow Baroque terraces, masked in shrubs and bordered by a gigantic hedge, ascend this in tiers towards the skyline. And here, seemingly among the clouds, is perched a massive fortress of red limestone – the medieval seat of Welsh princes and later the earls of Powis – crowned with battlements and lapped by domes of dark yew.

The appetite for exploration is whetted and there is no disappointment, for this is one of the Trust's richest flower gardens, with some of the most swashbuckling and sophisticated herbaceous planting to be seen anywhere in the country. The curving drive leads you on up the slopes, well wooded with oaks of such a size and quality that they were insisted upon by Admiral Rodney for his fighting ships during the American War of Independence. Groups of red and fallow deer can usually be glimpsed in the shadows.

You enter the garden just below the castle to be met by the reverse panorama: layers of herbaceous borders, topiaries, stairways and balustrades, descending to a 1ha (2½ acre) lawn; north of it, a large formal garden of fruit trees and rose beds; and opposite, another lower ridge, encased in oaks and yews, and backed by the patchwork of fields, villages and hills of the Welsh border countryside.

The grand terraces, incorporating an Orangery and Aviary, and an array of fine lead statuary from the workshop of the Flemish sculptor John van Nost, are a unique and remarkable legacy, having survived intact the destructive eighteenth-century taste for naturalistic landscaping. Legend has it (there is not shred of evidence) that Lancelot 'Capability' Brown visited and recommended that they be returned to the natural rock from which they were quarried, and that this was, therefore, a narrow escape.

Their exact history is something of a mystery. It seems most likely that they were designed by William Winde, the architect of

the terrace at Cliveden, and that construction began in the early 1680s, when William Herbert, the 1st Marquess of Powis, was at the height of his political career. The Glorious Revolution of 1688 sent the Herberts into exile with King James II, and work is then thought to have come to a standstill until after 1703, when the family returned. In its entourage was now a Frenchman by the name of Adrian Duval and he, perhaps under the continuing supervision of Winde, completed the design. This included an impressive Dutch water garden on the site of the Great Lawn below, dismantled by 1809; a recent geophysical survey has revealed that its foundations correspond to the design shown in surviving drawings.

The cue for the lavish overlay of flowers comes from Violet, wife of the 4th Earl, who, in 1911, set about transforming a 'gradually deteriorating' garden into 'one of the most beautiful, if not the most beautiful, in England and Wales'. However, the garden was once again in decline when it came to the Trust, and its present content – ever-changing and experimental in the spirit of Edwardian flower gardening – reflects the expertise of its head gardener and staff from the 1970s onwards.

The high, sheltering walls of the terraces, angled to the south-east, together with the comparatively mild climate, allow an adventurous range of shrubs and climbers. In late spring, deep blue ceanothus billow above the brick like thunderclouds, while against the Orangery, the buff-yellow roses *Rosa banksiae* 'Lutea' and 'Gloire de Dijon' pick up tones in the sandstone frontispiece, in the company of orange eccremocarpus and white abutilon. Later, there are curtains of flowering clematis, cream waterlilies from *Magnolia grandiflora*, a waterfall of pale green from honey-scented *Itea ilicifolia* and scarlet showers from wall-trained *Phygelius capensis*; less showy curiosities such as *Dregea sinensis*, *Rhodochiton atrosanguineus* and *Abutilon* 'Nabob' are to be discovered on every tier.

The display of tender perennials has been raised to the level of high art at Powis, where, with the backup of glasshouses, cuttings are grown on into bushy plants during the winter, brought into flower, hardened off and returned to the garden as early as April. Potfuls fill the pedimented niches in the upper terrace wall – the orange brick fringed with the compact form of silver artemisia, brought here in 1972 and subsequently named 'Powis Castle' – and punctuate almost every balustrade and stairway. Fuchsias, an Edwardian favourite, are a speciality, with both the petticoated hybrids and scarlet-tubed *Fuchsia fulgens* and *F. boliviana* and dark-leaved *F.* 'Thalia' presented in old basketweave pots. Elsewhere, you come upon glorious salads made from the likes of glaucous-leaved melianthus, crimson-red cestrum, trailing yellow bidens, double red nasturtium, and the most sumptuous of all the pelargoniums, the damson, crimson-edged 'Lord Bute'.

Each terrace border has its theme. Drier conditions on the narrow Aviary Terrace have suggested plantings of sun-loving Mediterranean, Californian and Southern Hemisphere plants, including cistus, carpenteria, broom, lavender, iris and *Artemisia arborescens*. The Aviary itself, its roof studded with lead urns and draped in Japanese wisteria, contains troughs of half-hardy, scented rhododendrons in the company of the giant-fronded chain fern and webs of creeping fig.

On the third terrace, the deep, heavy soil allows lush herbaceous planting, and either side of the Orangery, pairs of long, boxed-edged borders recede into the distance. They are at their peak in late summer, and because of the milder light and temperatures here, the plants have a freshness and length of season rarely met in more southerly gardens. On one side of the Orangery, the tints are

of violet, white and warm pink from perennials such as monkshood, cimicifugas, polygonums, asters and *Clematis* 'Jackmanii Superba', grown on balloon hoops; on the other side, the scene is of fire and brimstone, fuelled by orange crocosmias, yellow kniphofias, the vermilion hips of *Rosa moyesii* and *R. highdownensis*, and a plume of golden cypress.

The seasons of the lowest terrace's borders straddle this display, with one border focused on the euphorbias, galegas, verbascums and other perennials of early summer; the other on the chrysanthemums, sedums and Japanese anemones of early autumn – at which time the leaves of *Acer japonicum*, amelanchiers and euonymus on the adjacent grass slope are beginning to unite.

The yews are dramatic counterweights to this casual, ephemeral vegetation. The fourteen specimen 'tumps' that sit like jellies on the upper terrace, together with the stupendous,

**ABOVE LEFT** A view of the yew hedges that buttress the terraced gardens at Powis Castle. The garden was designed by Captain William Winde in the seventeenth century but the yew hedges have since swelled and subsided out of their original shape.
**RIGHT** The view from the terrace over the lower gardens and surrounding countryside.

bulging hedge at the northern end, were probably planted in the 1720s, with darker Irish yews planted as companions a hundred years later. The boxwood is hardly less impressive, and on emerging through a gap in the yew hedge, you meet a towering wall of it, running beside a sloping, serpentine walk. The smell is always intense.

This path leads down to the lower formal garden, made by the 4th Countess from the former kitchen garden. A long vine tunnel and lines of pyramidal apple trees are reminders of the earlier use – the latter including rare, old varieties like 'Mother' and 'Broad-Eyed Pippin', all set into silver and gold ground-cover plants, serving as permanent bedding. Beds of Floribunda and Hybrid Musk roses and other Edwardian favourites, including phlox, delphiniums, campanulas and hollyhocks, stretch away from the half-timbered gardener's bothy.

At the opposite end of the Orangery terrace, you are enticed out of the formal garden past an exposed face of rock, the path curving eastwards towards the opposite ridge. Paperbark maple,

evergreen eucryphia, a tall maidenhair tree and shrimp-tinted *Acer pseudoplatanus* 'Brilliantissimum' are among the trees on this bank. Remarkably, the ridge itself is formed of acid sandstone, in contrast to the limestone of the Castle ridge, allowing the 3rd Earl to indulge in the Victorian taste for rhododendrons.

The paths lead you to an ice-house and a Ladies' Bath, both probably dating from the nineteenth century, and here and there, you are given tree-framed prospects out to Long Mountain and the Breidden Hills and back across the daffodil and wildflower paddock and Great Lawn to the castle and its terraces. Few properties can offer such a variety of vantage points, or views of such breathtaking scale and detail. This is a garden that draws the visitor back again and again – several times a year, in my case.

**ABOVE** The red sandstone castle looms behind layers of trees, shrubs and topiaries.
**RIGHT** The Sham Bridge in the Wilderness at Prior Park, designed by Alexander Pope to appear as a bridge over a river although, in fact, it is on a pond with no watercourse running through it.

# Prior Park

**BATH, SOMERSET**

**AREA** 11ha (28 acres) • **SOIL** clay/loam • **ALTITUDE** 90m (295ft) • **AVERAGE RAINFALL** 762mm (30in) • **AVERAGE WINTER CLIMATE** sheltered, with frost pockets

An intimate Arcadian valley just 1.6km (1 mile) from the centre of Bath, Prior Park came to the Trust in 1993 in an advanced state of decay, but in its design remarkably little-changed since the death of its creator, Ralph Allen, in 1764. Thanks to generous bequests and donations from the public, and a large Heritage Lottery Fund grant in 2005, the major task of restoration has continued apace.

The 30 years of the park's development was a golden era in garden history, during which the new, 'natural' landscape style evolved from its early wooded, serpentine and allegorical phase to embrace the open, uncluttered panorama of lake and meadow. Allen responded, and his park both charts the changing fashion and preserves the work of some of the movement's most influential figures.

At the head of the combe stands the Palladian mansion built by John Wood from the honey-coloured stone that Allen, a self-made businessman, was quarrying in Combe Down for Georgian Bath; it has been a school since 1867. Below, the meadow sweeps down to a magnificent Palladian bridge and a chain of three ponds appearing as a curving lake, the whole prospect framed by woods. Beyond are the hills and skyline of Bath.

It is in the west woods that the oldest features of the garden are to be found. Here you come upon the Wilderness developed from the mid-1730s, where Allen was advised by his good friend Alexander Pope. Pope was one of the most persuasive advocates of the new style and of composing a garden as a sequence of varied, narrative and emotionally charged landscape pictures, influenced by the natural qualities of the site. He took a close interest in this garden, even loaning his own gardener, John Serle.

Previously overcast by branches, dense with evergreen shrubbery, punctuated by black ponds, and with only remnants of its many architectural surprises visible, the Wilderness has now been opened up and renovated with an attendant loss of historic atmosphere. But in time, the new stonework will mellow and the plantings mature.

From the garden's entrance, the first feature you come upon is Mrs Allen's Grotto. Grottoes, with their origins deep in the ancient world, were very fashionable in the eighteenth-century garden, with Pope himself having one of the most celebrated examples in his villa garden in Twickenham. Prior Park's, partly disintegrated and currently under restoration, is also impressive, with its floor a starburst of stones, bones and ammonites, and its walls and roof formerly a wonderland of glinting shells and minerals.

Beyond, the river-like Serpentine Lake, newly restored, curls artfully along a level terrace between the steep wooded banks, terminating in a low Sham Bridge with arched openings and vermiculated pediments, and a view of the house above it – both reflecting elegantly in the water. Below the lake, the water crashes down a 'natural' rock Cascade, with a weir plate enabling an increased flow when Allen wanted to impress his guests, who would have been assembled in the circular gravel arena known as the Cabinet at its base. Young oriental plane trees and decorative shrubberies of period plants – among them box, viburnum, phillyrea, ruscus, ferns, hydrangeas and magnolias – complete the scene.

This garden's main vista was refashioned several times. It began, in 1734, as a quite formal landscape, with a triangular lawn, circular basin of water and straight-edged woods. In the 1750s, it was greatly extended down into the combe, the woods were made to billow down the banks, the lower lakes were created by damming the stream and, in 1755, the Palladian bridge was built as its crowning ornament. After 1759, the naturalisation process was concluded, the circular basin with its accompanying cascade and plantations being removed to provide the present uninterrupted sweep of meadow. The leading landscape gardener was now Lancelot 'Capability' Brown, and it is possible that it was he who suggested the final alterations to Allen in the few years before his death.

The circuit of the park takes you around the meadow and down to the water by way of the eastern woods. In spring, there is a surge of wild garlic over the flank of the combe, and in among the trees there are many other ferns and wildflowers. An oak-framed summer-house, moved here in 1912, surveys one of the glades, and at one point you can walk out onto the adjacent field for a broader panorama of the city.

As you descend, the lake is gradually revealed as three ponds standing at different levels, with another dam made under the bridge, so that the water gushed through the arches. The architect of the bridge, one of only three Palladian bridges to survive in Britain (the earlier examples being at Stowe and Wilton House), is unknown, but it was probably a copy of Wilton's built by Allen's clerk of works, Richard Jones; the stone was brought down via a new driveway to the north-west, with a Chinese gate at its entrance.

From the bridge, you have the equally impressive view back up the combe. Until 1921, this took in not only the mansion but also the Gothic Temple of 1753, perched on the edge of the Wilderness. A replica may replace it in due course: it is one of the final missing or broken pieces of the jigsaw that the National Trust has been gradually reassembling.

**LEFT** Looking down over the lake with its Palladian bridge.
**ABOVE RIGHT** Snowdrops on the grass bank at Quarry Bank Mill, with the mill owner's house beyond.

# Quarry Bank Mill

**STYAL, WILMSLOW, CHESHIRE**

AREA 4.9ha (12 acres) • SOIL sandy loam/clay soil • ALTITUDE 96m (315ft) • AVERAGE RAINFALL 813mm (32in) • AVERAGE WINTER CLIMATE moderate

The Trust's acquisitions of Quarry Bank House in 2006, and the Upper Garden in 2010, in addition to its existing ownership of the adjacent working cotton mill, Apprentice House and other buildings and land on the Styal estate, have contributed two more colourful parts to what was already a remarkably complete picture of a community living through the early years of the Industrial Revolution.

The Mill, built in 1784, is a vast expanse of russet-red brickwork, sitting in an unspoilt and well-wooded valley beside the River Bollin, whose waters provided the necessary power to run the machines. Its owner was Samuel Greg, a wealthy young Manchester merchant, who took an enlightened and paternalistic interest in his workforce – though, to modern eyes, they still endured a very harsh existence both domestically and in the heat and dust of the Mill. It is a sign of his pride in his enterprise that in about 1800 he built his own house right beside the Mill, seeing it as an object of beauty and indifferent to the noise and smell which would later trouble the future Prime Minister William Gladstone, who visited in 1828.

A cream, bow-fronted villa of modest proportions, Quarry Bank House was intended as a country retreat, a periodic escape from the city for his wife and children, but eventually it became the family home. Its location, looking down a little river gorge, with red sandstone outcrops, high banks overhung with trees, and even a small cave – Disley Kirk, said to have once been inhabited by a hermit – perfectly suited the contemporary taste for romantic, layered, Picturesque landscape. The Mill itself was integral to it, its dominant architectural presence contributing much to the enjoyment of the views. As family and guests looked back towards the house, it provided that sublime uplifting drama of magnitude tinged with 'horror' which was so relished at the time, especially in mountain scenery.

Samuel Greg clearly developed a fine garden here – 'truly picturesque and cultivated to the greatest possible extent', noted the visiting American naturalist John James Audubon in 1826 – and the framework of it still survives. Many plantings and garden features were subsequently added by his son, Robert Hyde Greg, and his grandson, Edward Hyde Greg, so that the grounds attained a potent late Victorian overlay which the Trust – following a major programme of overgrown conifer and rhododendron clearance, painstaking path excavation and restoration, and garden renovation – is again fostering with the help of the 1872 Ordnance Survey map and old photographs.

The approach is through a girdle of iron railings and across the Tennis Lawn, created by Edward Hyde Greg out of the meadow parkland of the valley floor below the Mill, landscaped by his grandfather. The sloping banks above are thickly clad in tall beech woods, while elsewhere Scots pines and other specimen trees, including a weeping ash and a young Brewer's spruce with pendulous swags of needles, add craggy and cascade-like silhouettes to enhance the site's natural romanticism. The crashing waters of the weir and the smaller manmade waterfalls are the accompaniment which in the past would have helped to lessen the noise of the Mill and today mitigate that from traffic. Although only a mile from Manchester Airport, the garden is astonishingly tranquil and inhabited by a rich variety of wildlife. Dippers and kingfishers are often seen by the river, as are mink (which keep the rabbit population down), with northern divers and goosanders visiting in winter.

You cross into the Pleasure Garden via a rustic bridge over the water. The sloping lawns near the house (now privately tenanted and not open to the public) harbour further trees, including a huge purple Japanese maple, but the path leads you away from it down a long river terrace, flanked by formal gardens and shrubberies.

A principal highlight here, and indeed all up the steep banks and rich red sandstone undercliffs, are the azaleas and rhododendrons, which were an enthusiasm of Robert Hyde Greg and which he planted en masse between Quarry Bank House and his own house Norcliffe Hall, sited beyond the woods on this pathline. Spring therefore sees a terrific eruption of contrasting colours from thickets of yellow azalea, *Rhododendron luteum* (whose fruity scent fills the whole garden) to violet *R. augustinii*, blush-pink 'Loderi', and numerous carmine, pink, deep purple and blood-red hybrids, some of which were raised by Greg, who was a keen rhododendron breeder. Many await identification.

They are interspersed with lush plantings of hostas, daylilies, ferns and candelabra primulas along the side of the river, and on the opposite side of the path is a small formal parterre, appointed with cast-iron urns and bedded out in spring with tulips and forget-me-nots, followed by Victorian summer exotics such as castor oil plants and cannas. Above is the path to the Cave, with its steps hewn out of the rock, along which are more newly re-created circular beds and linear borders of herbaceous plants, shrubs and bulbs such as yuccas, lupins, peonies, iris and other Victorian favourites.

The path then zig-zags up the side of the gorge, past further trees and shrubs and a small lawn of sentinel yews, all the while giving attractive reverse views. Near the top, you are in the shadow of the overhanging oak, beech and Scots pines, where hydrangeas and ferns have been planted to join the carpet of bluebells sweeping under the yellow azaleas. Now 27m (90ft) above the river, you emerge into the upper parkland. There is a small Victorian orchard here, being replanted with pre-1830s fruit varieties, and in spring the meadow grass around is well studded with primroses. The adjacent paddock has some good trees, including a couple of enormous crab apples, *Malus hupehensis*, dating probably from the late 1940s, and on the corner is a massive and venerable beech tree, from which you are offered another fine prospect of the Mill and its landscape setting. In 2010, the Trust was also able to add another large section of this higher ground to its ownership, including the derelict, brick-walled kitchen garden, which still contains the shells of the 1820s glasshouses – with their early examples of curvilinear glazing bars – and a mulberry tree planted by Samuel Greg in 1795. Visitors will be allowed access during the restoration, and as well as fruit and vegetables, the Upper Garden will in due course also feature a long Regency shrubbery, a blowsy herbaceous border and a redwood walk. The surviving pathways offer further dramatic clifftop views.

This pleasant mill owner's world is in sharp contrast to that presented by the Apprentice House. The apprentices were indentured child labourers who, from the age of nine or ten, were forced to work a twelve-hour day, six days a week, for a period of some seven years. The Apprentice House was home to these children who had been drawn from local workhouses, and later, from distant city slums. It housed up to 100 apprentices in a plain, whitewashed building, accompanied by a cluster of brick outhouses, a cobbled yard, and a productive garden, in which, under the supervision of the superintendents, the children grew food for themselves and for sale. Today, restored by the Quarry Bank Mill Trust, the site once again displays humble plots of fruit and vegetables, neatly divided by picket fences, and, with a few weeds between the cobbles, the grass a little shaggy, and poultry around the yard, the rural nineteenth-century flavour has been recaptured.

One old apple and a few damson trees have survived; otherwise all the fruit and vegetable varieties now grown date from before the end of the nineteenth century, with many of local provenance. The garden is managed traditionally, using no chemicals. Among the apples are 'Irish Peach', 'Peasgood's Nonsuch', 'Lord Suffield' and the very rare, locally bred 'Withington Welter'; among the plums, 'Jefferson' and 'Imperial Gage' (syn. 'Denniston's Superb'); among the pears, 'Williams' Bon Chrétien' and 'Jargonelle'; and the damson is 'Cheshire Damson'. The currants in the soft fruit compound include an interesting collection of gooseberries donated by Manchester University. 'London', 'Catherina', 'Blucher', 'King of Trumps' and 'Hero of the Nile' are among them; all were prizewinners in the gooseberry shows held in nearby Wilmslow.

The free-draining soil, well-laced with manure, supports an extensive selection of vegetables, many grown from seed sourced from the heritage seed library at Garden Organic (formerly the Henry Doubleday Research Association) at Ryton-on-Dunsmore, near Coventry. These include the peas 'Champion of England' and 'Prince Albert'; the beans 'Early Warwick' and 'Green Windsor'; the kale 'Ragged Jack'; the carrot 'Altrincham'; the turnip 'Manchester Market'; the onion 'Southport Red Globe'; and the rhubarb 'Timperley Early'. The produce was stored in special tunnels.

There are also many herbs, which would have been used to make food more palatable, to treat minor ailments and, in the case of alkanet and woad, to act as dye plants. To add some cheer to the scene, there is a bed of cottage flowers, including stocks, pinks, columbines and dame's violet, which succeed the snowdrops, daffodils and cowslips that appear on the scythed grass bank in spring. This is a memorable place to visit.

**RIGHT** A view of the Mill showing its wooded setting.

# Rowallane

**SAINTFIELD, BALLYNAHINCH, CO. DOWN**

**AREA** 21ha (52 acres) • **SOIL** acid/loam • **ALTITUDE** 61m (200ft) • **AVERAGE RAINFALL** 914mm (36in) • **AVERAGE WINTER CLIMATE** mild

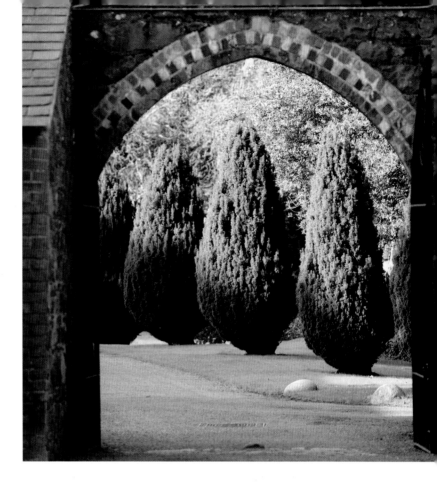

The land at Rowallane, Hugh Armytage Moore was told, was 'not fit to graze a goat'. This is rough drumlin country. The fields are boxed small by dry-stone walls and sheltering hedgerows, and stands of gorse and massive outcrops of rock break from the grass. But the rainfall is moderately high, the summers cool and the winters comparatively mild. From 1903, Moore began planting, and his legacy is a large plantsman's garden of striking scenic beauty and distinctive character. In parts of the grounds, a foundation of trees and walls had already been set out by his uncle, the Rev. John Moore, who bought the property in 1860. The long entrance drive, now richly coloured by immense arboreal rhododendrons, already had its close fringes of deciduous trees and its sinuous grassy glades shaded by specimen conifers. The stone seats and arresting cairns of giant's marbles were also in place, complementing the exposed rock.

Behind the modest apricot-painted farmhouse is the Rev. Moore's pleasure ground, a broad sweep of lawn and arboretum, featuring a pond and a circular stone dais, from which he is reputed to have delivered some of his sermons. This looks less odd now that it is the base for the iron bandstand from Newcastle promenade, given to the Trust in a derelict state in 1985. Many trees have been added over the past hundred years, but those planted by Rev. Moore still set the quiet mood. Monterey, Scots, bishop and umbrella pine, redwood, wellingtonia, cypresses, multi-stemmed western red cedar, Douglas fir, podocarpus, cunninghamia and *Fitzroya cupressoides* are among the many fine conifers framed by the beech trees.

The adjacent walled garden was also built by Rev. Moore, but although it retains its formal kitchen garden pattern of gravel paths, its planting is now very different. In place of some of the vegetable beds, Hugh Armytage Moore introduced borders of choice perennials, shaded by ornamental trees, and this theme has been seized and developed in red-blooded fashion by the Trust. The moist climate allows wonderfully lush plantings. Drifts of Himalayan poppies – in particular, the scintillating turquoise-blue *Meconopsis × sheldonii* 'Slieve Donard' – course between lime-green hostas and bronze and tropical-leaved rodgersias. Species peonies are displayed in variety, followed by primulas, daylilies and astilbes. Penstemons, phloxes and the Japanese *Kirengeshoma palmata* with its soft yellow shuttlecocks provide colour in late summer.

Low blocks of ornamental grasses, libertias and dwarf rhododendrons give contrasting flavours, while above and behind, ornamental trees, taller shrubs and climbers are providing backdrops, evergreen structure and, in many parts, a dappled, woodland atmosphere. Cherries and spring- and summer-flowering magnolias are prominent, including forms of *M. × veitchii* introduced in the early part of the twentieth century by the Veitch nursery in Exeter, from which Hugh Armytage Moore obtained plants. *Rhododendron cinnabarinum* in many guises, *R. hanceanum* and the superb *R. shilsonii*, with blood-red flowers and cinnamon bark peeling to reveal purplish branches, are highlights among the shrubs, with *Hoheria lyallii* (which self-sows freely) and eucryphias giving later blossom.

The compact form of *Viburnum plicatum*, raised from seed at Rostrevor but distributed from here and named 'Rowallane', grows in the centre of a small paved area, designed in the shape of a Celtic cross. The recently restored walls – unique in having projecting

**ABOVE** A procession of Irish yews at Rowallane.

pierced tiles incorporated, through which supporting wires for climbing plants may be threaded – shelter the New Zealand kowhai, *Sophora tetraptera*, *Acradenia frankliniae* from Tasmania and the conservatory rhododendron 'Lady Alice Fitzwilliam'.

The outer walled garden, formerly Hugh Armytage Moore's nursery area and currently being renovated by the Trust, springs further surprises, including *Helwingia japonica*, curious for producing its pale green flowers on the upper surface of the leaves. The unusual *Hydrangea aspera* subsp. *strigosa* is included in the large collection of hydrangeas, partnered with colchiums, and here also is the original plant of the popular garden japonica, *Chaenomeles* × *superba* 'Rowallane'. Crinums, watsonias, species dahlias and dieramas add some exotic herbaceous interest.

In 1903, the rest of the ground now covered by the garden consisted of rock-strewn fields. Gradually, as his experience and enthusiasm grew, Hugh Armytage Moore annexed them. But he did no taming, levelling or ploughing. He kept the dry-stone walls, the gorse and the spongy turf, made a feature of the rock, and had his planting follow the undulating rhythm of the land. The result is an extraordinarily heady mix of the wild and exotic, and a succession of images that could belong to no other garden. Wildflower management here is outstanding.

The fields retain their age-old names. From the Haggard, or stackyard (a remarkable sight in July when the falling cotton seeds of *Populus maximowiczii* envelop it in a local blizzard), a gate leads first into the Spring Ground, long valued for its early-warming, southerly orientation. In spring, you are greeted by swathes of flowers. The foreground ridge is heavily planted with daffodils, including many old Irish cultivars; they are succeeded by colonies of devil's bit scabious and other wildflowers.

The view down the bank, framed by pine, beech and oak, is punctuated by eruptions of rhododendrons. Large hybrids, such as white 'Dr Stocker' and 'Loderi King George', give way to stands of sun-loving azaleas and pink and purplish Triflorum species. Red Kirishima azalea, *Rhododendron* × *obtusum* and the scented *R. luteum* are prominent, the latter in its traditional garden partnership with wild bluebells. The white variety of *Magnolia campbellii* and summer-flowering *M. wilsonii* also grow here. Like many of the trees and shrubs in the garden, they have associations with the great plant-hunters of the early twentieth century. Moore corresponded with E.H. Wilson and George Forrest, and grew many of their introductions as they became available through Irish and English nurseries.

More rhododendrons, this time in the company of specimen trees such as Dawyck Beech, stewartias and deliciously fragrant *Malus toringo* subsp. *sargentii*, entice you through the New Ground to the famous rock garden. Here, Moore exposed a gigantic outcrop of grey whinstone, smoothed and striated by glaciers, and imported cartloads of soil to make beds around it. The rock, gravel and grass paths curl and plunge past a huge range of ferns, bulbs and herbaceous plants, among which runs of silver-leaved celmisias are memorable incidents. Mats of mouse plant, *Arisarum proboscideum*, lie at the bottom.

In fact, there are rhododendrons everywhere. The rock fringes and streamsides are home to *Rhododendron orbiculare*, *R. baileyi*, the aromatic *R. glaucophyllum* and hybrids such as 'Yellow Hammer' and 'Blue Tit'. In sheltered corners grow the tender *R. virgatum* and lily-scented 'Countess of Haddington'. A fine pieris, from Forrest's seed, gives a spectacular show, as does the thicket of *Mahonia japonica* Bealei Group and the collection of streamside perennials, which includes *Primula* 'Rowallane Rose'.

Wooded enclosures lie ahead. Once planted to act as wind shelter for the grazing stock, this matrix of forest trees is equally important for the protection of the garden. A young shelter belt of beech is gradually replacing the felled larches on Trio Hill above the rock garden; among them are fine groups of embothrium, berberis and *Enkianthus campanulatus*, this last delivering some sensational autumn tints. Recently rejuvenated plantings in Rock Garden Wood, composed with reference to Moore's diaries and correspondence, again feature rarified combinations such as *Boenninghausenia albiflora* with *Gentiana sino-ornata*, and meconopsis and primulas with *Arisaema griffithii*, as well as an assortment of tiny Himalayan rhododendrons overhanging the shady rocks.

Scots pine and beech form the mainstay of the plantations on the slopes running west towards the entrance drive. In these lower woods and glades, the contrast between the wild and the ornamental is at its most potent. For as you cross the bumpy terrain, past tree heathers, pieris and still more rhododendrons, between specimen maples, southern beeches, paulownia, davidia, sorbus, birch, chestnut and eucalyptus, you skirt the low boundary walls, over which you see land similarly contoured and compartmented, but empty. This is what Hugh Armytage Moore began with; behind you is what he made of it. Walks newly opened up through the surrounding farmland, meadows and woods heighten the contrast further.

# Scotney Castle

**LAMBERHURST, TUNBRIDGE WELLS, KENT**

**AREA** 12ha (30 acres) within parkland • **SOIL** neutral/sand, clay • **ALTITUDE** 76m (250ft)
**AVERAGE RAINFALL** 914mm (36in) • **AVERAGE WINTER CLIMATE** moderate to cold

*'Bless'd too is he who, midst his tufted trees, Some ruin'd castle's lofty towers sees / Nodding o'er the stream that glides below.'* In 1836, twelve years after the death of Richard Payne Knight, landscape gardener and the author of these lines, this same romantic vision began to take shape here. His friend Edward Hussey, the creator of Scotney, was determined to take advantage of the scenic potential of his site, and in that year he consulted W.S. Gilpin, the noted designer and nephew of the originator of the Picturesque style, William Gilpin. The 'picture' was to be fashioned in its entirety, with Anthony Salvin preparing plans for a new house, which was to command views across the ridge of hills to Goudhurst and down into the Bewl Valley.

The impulse for the composition lay below: a handsome 'medieval' castle, its surviving tower reflecting in a lake-like moat. Really a fortified manor, with sixteenth- and seventeenth-century additions, the castle was too cold and damp for habitation by the family, and Hussey had the walls selectively demolished to leave the present fairytale ruin. Gilpin's work centred on the terrace beside the new house, but Hussey's treatment of the entire valley landscape, with its planted quarry, sinuous sweeps of shrubbery and strikingly shaped trees dramatically sited, was clearly a red-blooded realisation of his and Knight's precepts.

Today, we see a post-1987 landscape, for the storm of that October ripped out many of the limes, beeches, oaks and yews that gave the slopes their curves, together with most of the cedar of Lebanon, Scots pines, incense cedars and Lawson cypresses that furnished the dashing horizontals and verticals between them. The long-term replacement trees, however, are now rising up, enabling fast-growing species such as Leyland cypress, installed as temporary accents, to be felled gradually and the landscape to recapture its old character.

From the bastion, you look out on a scene of great beauty, with the large numbers of deciduous trees and flowering shrubs ensuring a spectacular seasonal cycle. Bold and harmonious banks of shrubs, especially rhododendrons, were welcomed by the advocates of the Picturesque landscape. But for the array and succession of colour, much is owed to subsequent plantings by Christopher Hussey, the architectural historian, who, with his wife Betty, tended his grandfather's creation from 1952 until his death in 1970. Betty Hussey continued to have considerable influence at Scotney over the next 30 years.

Early in the year, waves of primroses and daffodils succeed the snowdrops, and large specimens of *Magnolia stellata* bloom in the quarry. This area, recently cleared and with its rock face exposed, has opened up many more dramatic planting opportunities. In late spring, it is the turn of rhododendrons and scented azaleas, in shades of yellow, cream and orange, accompanied by a mass of wildflowers. In June, the pink bells open on impressive mounds of *Kalmia latifolia*, to be succeeded in late summer by hydrangeas. And in autumn, the valley is filled with the mellow tints and flame highlights of leaves, furnished by Japanese maples, rhus, parrotia, liquidambar, nyssa and stands of royal fern.

The domestic garden is close to the new house and bastion, where Climbing, Shrub and Floribunda roses tumble about a Venetian font, and also in the forecourt of the castle, where Christopher Hussey set out a pattern of beds around the Venetian well-head installed by his aunt; its scheme of herbs was designed by Lanning Roper, who was Mrs Hussey's garden adviser after her husband's death. Herbaceous and bedding plants fill the border, and roses, vines and wisteria explore the ruined walls.

The octagonal walled kitchen garden, 0.4ha (1 acre) in size, is also now being brought back into production, with the help of a local school, a regular team of volunteers, and members of Centrepoint, a charity for the homeless. Around by the lake, the invasive *Rhododendron ponticum* and its hybrids continue to be cut down and cleared to make way for more interesting plantings. Waterlilies and marsh plants accompany the serene reflections of trees and castle, and a bronze figure, made and given by Henry Moore in tribute to Christopher Hussey, reclines on the isthmus. This is a powerfully atmospheric place.

**ABOVE LEFT** The new house, designed by Anthony Salvin in 1835 in the Elizabethan style.
**ABOVE** The plantings of vivid colour were designed to fill the valley between the old castle and the new house in the Picturesque style.

# Seaton Delaval Hall

**WHITLEY BAY, NORTHUMBERLAND**

**AREA** 5.2ha (13 acres) within parkland • **SOIL** slightly acidic sandy loam • **ALTITUDE** 30m (100ft) • **AVERAGE RAINFALL** 610mm (24in) • **AVERAGE WINTER CLIMATE** moderate

Remnants of a double lime avenue, over 1.6km (1 mile) in length and once accompanied by hefty gate piers, heightens the anticipation on your approach down the A190 (formerly the main estate road) and, turning the corner, you have the great house suddenly and theatrically upon you. A compact palace of now-blackened sandstone, bristling with architectural decoration, Seaton Delaval is one of the masterpieces of the English Baroque, and came to the Trust in 2009 following a major fund-raising campaign, with enthusiastic local support.

Constructed between 1719 and 1730, it was designed by Sir John Vanbrugh, the ebullient playwright and architect of Castle Howard, for Admiral George Delaval, whose Norman ancestor had been granted this estate in the eleventh century. For a more commanding presence and prospect over the sea, the coastal plain and the port of Blyth, Vanbrugh set the hall and its pleasure grounds on a raised platform, with a surrounding ha-ha and a three-quarter-circular bastion on each corner, a layout evocative of a Norman keep – as a former soldier, he frequently took inspiration for his designs from military fortifications. Each bastion sported a lead statuary group on a classical or Biblical theme from the workshop of John Cheere, some of which are now redistributed closer to the hall.

The earliest estate plan known to exist, from 1808 (the property's historical archive is far from complete), shows the hall standing in an asymmetric pattern of broad, formal grass corridors, framed by four large wilderness blocks of densely planted trees, and with a circuit walk above the ha-ha. Both Vanbrugh and Delaval died before the hall's completion, but the theatrical spirit in which it was conceived was savoured by those after them, for it was the setting for many parties and entertainments and the Delaval family were tireless and fun-loving hosts.

Today, as you stand under the rear, south-facing portico of the hall, remarkably little appears to have changed. Ahead, a sweep of grass, flanked by woody thickets containing old limes, beeches and sycamores, carries the eye to an obelisk 0.8km ($^1/_2$ mile) distant. You can still walk the perimeter from bastion to bastion, surveying the fields across the ha-ha, and, within one of the wilderness blocks, enter the little church that dates back to Norman times. The grounds are thus preserved as a rare and handsome survivor from the early transitional phase of English landscape gardening, when enclosed formality was giving way to an open parkland style.

Iron railings, however, now cut across the pleasure grounds close to the house. These were added later in the nineteenth century in Reptonian style to create an inner flower garden, safe from livestock. Its bones are visible in the Ordnance Survey plan of 1860, to which the present flower garden still adheres. The weeping ash, in the semi-circular lawn to the west of the portico, is presumed to date from this period, as do some of the box hedges in the adjacent parterre, which trace the footprint of a wing of the hall that was never built. The other wing to the East was destroyed in the fire of 1822, which also left the central portion of the hall the empty shell it remains to this day. For by then, the estate had transferred to the Astley/Hastings branch of the family, whose principal seat was in Norfolk.

After a long period of decline, culminating in the requisitioning of the hall for military use in the First World War and for prisoners of war in the Second, the flower garden was revitalised during the 1950s and '60s by the 22nd Lord and Lady Hastings with the help of the connoisseur plantsman James Russell of Sunningdale Nurseries, who, like Vanbrugh, has also left a legacy

**LEFT** A view over the box hedging in the rose garden.
**ABOVE** The Baroque house seen from the laburnum garden.

in the grounds of Castle Howard. The flower garden was revitalised again, after another lull, in the 1980s. A mixed border, featuring traditional favourites such as delphiniums, hydrangeas, alchemilla, orange alstroemeria and sweet peas, now curves around the lawn, backed by scented yellow and apricot azaleas and stands of red, pink and white Hardy Hybrid rhododendrons.

This kaleidoscope of summer colour is echoed in the rose beds of the parterre, which features *Rosa* 'Polar Star', *R.* 'Golden Wedding', *R.* 'Pink Peace' and other modern Bush roses in a maze-like pattern of box hedges and narrow gravel paths. Running behind it is a large border of irises, peonies, phlox and pink crinums, with shrubs and climbers such as lemon-scented verbena, jasmine, and purple-blotched white *Cistus* × *cyprius* benefiting from the warm, protective south-facing wall. An imposing statue of Samson and a Philistine commands the scene. In quiet contrast beyond is Lady Hastings' Garden, an intimate hedged enclosure with summerhouse, lawn, lily pool and azalea border, accompanied by a small, orchard-like area of ornamental trees. An unexpected laburnum tunnel leads towards the church, with a statue of the French Crown Prince Imperial by Bosio as its focus.

The principal set-piece scheme is the formal Sunken Garden. In alignment with the decorative wrought-iron gates and courtyard of the house's west wing, and with one of Vanbrugh's bastions forming one of its corners, this is also a nineteenth-century addition which was refurbished in the 1950s by James Russell. The central panel of lawn is flanked across broad gravel walks by side panels, patterned in box and infilled with silver santolina, white-variegated euonymus, hardy fuchsia and standard wisteria. These are backed by lines of grey-leaved whitebeams, clipped as mopheads, and the whole garden is contained within hedges of yew and beech. The central Haddonstone fountain was added in the 1990s.

Archaeological investigation continues across the estate, and there is much still awaiting repair, not least the abandoned walled kitchen garden, complete with its brick-lined pond and splendid stone Orangery. There is a good view across to it from Vanbrugh's north-east bastion.

**ABOVE** A view past the statue of David slaying Goliath over the Rose Garden at Seaton Delaval Hall.

# Sheffield Park Garden and Estate

SHEFFIELD PARK, EAST SUSSEX

AREA 49ha (120 acres) within 107ha (265 acres) parkland • SOIL acid/heavy clay
ALTITUDE 91m (300ft) • AVERAGE RAINFALL 889mm (35in) • AVERAGE WINTER CLIMATE
moderate

The reflections in the water of coloured leaves, soaring conifers, balustraded bridges, cascades and the towers and pinnacles of the gothick mansion give Sheffield Park an unmistakable sense of place. The axes of the garden are the four lakes, which are strung down the southerly slope below the house in an inverted 'T' formation. This is an ornamental landscape of dazzling scale and richness, planted above all for the drama of shape, trees, rhododendrons and autumn foliage, and encompassing nearly 162ha (400 acrcs) of meadow, marsh, woodland and glade.

The estate belonged to the Earls of Sheffield until it was purchased in 1909 by Arthur Soames, a Lincolnshire brewer, who had coveted the park since visiting it 20 years earlier. It was then that the rich overlay was applied. Scarlet oaks, Japanese maples, nyssas and amelanchiers were woven around the lakesides in the boldest drifts, complemented by new stands of giant conifers and seams of rhododendrons. But plant variety was always secondary to landscape impact, and Soames barely indulged in the new Chinese and South American introductions then being welcomed into other great woodland gardens.

These carefully conceived pictorial scenes were ravaged by the storm of October 1987. Shelter belts were devastated, ornamental trees brought down by the dozen, and much of the creative work of renewal and expansion carried out by the Trust over 30 years was undone. But the core of the garden survived largely intact, the native oaks were high-pruned and have regenerated splendidly and replanting has continued apace. Only those visitors acquainted with the previous landscape will now sense the loss.

The circuit of the park follows lazy figures of eight, and if all the tributary paths and glades are explored, and periodic pauses taken to savour the views, it lasts the best part of a day. No season is disappointing. In spring, the park wakes to camellias and a grass sward spangled with bulbs. You walk down banks sheeted with wild Lent lilies, *Narcissus pseudonarcissus*, and as the many old hybrid daffodils succeed them, there are the warm tints of amelanchiers and maples among the expanding greenery, and the scents of osmanthus on the air.

May brings the first great climax of colour, with pink and white dogwoods and the many thickets of rhododendrons and azaleas flowering in an ocean of bluebells. The palette is subtly graded, with the softer tones predominating through stands of tall, fragrant Loderi rhododendrons and other whites and pastels. Crimson, pink and purple Hardy Hybrids are grouped around the upper lake, and the more vibrant orange and gold Exbury azaleas (superb against copper beech), intense carmine and rose evergreen Kurume azaleas and electrifying violet-blue rhododendron hybrids (partnered with creams and lime-yellows) are gathered in their own glades. The zany group of 'Hinomayo' azaleas, clipped tight in late autumn and looking uncannily like a flock of brilliant pink sheep, is guaranteed especially to startle the eye.

By now, the purple beech and maples are reflecting sumptuously in the lakes, and the emerald leaves of the other deciduous trees have thrown the huge wellingtonias, redwoods, pines and cedars into deep relief. Every path has its quiet interludes, from sparkling glades of birch (the cream trunks looking well among the bluebells), to exotic and solemn groves of hardy Chusan palms, cypresses and hemlocks. Among these trees, the connoisseur will find rarities galore, including *Athrotaxis laxifolia* from Tasmania, *Pinus montezumae* from Mexico and *Fagus engleriana* from China.

One of the Trust's policies, as in many other woodland gardens, has been to enrich the summer display and, accordingly, an extensive collection of the late-flowering Ghent azaleas has been assembled (now the National Collection), together with hydrangeas – lacecaps in particular. There are no formal beds of herbaceous plants at Sheffield Park, but the lakes are edged in moisture-loving species and have their rafts of waterlilies. In 1979, the banks of the stream, west of the lowest lake, were also enriched.

The advent of the park's second climax is heralded by the red tints on spindle trees and *Prunus sargentii*. By mid-October, the landscape is alight with colour. At ground level, fiery hues break out among azaleas, fothergillas, enkianthus, blueberry and berberis, the flames rising through amelanchier, parrotia, Japanese maples, *Acer circinatum* and *A. maximowiczianum* (syn. *nikoense*), to engulf the American oaks, the celebrated grove of tupelos (*Nyssa sylvatica*), and, a little later, the liquidambars. Simultaneously, the numerous birches have turned to butter yellow, the columns of deciduous conifers (*Taxodium* and *Metasequoia*) to orange-brown, and the native trees to copper and russet. Added to all this are plumes of white pampas grass, sky-blue streaks of autumn gentians (linear beds of *Gentiana sino-ornata* – another quirky touch), complementary domes and spires of evergreens, the lakes and James Wyatt's fantasy architecture.

In spite of its exotic content, the park is a tranquil place to stroll, the underlying mood set by the expanses of grass and water, the native trees and wildflowers. Beyond the third lake, the exotics melt away almost entirely as you follow the Trust's new walk that takes you, via rustic bridges of hornbeam, across a marsh. Native sedges and bog plants grow here between thickets of alder and willow, and it is the haunt of kingfishers, grebe, marsh tits and several species of duck. The East Park, with its large population of spotted orchids, is tended as a wildflower reserve and is not at present open to the public, but the South Park, reattached to the estate in 2006 and spanning an additional 107ha (265 acres), is open and undergoing restoration. The park's cricket field, the scene of the first tour matches against the Australians between 1884 and 1896, has also recently been revived, with matches played throughout the summer.

**ABOVE** An almost perfect reflection of autumn colour in the middle lake.

# Sheringham Park

UPPER SHERINGHAM, NORFOLK

AREA 20ha (50 acres) within parkland • SOIL sandy, some clay • ALTITUDE 76m (250ft) • AVERAGE RAINFALL 508mm (20in) • AVERAGE WINTER CLIMATE mild

'After having passed nearly half a century in the study of Natural Scenery, and having been professionally consulted in the improvement of many hundred places in different parts of England, I can with truth pronounce that Sheringham possesses more natural beauty and local advantages than any place I have ever seen.' So declared the great landscape gardener Humphry Repton in his Red Book of proposals, watercolours and before-and-after overlays prepared for Sheringham's new owner, Abbot Upcher, in 1812.

Having lived in Norfolk on and off throughout his life (he is buried at nearby Aylsham), Repton had a special attachment to the county's landscape and knew this coastal estate well. When Sheringham came up for sale, it was his solicitor son William who handled its legal conveyance, and at the very moment Upcher came into William's office to sign the contract, Repton (by now wheelchair-bound following a carriage accident the previous year) was 'coincidentally' paying his son a visit. He secured the commission to design both the landscape and the hall, passing on the job of actually building the new house to another of his sons, the architect John Adey Repton.

Repton's skills were at their apogee, and this is considered one of the most complete and best-preserved of his commissions. Walking down the long entrance drive, you are taken over and around one of the wooded ridges and low hills that frame the hall and its pastoral coombe. The topography was well used by Repton to block and control the views and play with light and shadow, the upper ground being already well furnished with shelter belts, and the fields and slopes with old oaks, limes and beech which remain a feature of the estate.

As you descend, it is the sea that is first revealed, less than 1.6km (1 mile) away across the heathland, cliffs and shingle to the north, together with a windmill and coastguard cottages silhouetted against it. And then, as you veer east at a point known as The Turn, the hall comes handsomely into view, again with a flash of sea beyond. A large villa in the style of John Nash (its stone brought here by ship from Yorkshire), it looks inland across a ha-ha into meadow parkland, protected from the coastal winds by Oak Wood

Hill. There is a small pond nearby and, enclosed in iron railings, a small pleasure garden (the hall is privately tenanted and, with the garden, is not open to the public). On the opposite flank of hill, the hall has its architectural eye-catcher in the form of a small domed Temple, designed by Repton but not in fact constructed until 1975. It is a fine scene.

Knowing the local weather conditions, Repton persuaded Upcher not to contemplate siting the house on the exposed side of the hill, so there is no sea view from the hall. But if you penetrate Oak Wood Hill you will find a remarkable gazebo in the form of a high wooden stairway and platform, offering a panorama of the locality. It was erected in 1975 on the site of a look-out post built during the Napoleonic Wars.

Repton liked his landscapes to offer diversion and variety, and this encompassed human and agricultural activity. From the outset he suggested that 'proper persons' be allowed to walk the estate one day in the week and admire its views. No doubt he would also have enjoyed the white plumes, clatter and whistles of the steam trains of the North Norfolk Railway that run along the estate's coastline today. In front of the hall, he banished fences and cereal crops in favour of livestock roaming and grazing on a sweep of grass, which they continue to do. Nature also provides animation, the quiet habitats fostering a range of species from newts to nightjars (even, occasionally, golden orioles), with the orchids and wildflowers in the unimproved meadow grass attracting a diversity of butterflies, moths and other insects.

Sadly, Abbot Upcher died of fever in 1819 before the hall was completed, and it was not finally finished until 20 years later. But while Repton's vision for the broader landscape was adopted by successive members of the Upcher family, a major transformation took place in the woods flanking the main approach drive; from around 1850, and on through the twentieth century, the family indulged in the fashionable taste for rhododendrons.

The panoply of colour from some 20ha (50 acres) of hillside painted in purples, pinks, reds and assorted clashing tints is quite a spectacle, and there are two viewing towers that invite you to climb up among their cloud-like canopies. Many of the plants are so big and so densely packed that it is hard to appreciate them from below, until the flowers drop and create further carpets of colour on the ground. It seems puzzling that they would thrive so well in this dry climate, but the answer lies in the combination of overhead shade from the oaks, Scots pines, sycamores, sweet chestnuts and beech, their fine sponge-like root systems, and the high coastal humidity.

There is early action in the woods from groupings of shell-pink *Rhododendron* 'Christmas Cheer', together with thickets of camellias, but the climax comes in May and June when yellow and orange azaleas scent the air above the bluebells and red campion, and old hybrid rhododendrons such as blazing red 'Britannia', 'Pink Pearl', and purple-blotched white 'Sappho' are in full eruption, all merrily arranged with little concern for colour scheming.

The paths lead under towering forms of *Rhododendron arboreum* and *R. ponticum*. Over the years, the latter – together with many hybrids, grown on *ponticum* rootstock, which have reverted to type – have spread extensively, and are gradually being extracted and replaced, though the job has to be done judiciously as they are valuable windbreaks.

Numerous other rhododendron species and selections add exciting ambushes as you walk down the drive and explore the side tracks. Blotched pink and white *R. calophytum*, slender-leaved *R. strigillosum*, white *R. niveum*, and large-flowered, scented pink and white forms of *R. decorum* and *R. fortunei* are among the company, with yellow-belled *R. cinnabarinum* subsp. *xanthocodon* notable not only for its beauty but for its resilience to the fatal mildew attack to which its tribe is peculiarly prone.

Importantly, many of these rhododendrons are from wild-collected seed, which Henry Morris Upcher obtained by subscribing to the Chinese expeditions of the plant hunter Ernest Wilson in the first decade of the twentieth century. Other Wilson plants here are *Magnolia sieboldii* subsp. *sinensis*, handkerchief tree (*Davidia involucrata*), the pink-berried rowan *Sorbus hupehensis*, and *Dipelta floribunda*, a large shrub with blush-white, funnel-shaped flowers in late spring, and a programme to propagate them to preserve their genetic heritage is in hand. In the 1950s, Henry's grandson Thomas Upcher continued to plant rhododendrons enthusiastically, holding champagne parties at peak flowering time.

All this creates a much more ornamental approach to the hall than Humphry Repton envisaged, but beyond the woods there is little intrusion upon his landscape, which remains calm and green and which he would still recognise as 'my most favourite work'.

**BELOW** A mysterious tunnel of old rhododendrons.
**RIGHT** The Chinese House at Shugborough Estate was the first garden building erected by Lord Anson.

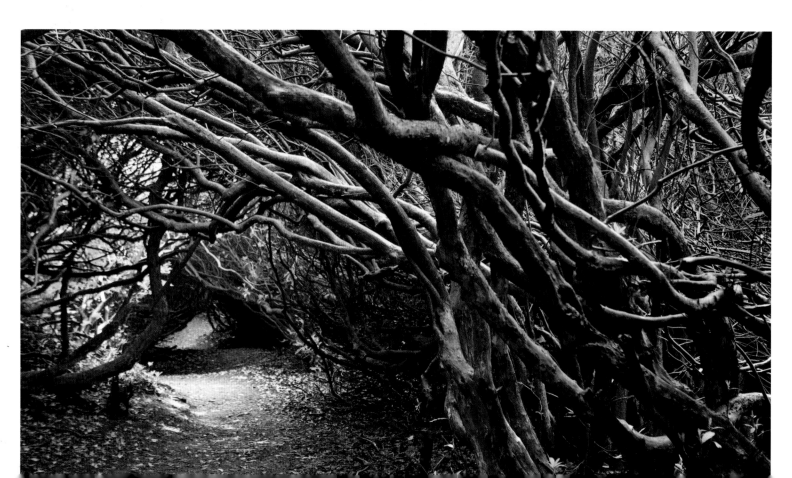

# Shugborough Estate

MILFORD, STAFFORD, STAFFORDSHIRE

AREA 9ha (22 acres) • SOIL acid/sandy loam • ALTITUDE 30m (100ft)
AVERAGE RAINFALL 686mm (27in) • AVERAGE WINTER CLIMATE cold

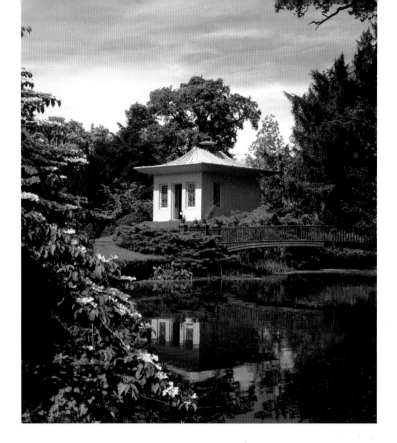

The capture of a Spanish treasure galleon in 1743 brought a fortune in prize money to Captain George Anson RN, later Admiral Lord Anson, and with this wealth, the fashionable improvements to the family estate at Shugborough, already being wrought by his older, bachelor brother Thomas, took on a new breadth and scale.

Entering the park through the belt of woodland beside the Stafford road (which is currently in the process of having its diseased and invasive understorey of *Rhododendron ponticum* eradicated), you get an immediate taste of the second phase of Thomas Anson's work. Down the drive, to left and right, three classical monuments appear in quick succession: on one side, the Lanthorn of Demosthenes, a cylindrical building with Corinthian columns, capped by a decorative tripod; on the other, mounted on a knoll, a Triumphal Arch, adorned with busts of Admiral and Lady Anson; and beyond, the Tower of the Winds, a slim octagon with windows and pedimented porches. The monuments are no longer part of a purely Picturesque landscape, for following a disastrous flood in 1795, which swept away many of Anson's other garden features, John Webb, a pupil of William Emes, was engaged to remodel the park, and with agriculture now the prime interest, its character altered. Trees, planted in great numbers in the 1820s and afterwards, have also changed the views. The setting is mellow and pastoral – flat, low-lying ground at the confluence of the rivers Sow and Trent (an attractive packhorse bridge crosses at the join), with the wild expanse of Cannock Chase rising behind.

The drive curves towards the east façade of the mansion, remodelled by Samuel Wyatt around the turn of the nineteenth century and rather ghostly in its milk-grey, ashlar-like cladding. But before you reach it, or explore the park, you are taken to the recently restored walled kitchen garden. Built in 1805, in its heyday this was one of the country's foremost productive gardens, with pioneering cultivation techniques, notably with pineapples. The gardening is now concentrated in the main 0.7ha (1³/₄ acre)

enclosure, but this would have been part of a sequence of walled and hedged compartments. The design is traditional, with four beds set around a central oval dipping pond, and many old vegetable varieties are grown in them, including golden and striped beetroot and 'Scarlet Emperor' bean. Early nineteenth-century apples and pears are espaliered on the walls. To fuel the mood, gardeners work in period costume.

The old head gardener's house within the garden looks appealing, but it had a major drawback. Smoke from the flanking glasshouse heating systems used to be channelled into its upper storey during the day, to be released at night, so as not to disturb the serenity of Anson's landscape. The glasshouses are no longer here, but it is hoped they can be rebuilt in the future.

The walk down to the house leads past the model farm. There are some fine wisterias on the coach house, and in the midden yard you will find the celebrated edible blue-flowered pea *Lathyrus nervosus*, brought from Patagonia by Captain Anson's cook and known as Lord Anson's Blue Pea. But the gardens lie behind and to the sides of the house, and it is here that you encounter Thomas Anson's earlier, more eclectic structures, absorbed into a nineteenth-century layout of formal lawns and flower schemes, and gently meandering pleasure grounds, all strung along an arm of the River Sow, which flows directly below the house. To the south, on the site of Anson's shrubbery, is the loop of the Ladies' Walk, leading between oak, beech and lime trees (including a particularly fine weeping silver lime), past banks of ornamental shrubs and on to open lawn beside the water, where massed daffodils are followed by a riverside fringe of meadowsweet, lythrum, cow parsley and other wildflowers. The Blue Bridge invites you over the river to explore the arboretum and its collection of American and Asian oaks – an enthusiasm of the late Lord (Patrick) Lichfield.

Rhododendrons used to abound in the pleasure grounds, but are now gradually being replaced by period shrubs such as philadelphus, species roses and laurels. Brooms, snowberry, osmanthus and the late-flowering buckeye *Aesculus parviflora* are also among the cast along the Ladies' Walk. Around the lawns and glades to the north of the house, the colour is boosted by fiery plantings of Ghent azaleas and a lavish new herbaceous border, and here you will also come upon an impressive weeping holly and a common yew of gigantic proportions, noted in 1898 as being one of the most remarkable in the country, and shading 0.2ha (¹/₂ acre) of ground.

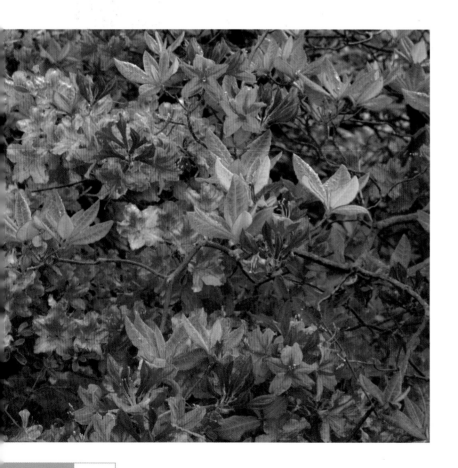

As you arrive in front of the house, the mood becomes strongly Victorian. A series of terraced lawns, set out by W.A. Nesfield in about 1855, replaces Anson's bowling green, and glowing cones of golden yew process down them towards the river, contrasting with the purple beech and plum woven into the backdrop of trees. This provocative yellow and purple contrast, much favoured at the time, has been intensified by beds of the canary-coloured Floribunda rose 'Bright Smile' and seams of 'Hidcote' lavender. Heliotropes, variegated helichrysums and blue lobelias are grown in the stone troughs and blue petunias in the urns. Close by, a rose garden in more delicate late nineteenth-century style has been reconstructed by the Trust. This takes the form of a pattern of small formal beds and ironwork arches arranged around a sundial, once more against the challenging backdrop of golden yew. But because of *Phytophthora* disease, the roses are now being replaced by clematis, accompanied by architectural blocks of herbaceous plants such as Japanese anemones, sedum and echinacea, in similar colours of pink, purple and white.

Beside the river, directly below the house, you pick up the first in the remaining series of garden buildings belonging to Anson's early phase of Rococo landscaping. Here stands the fragment of a ruin, with a rubble crag and the remains of a Coade-stone druid attached. At the turn of the river is the Chinese House, a white pavilion reflecting elegantly in the water; it was the first building Anson erected, in about 1747, and an early example of the new taste for chinoiserie. It is set off by a red iron bridge, and planting of an oriental flavour, including bamboo, stephanandra, berberis and Katsura tree (*Cercidiphyllum japonicum*). The scarlet lacquered stems of dogwood and some young dawn redwoods (*Metasequoia*) add to the atmosphere.

The Red Bridge leads you to an island between the two sections of the River Sow where, against a backdrop of yew, you meet the Cat's Monument – now widely believed to commemorate the ship's cat on Admiral Anson's circumnavigation of the globe in 1740–44. Returning to the main, curving gravel path, you encounter the Shepherd's Monument. A cryptic sequence of letters runs along its base, but the centrepiece is a marble tablet depicting a pastoral scene by Poussin and inscribed with a phrase that resonated in many an eighteenth-century landowner, *'Et in Arcadia ego'*.

**LEFT** Brilliant pink and red azaleas.
**ABOVE RIGHT** Statue of Dionysus in the Nuttery in spring at Sissinghurst Castle.

# Sissinghurst Castle

**SISSINGHURST, CRANBROOK, KENT**

AREA 2.4ha (6 acres) • SOIL neutral/clay • ALTITUDE 61m (200ft) • AVERAGE RAINFALL 737mm (29in) • AVERAGE WINTER CLIMATE moderate

The sudden view of Sissinghurst's twin-turreted tower, rising from the open farmland, always brings a surge of anticipation. The garden's reputation, reinforced by talented head gardeners, sails before it, and anyone who has been here knows it is not exaggerated. The Trust, which must cope with the wear and congestion caused by the large numbers of visitors, discourages publicity and occasionally uses timed tickets, but people still return in their droves. Over 30 years, I have been one of them.

'To Vita Sackville-West, who made this garden,' reads the tablet under the Tower. Vita saw the castle for the first time in April 1930. 'I fell in love; love at first sight. I saw what might be made of it. It was Sleeping Beauty's Castle; but a castle running away into sordidness and squalor; a garden crying out for rescue.' An aerial photograph of July 1932 shows the site cleared and the gardens laid out in front of the South Cottage and Priest's House. By May 1938, when Sissinghurst opened to the public for the first time, all the bones of the garden were in place and the new plantings maturing.

Her husband, Harold Nicolson, was responsible for the pattern of the design. A diplomat, biographer, journalist and politician, he was also, according to Vita, an 'architect manqué', delighting in the pleasures of 'square-ruled paper … stakes and string'. They decided upon a formal, emphatic structure: 'Long, axial walks, running north and south, east and west, usually with terminal points such as a statue or an archway or a pair of sentinel poplars, and the more intimate surprise of small geometrical gardens opening off them, rather as the rooms of an enormous house would open off the arterial corridors,' wrote Vita. Comparisons with Hidcote Manor are perhaps inevitable, though there is no evidence that Harold or Vita visited it before laying out their garden. The principal ingredient that distinguishes Sissinghurst from Hidcote, however, is the romance. At Sissinghurst are the ancient buildings, the moat and, above all, the fairytale tower, the garden's centrepiece, built shortly before Queen Elizabeth's visit in 1573; visible from most parts of the site, it lifts the eye from the enclosed spaces, and, from its roof, you have the opportunity of a bird's-eye view of the garden.

Then there is the all-pervading character of Vita herself. Her writing room in the Tower is much as she left it, with a cape primrose or other flowering pot plant on the table, for visitors intrigued by her intricate private life or admiring of her writing to come to inspect.

The tour begins in the courtyard, where Irish yews process from the entrance arch to the tower, between pads of tightly mown lawn. As at Hidcote, the mood of the beds and garden rooms is set by a clearly defined colour scheme. Here, there are plants echoing the salmon and copper tones of the brick: chaenomeles, evergreen magnolia with its suede-backed leaves, Climbing roses like 'Gloire de Dijon' and apple-scented 'Paul Transon', and, in late summer, the burnished foliage and orange hips of *Rosa moyesii* 'Geranium'. But there are also contrasting notes: in spring, bushes of rosemary, injecting a rich shade of blue at the foot of the tower (the variety, 'Sissinghurst Blue', occurred here as a seedling); in summer, *Solanum crispum* 'Glasnevin', hanging a lilac veil over the east wall. Then there are the troughs and pots, the former simply filled with trailing blue *Euphorbia myrsinites* or white osteospermums, and the latter perhaps with the damson pelargonium 'Lord Bute'. In the main, plants at Sissinghurst are not blended into salads, but displayed as individuals, in generous groups, and with partners that show off their shape and habit.

All this intensifies in the deep, south-facing border, where purple, violet-blue, mauve-pink and magenta perennials and climbers are assembled. The plant arrangement is masterly, with purple vine and clematis such as 'Perle d'Azur' and 'Ville de Lyon' cloaking the wall behind, and a well-matched succession of middle and foreground flowers, from tulips, wallflowers and dwarf irises to black-eyed *Geranium psilostemon*, platycodon (the campanula-like balloon flower), lythrum, and asters.

At midsummer, the first path to take is to the Rose Garden, now awash with the petal-packed, scent-drenched flowers of the old-fashioned Shrub varieties that were Vita's passion. For her, they were infused with the romance of legend, poetry and the East – with the bazaars of Constantinople, where one afternoon, 'the rugs and carpets of Isfahan and Bokhara and Samarcand were unrolled in their dim but sumptuous colouring and richness of texture for our slow delight'. Irises, peonies, violas, pinks and alliums spread a Persian carpet beneath them, and on the curved wall at the west end of the garden there is that much-photographed curtain of *Clematis* 'Perle d'Azur'; this feat is achieved by regular training and tying-in of shoots through the spring and summer months. Plantings of Rugosa roses, single-flowered Hybrid Teas and Hybrid Musks extend the rose season beyond mid-July, and in autumn there is a second flush from many others. Japanese anemones, sedums, caterpillar-like pennisetum grasses, caryopteris, lavatera and felt-leaved *Hydrangea aspera* Villosa Group are then in full bloom.

Much of the late summer colour comes from tender perennials – plants that must be propagated annually by cuttings and over-wintered under glass. Vita would have known few of the many varieties now used here to take over from the biennial wallflowers, honesty and foxgloves. Their greatest concentration is in the adjacent Cottage Garden – from spring to autumn, a cauldron of oranges, yellows and tropical reds. Wallflowers, tulips, irises, daylilies, euphorbias, helianthemums and coloured grasses fire up the garden earlier in the year, and then, from midsummer, it is the turn of Mexican salvias, argyranthemums, leonotis, cannas, dahlias and the sheets of the daisy-like arctotis hybrids, grown under the brick walls of the cottage. The contents of the verdigris laundry copper in the centre of the garden usually turn from the plum-splashed orange tulip 'Prinses Irene' to *Osteospermum* 'Orange Symphony'. Roses are ubiquitous partners. Together with figs and vines, Sissinghurst's old

walls seemed to Vita to cry out for them: 'I planted them recklessly, and have never regretted it'. Here, the glowing red 'Parkdirektor Riggers' partners orange honeysuckle, and, from the cottage wall, 'Madame Alfred Carrière' gives soft white backlighting.

Below, a strip of lawn runs down to the moat, flanked on one side by a bank of deciduous azaleas – as fiery in their autumn leaf tints as they are in their flowers – and an old plantation of Kentish cobnuts, below which is an idealised woodland understorey of shuttlecock ferns and perennials such as geraniums, trilliums and uvularia. The richest spring surprise is sprung in the pleached lime walk, where primroses, anemones, muscari, species tulips, narcissi and a host of other bulbs are planted in mixed colours and assorted groups at the base of the trunks, to the accompaniment of alpine clematis spilling from Italian oil jars. This was Harold Nicolson's personal garden, and his diaries record the many happy hours spent planning and improving the display each year, aided by visits to the Royal Horticultural Society's spring shows at Vincent Square.

Herbs, with their historical and poetic associations, were assured a home at Sissinghurst. They are formally arranged in their own enclosure, around a camomile seat and a lion-guarded bowl, and with rugs of prostrate thymes laid at the entrance: patterned pink, white and crimson in summer, these are perhaps my favourite single feature, but, like so much of Sissinghurst's planting, do depend on a very high level of maintenance – intricate hand-weeding and frequent renewal of plants.

From here, you walk past the moat wall, hung with white wisteria and lapped, from August to October, with the lavender daisies of *Aster* × *frikartii* 'Mönch', and into the orchard. This area, bordered on two sides by water, is the garden's only open and expansive compartment, and provides a welcome interlude. In spring, gold, citron, cream and white daffodils, in separate but interlocking drifts, appear en masse under the apple and cherry trees. In summer, there are wildflowers in the grass and Rambler roses foaming in the branches.

Returning to the walls and hedges, there is still much to see. There is the Tower Lawn, with its 'Albertine' roses and a shady sunken garden; there is Delos, with its magnolias and ferns; and there is the most famous compartment of all. 'I am trying to make a grey, green and white garden,' wrote Vita in one of her weekly gardening articles for the *Observer* in January 1950. The idea transported her readers, and the garden itself prompted countless imitations. The

**RIGHT** Agapanthus and anemone in the Rose Garden with the Tower in the distance.

images hardly need describing: *Lilium regale*, white delphiniums, irises, eremurus, galtonias and *Onopordum* thistles rising above cushions of artemisia and hosta; a weeping silver pear (the original fell in the great storm of October 1987; the present one is a replacement) sheltering the lead statue of a virgin; an ironwork bower covered in the white Rambler rose *R. mulliganii*, and the Priest's House in *R.* 'Madame Alfred Carrière' and *R.* 'Cooperi'. The colours span every tint and tone, with each plant sited for maximum impact of shape, height and leaf size.

'It may be a terrible failure,' added Vita with her customary modesty. 'All the same, I cannot help hoping that the great ghostly barn owl will sweep silently across the pale garden next summer in the twilight, that I am now planting under the first flakes of snow.' Whether or not it is twilight when you leave Sissinghurst, I recommend this enclosure as your departing image: a sorbet after the feast of colour.

Staffed separately from the main garden, and with the help of volunteers, Sissinghurst's new vegetable garden is now supplying large quantities of organic produce to the restaurant. A variety of crops is grown in large beds, edged in grass paths, including salads, leeks, potatoes, courgettes, brassicas and soft fruit such as gooseberries, raspberries, currants, rhubarb and strawberries. A new orchard has also been planted recently, adjacent to the car park, comprising apples, pears, cherries and plums.

**ABOVE** A carefully colour-schemed display of old roses and geraniums.
**RIGHT** The Rock Garden at Sizergh Castle is a tapestry of conifers, ferns and Japanese maples.

# Sizergh Castle

KENDAL, CUMBRIA

AREA 7.3ha (18 acres) • SOIL neutral/shallow loam overlying limestone • ALTITUDE 61m (200ft) • AVERAGE RAINFALL 1,270mm (50in) • AVERAGE WINTER CLIMATE mild to moderate

Just to the east of the castle's fourteenth-century tower is one of the most impressive rock gardens in the Trust's hands. Built in 1926 by the noted Ambleside firm of T.R. Hayes & Sons, it is an 0.1ha (½ acre) bowl of rough limestone terraces, contained within a dell and watered by streams, pools and falls fed from the natural pond above. Originally more open, the garden now has a fringe of sizeable conifers, including Bhutan, Arolla and mountain pines, maples and other ornamental trees, creating a quieter, leafier, more secret world within. On the lower banks, many of the dwarfer conifers, which punctuate the various meandering walks with numerous green and purple Japanese cut-leaved maples, have been allowed to mature into magnificent specimens.

The semi-prostrate Caucasian fir, golden Westfelton yew and weeping hemlock are among the most memorable, but every path takes you past curiosities in the form of miniature Norway spruce, noble fir, junipers and chamaecyparis, interspersed with taller gems such as the Japanese umbrella pine, *Sciadopitys verticillata*. A number of outsized conifers have been selectively felled to make room for them, to expose the contours of the bowl and to let in the sun. But as the high-altitude alpines have been shaded and elbowed out, the bowl has become filled with an alternative cast, appreciative of moisture and dappled light. The prime sources of flower colour are no longer the rock plants but the woodland geraniums and the bog and aquatic plants along the watercourses. Cool and moist, the dell has also become a paradise for ferns ranging from shield and sword ferns (*Polystichum*), bladder ferns (*Cystopteris*), delicate maidenhairs (*Adiantum*) to elegant forms of the royal fern, including the miniature *Osmunda regalis* 'Gracilis'. Sizergh can now boast one of the finest plant collections in the country, including four National Collections.

Part of the success of the rock garden is that it is a locally inspired feature. This is limestone country and Sizergh's 607ha (1,500 acre) estate encompasses screes, cliffs and pavements, as well as panoramic views of the distant Lakeland fells (the walks also take in some fine tracts of ancient woodland). These habitats are rich in wildflowers, and there is a taste of this abundance on the bank east of the castle and in the meadow below the rock garden, where the wild Lent lily, *Narcissus pseudonarcissus*, is followed by a kaleidoscope of local species, including early purple, twayblade, fly and butterfly orchids, meadow geranium, ladies' smock, quaking grass, vetches and ox-eye daisies – the colours augmented by orange-tipped butterflies and much other insect life.

Elsewhere, natural themes are pursued with more decorative plants. The thin shady grass above the rock garden is lit in spring with crocus, scillas, dog's tooth violets and double white anemones, to the accompaniment of the white Mount Fuji cherry, *Prunus* 'Shirotae'. Thousands of daffodils bloom under the orchard's fruit trees, which include many northern apple varieties such as 'Keswick Codlin' and 'White Melrose' as well as plums, damsons, quinces and medlars. The nearby kitchen garden was opened in 2003 and comprises beds of cut flowers, herbs, soft fruit and vegetables, structured by hedges of step-over apple trees. To the west of the house, you walk through a pyramid-shaped avenue of yews into an area of grassy glades, shaded by magnolias, handkerchief tree and more flowering cherries.

The castle itself, built originally as a defence against the marauding Scots and the home of the Strickland family for over 750 years, rises above the garden lake. Alternate pears and vines have recently been planted along the brick-faced hot wall beside the massive grey edifice, fronted by a narrow bed filled with bulbs for a long succession of colour. Thousands more bulbs accompany the cherry avenue on the second grass terrace below, formerly an elaborate Dutch parterre, which runs between a summer-house and flights of stone steps. The second stairway descends to a bastion over the garden lake, created from the former moat. Much of this is also the work of T.R. Hayes.

Everywhere, the walls, balustrades and paving are decorated with plants: fuchsias, honeysuckle, *Clematis montana* and big-leaved *Vitis coignetiae*. The mauve *Erinus alpinus* colonises the castle's own stairway, and the pink and white daisies of *Erigeron karvinskianus* has seeded high into the wall crevices. These details play against the grander scenery: the still sheet of water, in which the castle and fringe of manna ash, willow, sumach and weeping hornbeam are reflected; the rolling parkland, with its fine walnuts and field maples; and beyond, the looming Howgill hills.

**ABOVE** Plumes of aruncus in the herbaceous border in June.
**RIGHT** The garden at Snowshill looking towards the dovecote, with poppies and Canterbury bells.

# Snowshill Manor

SNOWSHILL, BROADWAY, GLOUCESTERSHIRE

AREA 0.8ha (2 acres) • SOIL neutral to lime/light loam • ALTITUDE 229m (750ft)
AVERAGE RAINFALL 660mm (26in) • AVERAGE WINTER CLIMATE cold

From the mid-nineteenth century, the honey-coloured villages of the Cotswold hills – unspoilt, harmonious, rich in vernacular detail and an alluring antidote to the growing Victorian industrialisation – became an idyll and inspiration to a succession of painters, illustrators, craftsmen and other adherents to the Arts and Crafts creed. Charles Paget Wade, an architect, artist and woodworker, and a tireless collector of curios, saw a *Country Life* advertisement for the sale of Snowshill Manor in 1919. His legacy is one of the most extraordinary houses in the country, and the garden, anchored to the steeply sloping hillside below, is no less absorbing.

Here you will find a gold and green patchwork of intimate walled courts, narrow corridors, terraces, ponds and rustic outbuildings, idiosyncratically ornamented and sensitively planted. In spring and summer, a lively mix of cottage flowers, dispersed in repeated stands down the long outer path, injects a swathe of bright colour across the mellow composition: tulips, oriental poppies, lupins, foxgloves, veronica, lime-green alchemilla and purple sage are among the company. With white doves disporting on the roof of the medieval dovecote, the tops of clematis and roses visible beyond, and the fresh greens of the countryside all about, this is traditional England at its picture-postcard best.

All parts of the garden have their flower-filled moments. Here and there, you will come upon mixed beds of hellebores and Japanese anemones (an excellent, long-lasting partnership for part shade), peonies, phloxes, lavender, acanthus, thalictrum and viola; steps fringed with red valerian; grass strewn with daffodils; and walls hung with roses. Wade found blue, mauve and purple toned best with the stone, and these he allowed to predominate, with secondary use of salmons and creams, and sparing use of reds and yellows. Orange was banished.

This is emphatically an architect's garden. 'A garden is an extension of the house, a series of outdoor rooms,' Wade wrote, echoing contemporary philosophy. 'The plan is much more important than the flowers in it. Walls, steps and alleyways give a permanent setting, so that it is pleasant and orderly in both summer and winter.' Each room has its rustic details and crafted ornament: gate-piers, troughs and cisterns carrying the sound of water, a gilded armillary sundial crowning a stone column, a Venetian well-head, a bellcote with figures of St George and the Dragon, a shrine for a Madonna on the byre roof and a wall-mounted astrological dial. These last, like all the garden's wooden furniture, are painted in Wade's preferred shade of turquoise-flushed French blue, which, as with his favoured slice of the floral spectrum, he found the most satisfactory foil to stone and grass.

Beyond the walls and tiled roofs, there is the sweeping contrast of the Cotswold landscape. Though independent of it, the garden nestles into it as comfortably and organically as does the village, and any sense of claustrophobia engendered by the passages and small, introspective rooms is dispelled by the open views offered by others. Areas of rough grass, native trees, hedgerow shrubbery and wildflowers also create a bond. Common ivy, ferns, boxwood and ash are among the garden flora, and a dark tunnel of guelder rose, *Viburnum opulus* (a replacement for the aged elders planted by Wade), leads from the byre at the head of the Well Court; scillas, snakeshead fritillaries and primroses spangle the ground here in spring, followed by the pink and white Turk's caps of martagon lilies. This all adds to the rustic mood, and in sympathy, the National Trust maintains the garden entirely on organic principles. A small kitchen garden also provides organic produce to the restaurant.

# Stourhead

STOURTON, WARMINSTER, WILTSHIRE

AREA 38ha (93 acres) • SOIL acid/greensand • ALTITUDE 213m (700ft)
AVERAGE RAINFALL 1,016–1,118mm (40–44in) • AVERAGE WINTER CLIMATE moderate

Here we have probably the most bewitching and beautiful of this country's landscape gardens, an eighteenth-century arcadia of hills and hanging beechwoods, water and classical architecture, but dashingly overlaid with a later collection of exotic broad-leaved trees, conifers and richly coloured rhododendrons. A few purists balk at the combination, but they are in the minority. The balance, however, is fine, and the Trust has been working to recapture more of the flavour of the earlier phase by reopening vistas and reordering the planting, eliminating disjointed patches of colour and strong contrasts in favour of gentle harmonies and smooth transitions.

The valley landscape is the work of various members of the Hoare family, beginning in the early 1740s, with Henry Hoare II, son of the founder of Hoare's Bank. Motivated by the new-born idea of garden-making not as an exercise in geometry but as a branch of landscape painting, and freshly returned from a three-year tour of Italy, he set about creating a poetic landscape inspired by the Roman Campagna – scenes from the much-admired era of peace and artistic accomplishment under Augustus, alluding allegorically in part to the epic journey of Aeneas. Hoare's architectural advisor was Henry Flitcroft, an associate of William Kent, the new landscape movement's leading designer, and the scenes are very much in his style. It was his grandson, Richard Colt Hoare, who, responding to the current influx of new plants from America and Asia Minor, introduced *Rhododendron ponticum*, cherry laurel and the tulip tree into the landscape, and the exotic planting continued in the late nineteenth and early twentieth centuries, under the direction of Sir Henry Hoare.

The valley is tucked between folds of chalk downland and divorced from the grand Palladian villa, which stands back on the ridge to the north. One way of entering is to bypass the house by walking immediately downhill from the car park and arriving at the lakeside through the little estate village of Stourton, with its inn, church and row of cottages. The most dramatic approach, however, is to descend the wooded hillside across the lawn from the house, and have the first surprises sprung from above.

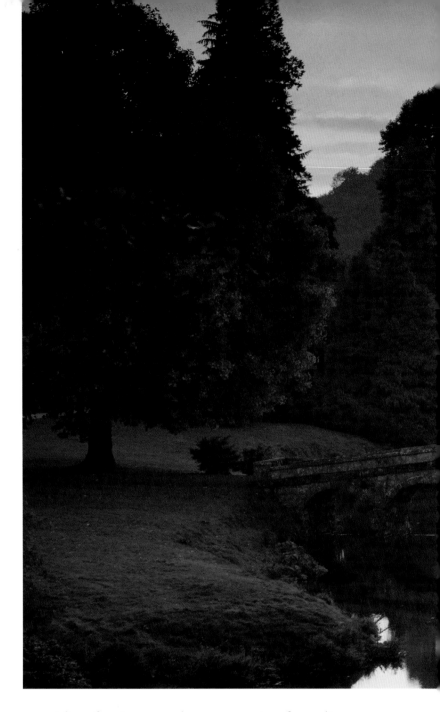

A line of ancient sweet chestnuts, a vestige of an earlier avenue to Stourton Castle, flanks part of the curving driveway to the mansion, and to the left are the old stable yard and walled kitchen gardens, currently being renovated by the Trust with the active involvement of students, community groups and volunteers, and planted with a wide variety of fruit, vegetables and ornamental plants. A Foster and Pearson glasshouse, dating from 1902, stands in the lower walled garden and houses a fine collection of pelargoniums. Ahead looms the house, designed by Colen

Campbell for Henry Hoare I, but with a later portico and flanking pavilions; the backdrop is of tree belts and open countryside carrying the eye across the edge of Salisbury Plain.

Opposite the south front, across a lawn lined with rows of beech trees, Edwardian-style shrubberies of purple, red and white rhododendrons – hybrids such as 'Britannia', 'Mrs Charles E. Pearson' and 'Loder's White' – colour the way, and there is a particularly good ice-house concealed down a laurel passage. Specimens of Persian ironwood (*Parrotia persica*), *Philadelphus*

'Belle Etoile' and *Ligustrum compactum* (syn. *L. chenaultii*) feature among the trees and in the eighteenth-century shrubbery on the lawn edges.

Magnificent tulip trees mark the beginning of the valley landscape. First, there is a view down to the village church, past sweet chestnuts and Himalayan whitebeam, and then you enter the wood, the path winding downhill between the beech and the rough

**ABOVE** The Palladian bridge and Pantheon at Stourhead, lit by an October sunset.

carpets of ferns, grasses and wildflowers – the browns and greens seasonally washed with snowdrops, bluebells and the native Lent lily, *Narcissus pseudonarcissus*. An obelisk, surmounted by a gilded solar disc, is the focal point for Richard Colt Hoare's broad, straight Fir Walk, now regenerated with young western hemlocks. Cherry laurel, kept low by annual pruning, gives a glossy evergreen understorey to the woods, with the more interesting rhododendrons appearing in loose drifts: Ghent azaleas and large-leaved Himalayan species; cool-coloured Hardy Hybrids like 'Blue Peter', 'Cynthia' and 'Nobleanum Venustum'; *R. barbatum*; and fragrant yellow *Rhododendron luteum* continuing into high summer with *R. auriculatum* and 'Polar Bear'.

Between the trees, two garden buildings suddenly appear – first, the Temple of Apollo, a pale cylinder with domed roof and Corinthian columns, perched on its hill across the valley, and then, on the far bank of the lake, the portico and rotunda of the Pantheon. No sooner glimpsed than lost; enveloped by the wood, you continue down to the valley floor, where a more ornamental cast of trees again takes over from the beech and oak – handsome flowering species such as snowdrop tree, handkerchief tree, Italian maple (*Acer opalus*) and tree magnolias, including a champion *M. campbellii* subsp. *mollicomata* and *M. denudata* (syn. *M. heptapeta*); conifers such as Macedonian pine, cryptomeria, dawn redwood and noble fir.

This assortment of exotics, backed by the hanging woods, extends around the lakeside. There are the evergreen rockets of wellingtonias and thujas (an immense broad-skirted specimen awaits across the water); the elegant uprights of tulip trees, punctuating the banks and rising from the central island; a number of purple beech trees; blasts of springtime rhododendron colour; and an exciting autumn panorama of red Japanese maples, American oaks and russet cypresses. Inside this rich canvas, you follow the circuit walk from one poetic building to the next, passing from sunlight to shadow. The reflections in the water add greatly to the composition, not only of the main lake but of the flanking pools – to the west, a lily lake, with a view beyond, up Six Wells Valley, where the River Stour rises; to the east, Turner's Paddock Lake, fed by a cascade and married with trees and a newly restored water wheel.

The path leads through a tunnel of yew, under a rustic stone arch, and into one of the most impressive of English grottoes, dank and gloomy but alive to the sound of water splashing from the natural springs; a nymph sleeps above the cascade, and from the opening in the lakeside wall there is a view across the water to the village church and arched bridge, framed in limes and sugar maples. A river god in the adjacent cave points in the direction of the Pantheon, and you leave by way of a rustic stairway, edged in hart's tongue fern. Now you come to the old Watch Cottage, Gothicised by Richard Colt Hoare in 1806 and with a good Japanese maple, *Acer palmatum* 'Osakazuki', beside it. From here, an array of features is visible – the Temple of Apollo on its mount, the slim and skeletal sculpture of the Bristol High Cross in the village and, on the opposite bank, the pediment and Doric columns of the Temple of Flora.

A statue of Hercules and other classical figures stand inside the rotunda of the Pantheon, and thence it is around the edge of the lake, and on to temples of Apollo and Flora, from where you obtain the equally glorious reverse views of the lake, trees and architectural ornament. These vistas are as close to perfection as any artist gardener can compose, and, thanks to their exotic plant content, they pass through a breathtaking sequence of colours. This is a landscape to visit at every season.

**LEFT** Autumnal bronze foliage in the trees by the water.
**RIGHT** View across the Octagon Lake towards the Lake Pavilions and Corinthian Arch at Stowe Landscape Gardens.

# Stowe Landscape Gardens

**BUCKINGHAM, BUCKINGHAMSHIRE**

**AREA** 101ha (250 acres) • **SOIL** alkaline/clay and gravel • **ALTITUDE** 120m (394ft)
**AVERAGE RAINFALL** 660mm (26in) **AVERAGE WINTER CLIMATE** cold

'The visitor should prepare to be impressed,' wrote John Martin Robinson in a past Stowe guidebook. This is one of England's foremost landscape gardens. At the Buckingham entrance, the scale is immediately heroic – 2.4km (1½ miles) of beech and chestnut avenue splicing across the undulating, wooded ridges of the countryside and carrying you to a triumphal Corinthian arch, the landscape's crowning monument. The New Inn to the side of it, built to accommodate Stowe's eighteenth-century visitors, is newly restored and reopened, and soon visitors will also be able to enter the grounds through Bell Gate, which provides one of the most celebrated views, across the Octagon Lake to the Palladian mansion, now Stowe School, which is the centrepiece of the 101.1ha (250 acre) garden. The school is periodically open to the public for guided tours by the Stowe House Preservation Trust.

This stupendous composition is the work of the socially and politically ambitious Temple-Grenville family, beginning with General Sir Richard Temple, later Viscount Cobham, who, funded by his marriage in 1715 to a wealthy heiress, Anne Halsey, set about transforming his father's small terraced garden in splendid style. This was a momentous period in landscape design, with the pendulum about to swing towards more natural and less formal composition. Stowe would not only reflect but pioneer the change in taste, with many of the leading architects, designers and sculptors employed here.

The early phase was executed by the royal gardener, Charles Bridgeman, and adorned with buildings designed by Sir John Vanbrugh, the architect of Blenheim Palace and Castle Howard. Very little of this layout remains today, for it was gradually dismantled in the 1740s, and then, in the 1750s, finally converted by Cobham's nephew, Earl Temple, into the more confidently sweeping style of the time, in harmony with the later parts of the landscape.

The main garden axis, below the majestic south façade of the house, is now broad and open. Where once the eye would have been channelled over an elaborate parterre, between an avenue of poplars and across an octagonal pond, there is empty lawn, informal flanks of forest trees, and a seemingly natural pool of water, strewn with the native white waterlily. Beyond, Earl Temple widened the axis between Vanbrugh's pavilions, giving the present grand vista into the park, terminated by his masterstroke, the Corinthian Arch. To the west of the house, Vanbrugh's domed rotunda, once the centre of radiating gravel walks, was set into a more informal wooded glade.

Bridgeman's principal legacy is the ha-ha. This French device of a sunken ditch, giving gardens protection from grazing animals yet allowing them to merge uninterrupted with the countryside, had a decisive impact on the development of the landscape garden. Stowe was the first English property in which it was used extensively. The runs were constructed like military fortifications and punctuated by projecting bastions, and on the south-west and south-east corners, these are adorned with monuments, a Palladian Temple of Venus and a Tuscan Temple of Friendship added by Earl Temple and now a ruin, following a fire in the nineteenth century.

The second phase of the garden's development under Lord Cobham took place from 1734 and is centred in a narrow dell, a little to the east – once occupied by Stowe village and its public road, of which only the fourteenth-century church remains. Garden design was now being compared to landscape painting, with landowners beginning to yearn for the sort of pastoral landscapes depicted by Claude Lorraine and Salvator Rosa. The pioneer of this Picturesque style was William Kent, who was engaged by Lord Cobham to create these Elysian Fields (the Romans' mythological paradise) here at Stowe.

It is the most intimate portion of the garden. Access, as in the myth, is across the serpentine River Styx, spouting from a newly restored grotto and created by damming the existing stream (the upper dam being the Shell Bridge). You enter into bright glades, fringed by trees and filled with monuments, but presided over, on the west bank, by the Temple of Ancient Virtue, an Ionic rotunda erected in 1736, and on the east, by the Temple of British Worthies, a curved screen in which the busts of distinguished men of action and of contemplation are displayed in niches (along with that of one woman, Queen Elizabeth I). The cast ranges from King Alfred and Walter Raleigh to William Shakespeare and Isaac Newton, and includes Cobham's friend Alexander Pope, the poet and influential landscape theorist – all Whig heroes. This was one of the first monuments intended to be 'read' by visitors, who would have noticed the pointed omission of Catholic priests. Exploring the Arcadian landscape was intended to be as much an exercise for the mind as for the feet. Here at Stowe, there are not only classical and literary references to pick up but also the family's strongly held beliefs and prejudices, often conveyed with satire.

At the base of the Elysian Fields, you are enticed further east, across Hawkwell Field, which rolls down to another naturalistic stretch of water, spanned by one of the garden's best-known monuments, the Palladian Bridge by James Gibbs. Lord Cobham began developing this area in the late 1730s as ornamental pasture, combining classical decoration with agricultural use; it was an early example of *la ferme ornée*, and is still grazed today. Presiding over the scene, on a ridge far to the north, stands the Queen's Temple, a Corinthian temple built as a summer-house for Lady Cobham, and on the same axis, halfway to the water and flanked by young and old cedar trees, the Gothic Temple, a monument to the 'Liberty of our Ancestors'.

The last part of the garden to be completed was the Grecian Valley, north-east of the house. A carefully contoured sweep of hay meadow – full of wildflowers, including massed cowslips – and framed by broad and muscular banks of deciduous trees, cedars and pines, this marks the arrival of a more open and bold style of naturalistic landscaping. It was begun in 1746, by which time Lord Cobham's head gardener was none other than the young Lancelot, later 'Capability', Brown.

The Grecian Valley contains one of the most impressive of Stowe's monuments – the Ionic Temple, completed by Earl Temple with the addition of a magnificent carved pediment, showing Britannia receiving the tribute of the world; it was transferred here from the Palladian Bridge, structures being moved about the garden like chess pieces. Named the Temple of Concord and Victory in line with Earl Temple's development of the garden on still grander lines, it embraces not only national but imperial achievements.

Stowe is the most complex of English gardens, but no deep understanding is needed in order to appreciate its beauty – the open meadows, the lofty plantations of beech, lime, oak and chestnut

with their yew, holly, cherry laurel and box understorey, the waterside fringes of alder and ash, and the golden architecture. It presents a succession of magnificent landscape pictures, changing in response to every phase of light and season.

Only after the Second World War, when the study of garden history grew, did Stowe School begin to realise the landscape's true significance and the scale of the rescue work demanded. Repairs were tentatively begun, gathering momentum in the 1960s. But the scale of the declining landscape and the sheer quantity of crumbling buildings was alarming. In 1990, following offers of support from a benefactor, English Heritage and the National Heritage Memorial Fund, Stowe School conveyed the gardens to the National Trust, and a major appeal was launched. Numerous individuals and public and private bodies have contributed subsequently, a comprehensive historical survey has been commissioned, and lake by lake, plantation by plantation, and temple by temple, the work has proceeded, involving archaeology, dredging, skilled stonemasonry and the planting of thousands of trees. It has been one of the most ambitious garden restoration projects ever undertaken.

**ABOVE LEFT** The Oxford Bridge on a frosty day at Stowe Landscape Gardens.
**RIGHT** The Palladian Bridge, built in 1738, with the Gothic Temple designed by Gibbs on the skyline.

# Tatton Park

KNUTSFORD, CHESHIRE

AREA 24ha (60 acres) • SOIL acid/sand • ALTITUDE 60m (197ft) • AVERAGE RAINFALL 28in (711mm) • AVERAGE WINTER CLIMATE cold

'A grand domain of great verdure, and with a noble lake; these are the charms: the per contra, no inequality of ground; the timber of neither stature nor girth,' wrote the diarist Lord Torrington in 1790. The terrain is certainly flat; the estate lies at the northern end of the Cheshire plain, amid pastureland and meres. The trees, however, have become one of the chief assets. Before Lord Torrington's visit, and in the decades after, a considerable number were planted as clumps and woods, and these, with their replacements, now bring shape and texture to the setting; an extensive arboretum has also grown up beside the house. Herds of red and fallow deer graze the meadows, together with sheep, and there is further animation from the boats coursing the lake – sailing being one of many recreational activities for which the park is available to the public.

A varied landscape thus presents itself, much in the style of Humphry Repton, who paid a visit here in 1791 and prepared one of his Red Books of proposals the following year, though, in fact, it owes more to one John Webb, a pupil of William Emes, who worked here in the second decade of the nineteenth century, and to planting by the 1st and 2nd Lords Egerton in the 1870s and 1880s.

Surveying the scene is an imposing Neo-classical mansion of pinkish-grey sandstone, built by Samuel Wyatt and his nephew Lewis Wyatt, between 1790 and 1812. And to accompany it are gardens: the full panoply of parterre and croquet lawn, herbaceous borders and topiary, glasshouses and aviaries, kitchen gardens, shrubberies, water gardens and pinetum, which would provide a string of diversions for the leisured Victorian and Edwardian family and their guests.

Below the portico, terraced lawns flow down to the Italian Garden, constructed in the 1880s and restored by the Trust a century later, using archive photographs. Grass, gravel, box and bedding (polyanthus and forget-me-nots, followed by armeria, ageratum and mauve pink 'Princess Marie José' dahlia) provide the pattern, sculpted around marble vases and a Neptune fountain. The upper parterre has also recently been restored, with the bedding set among ribbons of armeria and the original top-dressings of white marble and red shale.

The decorative glasshouses stand to the west. The Conservatory, built by Lewis Wyatt in 1818, is stocked with oranges and lemons.

These would once have stood outside on the terrace for summer, but now they are permanent inhabitants accompanied by clivias, passion flowers and mimosa. Many other gardens have a conservatory on this scale, but none has as impressive a fernery. Dating from the 1850s, its architect was probably Joseph Paxton, designer of the Crystal Palace and the conservatory at Chatsworth. The speciality is the Australian tree ferns collected on his travels by Captain Charles Randle Egerton RN, the brother of the 1st Lord Egerton. The path curves under their crowns – mesmerising traceries of emerald, as you look through them towards the roof glass – passing a dry-stone wall studded with maidenhairs and cyrtomiums, while the enormous fronds of the chain fern, *Woodwardia radicans*, brush against your legs. The connecting conservatory, also rebuilt, is now a traditional riot of colour.

Beyond are further flower gardens: a long L-shaped border, colour-coded within buttresses of yew, and backed by walls densely clothed in climbers and shrubs (including the rare *Magnolia acuminata* var. *subcordata*, which gives a good show of yellow flowers in summer); a garden partially restored in the sinuous and curious gardenesque style of the early nineteenth century, where specimen plants are shown

ABOVE The Japanese Garden at Tatton Park with the 'flying goose' bridge and the ornamental tea house in the background.

off as individuals in small beds; and a walled enclosure of roses and scented plants set beside a pool. Topiary yews, a fountain, a shady pergola and trellis arbour, and a castellated sheep-watcher's tower, dating from before 1750, add further incident.

The walled kitchen and orchard gardens, each 1ha (2½ acres) in size, have been the subject of major restoration and are now very impressive. In the kitchen garden, heritage and unusual vegetables such as salsify and scorzonera are grown on a rotation system in four beds. A central cross of apple tunnels, fig houses with twelve varieties of fig, including the very early 'White Marseilles', and forcing pots, used for sea kale as well as rhubarb, add to the scene, all presided over by the tea house of the adjacent rose garden.

The orchard garden now boasts restored glasshouses for vines, tomatoes, peaches and even pineapples, whose three-year fruiting cycle is once again being mastered. There are also glasshouses for begonias and orchids, the latter comprising four temperature-controlled sections, restocked with the help of the North of England Orchid Society. Outdoors, the hardy fruits are all varieties grown in Cheshire before 1900. The soft fruits are set around the central pergola and twin herbaceous borders, and the tree fruits are grown in an array of goblet, fan and espalier shapes. These demonstrate and conserve old pruning and training skills now rarely encountered in Britain.

The view from the house towards the distant hills beyond Congleton encompasses fine evergreen and Turkey oaks and cedar of Lebanon, and, in the dell below, high conifers, beeches and sweet chestnuts (the twisted, deeply fissured trunks are a memorable motif). Around the lawns of the flower gardens, you will have come upon handkerchief tree, *Malus hupehensis*, *Magnolia obovata* syn. *M. hypoleuca*, large-leaved *Emmenopterys henryi*, blue-podded *Decaisnea fargesii* and choice conifers such as Brewer's weeping spruce and the red-coned Chinese spruce, *Picea likiangensis*.

These are a taste of what awaits in the arboretum's many hectares of grassy and pool-side glades. The cast is arranged fairly erratically, and often very closely packed, but it is an interesting catalogue of what will thrive in a northern climate and there are some magnificent specimens, not least among the conifer collection.

The pinetum was well established by 1795, though the oldest of the present plants date mostly from the late nineteenth and early twentieth centuries. In addition to the extensive range of tall American and Far Eastern species, such as *Pinus jeffreyi*, *P. wallichiana*, *Abies recurvata* var. *ernesti* and *Picea purpurea* syn. *P. likiangensis* var. *purpurea*, there are contrasting plumes from Sawara cypresses (*Chamaecyparis pisifera*) and cryptomeria, dawn redwoods grouped in a glade, and swamp cypresses (*Taxodium distichum*) beside a stretch of water. Among deciduous trees, there are cherries and parrotia, styrax and halesia, a very tall bay willow (*Salix pentandra*) and a prickly curiosity in the form of *Kalopanax septemlobus* syn. *K. pictus*, whose maple-like leaves are among the last to drop in autumn.

In summer, the glades are predominantly green, but in spring, there are blasts of colour from massed rhododendrons. The collection was built up by the last Lord Egerton in the 1940s, during his enforced confinement in Britain away from his beloved estate in Kenya. The walls of the Tenants' Hall are covered with the heads of game that crossed his path, and at one point in the garden tour you come upon a heather-thatched African hut.

*En route*, you encounter two surprising vestiges of an earlier layout. One is a small beech maze, a rare feature established before 1795 and said to be the same plan as at Hampton Court. The other, splicing the arboretum into two parts, is the Broad Walk, an avenue predominantly of beech. It dates from the 1730s, and in the 1820s the family installed a grand monument at its head, inspired by that to Lysicrates, the chorus or storyteller, in ancient Athens. This marks the boundary of the garden, from where you can look out over the park.

I have left the jewel in Tatton's crown until last. The opening of Japan to foreigners in the late nineteenth century brought a fascination with all things Japanese, culminating in the Japan-British Exhibition of 1910. Almost immediately, the 3rd Lord Egerton embarked on a Japanese garden at Tatton. It is probably the finest in the country. A fusion of the various styles of classical garden, it has a dark pool as its centre, fed by four streams that flow over cascades, under flat bridges, past stone lanterns and between a carefully placed cast of plants, including maples, bamboo, water iris, cherry, and fine specimens of *Picea pungens* Glauca Group. Cranes and other mythically charged animals are met on the way, and the centrepiece, on the Master's island, is a thatched tea house. Beyond the arched bridge a Shinto shrine, brought from Japan, adorns the island on the adjacent lake – made for Lady Charlotte Egerton, wife of the 1st Baron, out of disused clay pits. The symbolism of these Japanese features passes most of us by, but the craftsmanship and tranquillity of the setting are there for all to savour. A Japanese gardener may have supervised the original work, and the garden has been comprehensively restored under Japanese guidance.

So there are large and varied gardens at Tatton, full of interest and reflecting the enthusiasms of many generations of the Egerton family, who lived here from 1598 for more than 350 years.

# Tintinhull Garden

TINTINHULL, YEOVIL, SOMERSET

AREA 0.8ha (2 acres) • SOIL neutral/loam over marl clay • ALTITUDE 30m (100ft)
AVERAGE RAINFALL 762mm (30in) • AVERAGE WINTER CLIMATE moderate

The west front of Tintinhull House, part-hidden by a high wall at the edge of the village, is as dreamy a façade as you are likely to come upon. Compact, symmetrical, built of a warm and welcoming honey-coloured stone (quarried at nearby Ham Hill), and adorned with pediment and pilasters, mullioned windows and carved scrolls, it is the picture of early eighteenth-century elegance. The lines and proportions of the manor have been extended to create an equally exceptional garden: an open and varied sequence of rooms, or courts, formally set out over the more or less flat terrain, and decorated with a varied but discerningly chosen range of plants. 'Nothing is out of place, and the result is a garden that is the embodiment of peace,' wrote the cottage gardener Margery Fish.

From the sitting-room door, a long, straight path, flanked by low domes of clipped box, invites you west through three enclosures. The first, Eagle Court (named after the pair of birds mounted on its gate-piers), is the oldest part of the garden, dating from the eighteenth century, with the stone paving added, and the further enclosures formally connected and shaped, some time after 1905, probably by Dr S.J.M. Price, a churchman of private means who was then the tenant.

But the planting, the design of the larger courts and the character of the present garden is the inspiration of Phyllis Reiss, who, with her husband, Captain F.E. Reiss, came to live here in 1933, having already made a garden near Cheltenham – not far from Hidcote, to which Tintinhull owes more than a passing acknowledgement. She had an ordered and distinctive approach. 'Her special gift,' wrote the garden designer Lanning Roper, was 'for selecting and placing plants to create an effect … If a plant is distinguished in form and texture it is used boldly and often repeated, this making a unity of design.'

Within the parameters of colour and mood set by Mrs Reiss, the Trust's former tenants, the distinguished garden writer Penelope Hobhouse and her husband the late Professor John Malins, continued to experiment and rejuvenate. As at Hidcote, there is an exciting tension between the plants and their trim and emphatic framework. The design is very firm, with the new courts running parallel with the old, and bound together with strong east-west and north-south axes in the form of stone paths, terraces and channelled views leading to a seat or other ornament.

Thus, from the central old court, you gain a prospect down the length of a rectangular waterlily pond to a stone loggia; this garden was made from the old tennis court in 1947, and the loggia erected by Mrs Reiss in memory of her nephew who was killed in the Second World War. From the Fountain Garden beyond, the eye is led between rivers of catmint down the centre of the Kitchen Garden, to a farm gate and then out into a woodland walk, edged in bulbs. The Kitchen Garden itself is full of unusual crops, many from the Heritage Seed Library of Garden Organic (formerly the Henry Doubleday Research Association); 'Rat's Tail' radish, 'Tiger Tom' tomato and the chilli pepper 'Long Green Buddha' are among the curiosities.

Often, the symmetry of Tintinhull's design is reinforced in the planting. Lavender is repeated either side of the Eagle Court's terrace steps, for example, and beds of the Apothecary's rose, *Rosa gallica* var. *officinalis*, either side of the southern entrance to the Kitchen Garden. A clump of variegated flag iris stands in each corner of the waterlily pool; and a pair of white-tiered *Cornus controversa* 'Variegata' (introduced by the Trust, and perhaps a touch too flashy for Tintinhull) preside over the extension to the Fountain Garden, teamed with foliage plants.

But everywhere, there is the contrasting exuberance: hellebores filtering between evergreen *Itea ilicifolia* and *Mahonia × media* 'Winter Sun', oak-leaved hydrangea and mock orange, in a north-facing bed; *Iris sibirica* 'Flight of Butterflies' interplanted with *Allium christophii*. As at Hidcote, colour is the medium that orders the mixed cast of plants. The beds around the circular pool in the Fountain Garden have a crisp white theme, founded on the flowers of tulips, roses, penstemons, argyranthemums and cosmos, and set off by silvery foliage and a dark backdrop of yew hedges.

The large north-eastern court has a border of smouldering crimson and bronze-red leaves, provided by various berberis and the young growth of Bush roses, partnered with the magenta-red flowers of *Rosa* 'Zéphirine Drouhin' and 'Rosemary Rose', alliums and penstemons; a more subdued, old-world mood than the red borders at Hidcote, with their brilliant scarlets and oranges. Flanking the rectangular waterlily pool is a contrasting pair of schemes, one with the soft, feminine tones of pink and lavender phlox, veronica and aster, and the other with the more potent, advancing shades of blood-red 'Frensham' roses, dahlias and yellow achilleas, but harmonised by the presence of white and silver in the form of stachys, crambe, sweet rocket and *Clematis recta*.

Because most of the garden is seen from the upstairs windows of the house, Mrs Reiss planned the borders for an all-year display, and wherever possible, bulbs, annuals and biennials are used to give each piece of ground a second season of colour. Thus, snowdrops, winter aconites, anemones, chionodoxas and scillas are ubiquitous (the blues particularly striking beneath plants whose young leaves are in shades of red); tulips and daffodils appear in advance of roses; pink and white cyclamen follow the spring magnolias. There is an additional boost from pots, notably around the waterlily pool, where tulips perform ahead of pink verbena and *Anisodontea*, white *Argyranthemum* and grey-leaved marguerites. In the cool shade of the loggia stand pots of hostas and ferns.

In every enclosure, large and small, there is a sense of space and tranquillity, an impression fostered by the central uncluttered expanses of lawn or water. The terraces are generous, appointed with steps wide and shallow to 'emphasise the change of level on what is a relatively flat site', as Lanning Roper observed. The trees are also of an unexpected scale: there are just a handful to lift the eye and draw in the sky, including yew, cedar, and holm oak, *Quercus ilex* – all evergreen and nicely in period with the house.

All this, together with the various sub-divisions and wealth of detail, makes it very hard to believe that the entire composition encompasses only about 0.8ha (2 acres), as many writers have commented. The ideas and lessons here for all owners of small gardens are legion.

**ABOVE** Evening light streams across catmint and lime-green smyrnium in the Kitchen Garden.

# Trelissick Garden

FEOCK, TRURO, CORNWALL

**AREA** 10ha (25 acres) • **SOIL** acid/loam • **ALTITUDE** 30m (100ft) • **AVERAGE RAINFALL** 1,016mm (40in) • **AVERAGE WINTER CLIMATE** frost-free, mild

Cornish gardens spring many surprises, but the apparitions at Trelissick take some beating. Detached from the Neo-classical mansion, the grounds are on an intimate scale, a tranquil composition of plunging lawns, specimen trees, shady paths and stream-fed dell framed by woods and the expected masses of rhododendrons and camellias. There are occasional glimpses of the River Fal below, a ribbon of light between the tree-clad banks. But as you emerge from the shrub walks to the north, the jaw drops – for the water near the river mouth is deep, and at anchor on the garden's boundary is likely to be a substantial cargo ship. Like the land approaches to the Suez Canal, where great tankers suddenly appear, gliding between folds of empty desert, not only their size but their very presence is a shock.

It would be more appropriate if the ships were galleons, for this is a country of creeks and secret coves, of smugglers' legend and historical romance. The house commands an excellent view of Carrick Roads and beyond to Falmouth Bay, while the road that bisects the garden drops to the King Harry Ferry, connecting Truro with the isolated Roseland Peninsula. The garden acquired its present richness after 1937, when the estate became the home of Mr and Mrs Ronald Copeland. Since 1955, the Trust has developed the grounds considerably in response to various losses from drought, frost and storm by extending the shrubberies and tree collection into Carcadden, the land across the Ferry road, as well as boosting the post-spring displays.

Entering the garden beside the walls of the old kitchen garden, you plunge immediately into flowers. In spring, Chinese and Japanese wisterias, with violet abutilon, accompany clove-scented *Viburnum × juddii*, while in summer, hot-coloured cannas, dahlias, hedychiums and heliotrope are backed by scented evergreen *Trachelospermum jasminoides* and *Magnolia grandiflora* 'Galissonière'. There is also a collection of figs further on, near the shop.

The climate, though not quite as benevolent as at Glendurgan or Trengwainton, is mild and moist, and the shrub display that draws you into the woodland walks begins early. Brazen stands of 'Cornish Red' rhododendrons and the blood-red form of *R.*

*arboreum* give way to groves of *Camellia japonica* and *C. × williamsii* in their many red, pink and white cultivars. There are splashes from blush-pink *Rhododendron sutchuenense* and red *R. thomsonii*, the pink *R. williamsianum* cultivars and other Cornish hybrids such as 'Penjerrick' and 'Beauty of Tremough'. And so the succession continues, with appearances from evergreen azaleas, violet-blue *R. augustinii* hybrids, scented white 'Avalanche', scented deciduous azaleas, numerous Hardy Hybrids and a large collection of blood-scarlet rhododendrons from early 'Little Bert' and 'Earl of Athlone' to 'May Day' and 'Romany Chai', and the Trelissick speciality 'Gwilt-King'. The more tender varieties, such as *R. magnificum*, grow on the sides of the dell, on the far side of the main lawn. The huge Australian tree ferns inevitably steal the show here, but the collection of white, lily-scented *maddenii* rhododendrons is bewitching. The shelter and moisture is also enjoyed by large-leaved species, such as the rose-tinted form of *R. rex* subsp. *arizelum* and by the beautiful sulphur-yellow hybrid 'Mary Swaythling'.

The wet ground below is at its most brilliant in early summer, when awash with variously coloured candelabra primulas, but earlier it is lit by the yellow flares of skunk cabbage in spring, and, later in the summer by lemon-scented *Primula florindae* and astilbes. The accompanying fern and hosta leaves are as large and lush as you will see anywhere.

Hydrangeas, extensively planted by the Copelands, have been still further exploited by the Trust, so that now the banks of spring shrub colour have their match in summer and autumn. A walk of blue and white hydrangeas, overhung with cherries and the snowdrop tree, *Halesia carolina*, skirts the dell, and more white varieties, grown near eucryphias and orange kniphofias, illuminate the view over the river to the gothick mansion of Tregothnan. Hydrangeas are also massed in Carcadden. This young arboretum, reached by a new bridge – the original of which was part of the system of carriage rides set out in the early nineteenth century – is a former orchard and nursery, and was brought into the garden in the 1960s. Magnolias and viburnums, as well as rhododendrons, camellias and cherries, now feature here, together with a range of unusual trees and larger shrubs, including two fine plants of the Chilean hazel, *Gevuina avellana*.

Much of the garden's attraction comes from the vistas, across from one side of the plant-filled valley to the other, along the undulating lawns and meandering paths, and, of course, down over the River Fal and the estuary. Daffodils, anemones and wildflowers carpet these views in spring and summer, and the mixed deciduous and evergreen trees provide an ever-changing frame; the highlights include *Acer platanoides* 'Cucullatum' in Carcadden and, most memorably, C.D. Gilbert's Japanese cedar, *Cryptomeria japonica*, stretching its many limbs in the centre of the main lawn, surrounded by deep exotic borders of cannas, ginger lilies and bananas.

**ABOVE LEFT** Wisteria in flower on the Entrance Walk, with the Water Tower beyond.
**ABOVE** The new entrance and landscaping at Trelissick Garden in May.

# Trengwainton Garden

MADRON, PENZANCE, CORNWALL

AREA 10ha (25 acres) • SOIL acid/loam over granite • ALTITUDE 75–120m (246–394ft)
AVERAGE RAINFALL 1,220mm (48in) • AVERAGE WINTER CLIMATE mild to moderate

The south-west corner of the Cornish peninsula enjoys one of the mildest climates in Britain, and in some of the dappled glades and old walled enclosures at Trengwainton you feel you could be in some lush subtropical garden. The long growing seasons, high rainfall and moist sea air promote fast growth, mosses and lichens, and the soft winters allow trees, shrubs and climbers from some of the world's temperate regions to flourish. The exotic flavour is appropriate, for it was wealth from his family's Jamaican sugar plantation that enabled Sir Rose Price to lay the foundations of the garden in the early nineteenth century.

It was he who built, in about 1820, the series of small walled compartments close to the entrance lodge, of great interest to garden historians for their sizeable raised brick vegetable beds, specially angled to take advantage of the winter sun; though known to have existed elsewhere, these are thought to be the only survivors. The southernmost compartments are now mysterious and jungly plantsman's plots, with wild ferns running through the grey granite walls, primroses and anemones spreading around the skirts of shrubs, and old, spring-flowering tree magnolias, *M. × veitchii* and forms of *M. campbellii*, shading a mossy carpet patterned with scented plants and areas of wildflower meadow.

The micro-climates here suit a mouth-watering range of tender trees and shrubs. *Eucryphia moorei* and *Panax laetus* syn. *Pseudopanax laetus* from Australia, *Magnolia doltsopa* syn. *Michelia doltsopa* from China and the Himalayas, and the South American *Fuchsia excorticata* have all grown into fine specimens, as have hardier Asian species such as *Enkianthus campanulatus* and *Stewartia sinensis*, appreciative of the additional warmth, shelter and moisture.

Tender rhododendrons abound, among them the Formosan azalea *R. oldhamii*, and white-flowered, lily-scented species and hybrids of the *maddenii* series. The soaring biennial *Echium pininana*, from the Canary Islands, is a luxurious sight, as is *Geranium palmatum* from Madeira. The abundance of broad-leaved evergreens and scarcity of conifers contributes much to the balmy flavour of the gardens, but a few Southern Hemisphere coniferous species add exotic notes, among them *Podocarpus salignus* from Chile and *Athrotaxis selaginoides* from Tasmania.

Trengwainton began sampling such treasures after 1925, when Lt Col Edward Bolitho (who gave this garden to the Trust in 1961) inherited. The foundation for his collection of rhododendron species was Frank Kingdon-Ward's 1927–8 plant-hunting expedition to north-east Assam and the Mishmi Hills in Upper Burma, in which he was offered a share of the spoils by G.H. Johnstone of Trewithen. A number of species, including *Rhododendron macabeanum*, *R. elliottii* and *R. cinnabarinum* subsp. *xanthocodon* Concatenans Group, flowered here for the first time in the British Isles. Over a long spring season, their flower trusses colour the woodland fringes and grassy glades through which the curving drive and its parallel long walk climb towards the house, following the old carriage drive.

At the height of the display, strong patches of magenta and pink Kirishima and Kurume azaleas draw the eye through the softer rose tones of *R. vaseyi*, the violets of 'Penheale Blue' and 'Saint Breward', and a great many other handsome selections, some bred here and most growing in the company of daffodils or wildflowers. The scents are rich and heavy, from deciduous azaleas and tender

**ABOVE** Tree ferns surround the pond at Trengwainton.
**RIGHT** Colourful azaleas and rhododendrons.

rhododendrons such as *Rhododendron johnstoneanum* and *R.* 'Lady Alice Fitzwilliam', and in the shadows and moist troughs, you come upon the elephantine foliage of *R. grande, R. magnificum, R. falconeri* (layers from the original specimen dating from the 1880s), and, of course, *R. macabeanum*.

Camellias are also here in quantity, massed into *allées* and scattered in drifts; and, later in summer, the drive and woodland walks are flushed blue and white with hydrangeas. Shortly after beginning the walk up the hill, you hear the sound of water. The hills are laced with underground springs, and the stream beside the drive is fringed with lysichitons, candelabra primulas, astilbes, polygonums, arum lilies, hydrangeas and crocosmias. This contrasts with the jungle mood recaptured in the shady, sheltered pockets between the trees and rhododendron thickets, where

wooden bridges cross the water and the mossy streamside banks support self-sporing colonies of Australian tree ferns; the open zones of bamboos, grasses and phormiums give a special theme to the Jubilee Garden.

In front of the Victorian house, the trees give way to falling lawns and, from the terrace, a stunning view of St Michael's Mount rising from the sea. The garden's chief threat – the wind – may also become apparent. The westerlies can be savage, and without extensive tree planting to protect the slope, little ornamental gardening could have been attempted. The shelter belts need continual management, and much restoration has been necessary following the severe gales of January 1990. Unusual plants continue to be sampled at Trengwainton, ensuring that the collection retains its pioneering flavour and can always spring exotic surprises.

# Tyntesfield

## WRAXALL, SOMERSET

**AREA** 18ha (45 acres) • **SOIL** neutral/loam over limestone • **ALTITUDE** 40–78m (131–256ft)
**AVERAGE RAINFALL** 1,054mm (41¹/₂ in) • **AVERAGE WINTER CLIMATE** mild

In April 2002, this High Victorian timepiece – a complete estate and ensemble, just 11.3km (7 miles) from the centre of Bristol – came blinking into the limelight, secured for the National Trust by a grant from the National Heritage Memorial Fund and a fundraising campaign to which 70,000 donors contributed. It had been a well-kept secret even in its locality, with Richard Gibbs, 2nd Lord Wraxall, guarding his privacy.

Although Lord Wraxall kept the walled kitchen garden in continuous production and the pleasure grounds mown and clipped, the decorative buildings, greenhouses, boating lake, tennis court and flower gardens were allowed to deteriorate. So the grounds required major restoration, and, in a departure from traditional practice, the Trust has been sharing this complex and fascinating task with trainees, volunteers, schoolchildren, and other members of the public wherever possible.

Walking onto the terrace, you are met by the wide, tranquil landscape of the Yeo valley, seen over layers of shapes and silhouettes – Irish yews against deciduous trees and trees against distant hills – while behind bristles the Gothic fantasy of the house, with golden towers, turrets and chimneys. The house was rebuilt in the 1860s for William Gibbs, whose virtual monopoly of the Peruvian guano trade (the bird dung used as an agricultural fertiliser) made him the richest commoner in England. His principal architect, John Norton, may also have designed the terrace, which wraps around two sides of the house, bounded by a balustrade.

Before 1917, the terrace culminated in a great conservatory, with a domed roof modelled on St Mark's in Venice, and its footprint is still visible, together with its camellias, magnolias and Chusan palm, which has soared high in the open air. A mature lemon verbena, growing near wisteria and yellow Banksian roses elsewhere on the terrace, indicates the mildness of the climate here.

As you would expect, the High Victorian taste for artful, 'unnatural' gardening finds expression in bedding schemes, formality and coloured foliage. The central feature of each of the ten patterned terrace beds is a circle of green or golden hollies,

topped by a stone urn; these are accompanied by rich, ever-changing displays of spring and summer bulbs, annuals, biennials and hothouse exotics, which, it is hoped, will be increasingly innovative and experimental over time. The formality then extends down a double stairway into a grand avenue of Irish yews (formerly interplanted with yuccas), and between topiary spheres of Portugal laurel. Off to the west, a procession of hollies, pruned into mushroom mounds, leads you past an ornamental wooden aviary and into the pleasure grounds. The other decorative elements in the surrounding woods and farmland are part of an extensive designed landscape, while the pleasure grounds' tree collection is the nucleus of a vast planting scheme. Its sloping lawns are dotted with favourite Victorian curiosities, from blue cedar, monkey puzzle and variegated cypress (a fine pair of *Thujopsis dolabrata* 'Variegata') to gingko, oriental plane, and cut-leaved lime. There are also trees of champion size, including *Acer triflorum*, *Cercis siliquastrum* and *Zelkova serrata*. New plantings are being influenced by the discovery of some 400 zinc and terracotta tree labels, though curiosities such as Wollemi pine are also being added.

A High Church man (with his own resident chaplain), William Gibbs funded the building of the chapel at Keble College, Oxford, and this is commemorated in the planting of a hybrid Algerian oak, *Quercus canariensis* × *robur*. The cedars of Lebanon were grown from seed brought from the Holy Land. Frequently, the lawn dissolves into wilder areas, with colonies of daffodils, cowslips and other wildflowers, or thickets of bamboo and pampas grass. Indeed the lawns, which are presumed never to have been treated with fertiliser or weedkiller, are themselves rich wildflower habitats and home to orchids – twayblade, bee, green-winged, early purple and hundreds of autumn ladies' tresses. They are also rich in fungi, notably waxcaps.

Stone seats invite you to pause and survey the scene, one flanked by a pair of slim columnar cypresses, *Chamaecyparis lawsoniana* 'Wisselii'. Below the terrace, you meet rhododendron clumps and a little maze of yellow azalea. Another surprise among the trees is a large terraced rose garden, patterned in box hedges and ironwork tunnels, and with a pair of Minton-tiled gazebos (currently being restored) as architectural eye-catchers. Deer make rose-growing difficult here, so bedding and other plants make up today's palette. Lavenders and pink peonies, disliked by deer, present a good display, while to the side is a fernery and a rock bank, which will be developed as an intricate alpine garden. A sloping theatre lawn, backed by a hedge, rises behind the rose garden.

The walled kitchen garden is downhill from the house, the curving drive taking you past more rhododendrons and specimen trees, including yellow buckeye, *Aesculus flava*. After 1896, when it was redesigned by architect Walter Cave, the kitchen garden was on show to guests as part of the garden tour and suitably ornamented with wrought-iron gates, a small flowery entrance garden, and an Italianate loggia in brick and sandstone, a classical contrast to the Gothic of the house, which would have been filled with seasonal pot plants, such as carnations and pelargoniums. The accompanying Lady Garden sports the exotic foliage of tetrapanax, paulownia and hedychium.

Beyond is the range of glasshouses, already restocked with peaches, vines, tomatoes and cucumbers, and gardeners' sheds (including a packing room, where produce would have been prepared for the kitchen and for dispatch to London in boxes embossed with the family coronet). The Cut Flower or Dial Garden is lively with dahlias, sweet peas and other cutting flowers, and there is an extremely decorative classical orangery, currently being renovated. This would probably have been used as much for entertaining as for growing plants.

The main walled garden has a central dipping pool, and glasshouses on its southern side for figs, peaches and other tender fruits. With a full range of vegetables being returned to its beds, and hardy fruits newly trained on its walls (which were inset with vine-eye supports as they were built), this is once again reaching full production. Outside, the derelict orchard house and other outbuildings are projects for the future.

**LEFT** Agapanthus flowers on the terrace with formal beds beyond.
**ABOVE** A display of dahlias in the Cut Flower Garden.

# Uppark

SOUTH HARTING, PETERSFIELD, WEST SUSSEX

**AREA** 22ha (54 acres) • **SOIL** alkaline/brown earth, chalk • **ALTITUDE** 150m (492ft)
**AVERAGE RAINFALL** 940mm (37in) • **AVERAGE WINTER CLIMATE** cold

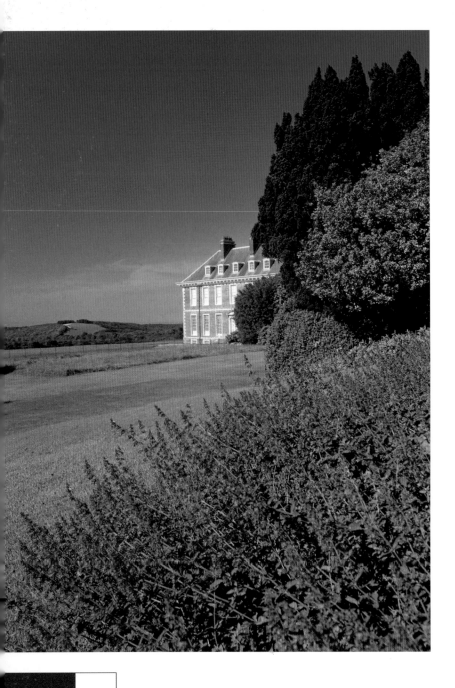

Uppark suffered more than its fair share of calamity at the end of the twentieth century. In October 1987, and again in January 1990, its garden, park and woods were devastated by gales. In August 1989, when the restoration of the house was nearing completion and while the roof was being leaded, the building caught fire and was severely damaged. But the house has been painstakingly reconstructed, plaster wall by ceiling, door hinge by bracket, and looks uncannily unchanged; the scars suffered by the garden from the building works are gone and trees are growing up to re-create the former wooded setting.

Its position, high on the South Downs with a view between flanking hills to a distant band of sea, is the chief delight. The house stands proud in this landscape, an elegant Dutch-style building with steeply pitched roof, pediment and red-brick walls, dressed in pale stone. It was built in about 1690 for Lord Grey of Warke, later 1st Earl of Tankerville, and in the mid-eighteenth century was given its supporting pair of large brick outbuildings, a stable block and kitchen-laundry range (later becoming the Orangery), each with a clock tower. Your first sight is of its rear, north façade and portico, at the head of a short drive, informally bordered by grass glades, groups of free-growing yew and other evergreens, and a young avenue of Norway maple.

Clearly, this is not a 1690s setting. The early, grander formal gardens, which seem to have had terrace walks, courts, orchards and a bowling green, had mostly disappeared by about 1730 in favour of parkland sweeping up to the house walls. The present rear garden of sinuous lawns, meandering gravel paths and shrubberies evolved afterwards. It may well be that they were worked on by Lancelot 'Capability' Brown, for there is a plan dating from about 1750 attributable to him. But the principal protagonist behind today's garden is Humphry Repton, who advised Sir Harry Fetherstonhaugh from 1793, and produced one of his celebrated Red Books of proposals and sketches in 1810. He redesigned the north approach drive and portico, and most likely designed the game larder, the pathway to which is gruesomely inset with deer vertebrae. He probably also designed the iron gratings in the light wells over the intriguing underground service passages in the rear forecourt, which link the house to the kitchen, laundry and stables. The upstairs-downstairs world here was experienced at close hand by the young H.G. Wells, whose mother was housekeeper for twelve years until being dismissed for incompetence in 1892.

In the flower gardens and shrubberies either side of the drive, the Trust has embarked on a programme to capture more of the flavour of Repton's Picturesque style. To the east, broad grass walks and glades curve around belts and island beds of loose, serpentine planting, the ingredients arranged in defined groups of gently contrasting form and habit, and graded in height for theatrical effect and plays of light and shade. To the west, there is a small scented garden. Repton commented on the 'atmosphere of sweets': 'I may truly say that in no place have I ever seen such accurate attention given to olfactory joy as at Uppark – every window has its Orange Tree or Tube roses – and admits perfume from the surrounding beds of Mignionette and Heliotrope.' Everywhere, the

emphasis is on shrubs and perennials of Repton's period, such as Shrub roses, lilacs, philadelphus and strawberry tree. There is a good show of bulbs, and also of chalkland wildflowers which thrive in the unimproved grass of the lawns and meadows and, with the trees, connect the garden to its breathtaking setting.

**FAR LEFT** A distant glimpse of Uppark, a late seventeenth-century house set high on the South Downs.
**ABOVE** Red valerian edges one of the island beds, planted in the Picturesque style.

# Upton House

**BANBURY, WARWICKSHIRE**

**AREA** 15ha (37 acres) • **SOIL** neutral/iron-sandstone • **ALTITUDE** 211mm (693ft)
**AVERAGE RAINFALL** 686mm (27in) • **AVERAGE WINTER CLIMATE** cold

Upton stages one of the great *coups de théâtre* of English gardening. The opening scene is sober, even austere. The house, a wide, plain and symmetrical building, constructed of the local honey-brown Hornton sandstone, stands at the head of a straight drive, enclosed by tall beech and Scots pine, holly and yew. Its core was built by Sir Rushout Cullen, the son of a London merchant, in 1695; its additions date from the late 1920s, when the estate was bought by the 2nd Viscount Bearsted, a noted art collector and philanthropist.

The garden front is cheerier. There is clematis, wisteria and pink 'Albertine' rose on the walls; a succession of bedding plants, including wallflowers, tulips, Canterbury bells and seed-grown dahlias, fringing and spilling over the flagged terrace; and a stand of the hybrid Scots briar rose *Rosa × harisonii* 'Williams Double Yellow' complementing the stone. Opposite, a broad platform of lawn, framed on one side by yews and on the other by eighteenth-century cedars of Lebanon, sweeps to a ha-ha, beyond which the land climbs up a hillside, dotted with sheep and clumps of trees. It is a gentle and pleasing scene. Some visitors may look out upon it

and turn back. On my first visit, I nearly did, but luckily decided to continue to the lawn edge.

As you peer over, the contents spring up at you like a jack-in-the-box. A valley is revealed, the nearside bank tamed by terraces of flowering shrubs and perennials, double herbaceous borders running down to a copper beech tree, a garden of roses, sloping yew hedges, a grand Italianate stairway, a large fruit and vegetable garden and, at the bottom, a rectangular lake. A complete garden landscape is hidden here. The walls are contemporary with the older part of the house, and it seems that for three centuries the slope has been providing fruit and vegetables for the household. Angled to the south, the plots absorb all the available warmth, and they are still managed intensively, with greenhouses used to raise seedlings and cloches to protect young plants. The gamut of vegetables, grown on a four-year rotation, runs from French beans and Brussels sprouts to kohlrabi and onions. Falling rows of salad crops, asparagus beds, apple trees and blocks of soft fruit, including worcesterberry and jostaberry, complete the scene.

But while this productive section remains as the centrepiece, and a reminder of the priorities in the late seventeenth- and early eighteenth-century garden, the remainder of the slope has been developed for purely ornamental purposes. This was undertaken for Lord and Lady Bearsted by their architect, Percy Morley Horder, and the plantswoman and garden designer Kitty Lloyd-Jones, whose practical skills and artistry were employed by clients on both sides of the English Channel. In the present five-year refurbishment of the garden, the Trust is intending to reflect more of this 1930s flavour in its plantings – notably Kitty Lloyd-Jones's colour drifts in the Gertrude Jekyll style, and use of bulbs, annuals and tender perennials to extend the season. Family photographs and other archive material are helping in this.

With the construction of the stone stairway, the Baroque grandeur of the house was extended into the composition. The flights descend elegantly either side of a crown of wisteria, and at the base, where once the greenhouses stood, you come to the formal rose garden with beds of China and Hybrid Musk roses around a statue of Pan; Lady Bearsted's paved garden with pink and white perennials, shrubs and bedding plants; and a garden of blue flowers, woven around *Hibiscus syriacus* 'Oiseau Bleu' (syn. 'Blue Bird'), and framed again by double yellow hybrid Scots briar roses.

Soft and carefully focused associations of colour distinguish the planting here on the terraces, with blue and yellow, alone or in partnership, as a principal motif. There are many memorable passages: Dutch lavender, running beside the upper grass walk, accompanied by ceanothus, romneya, laburnum, salvia and agapanthus; a wave of creamy, iris-like *Sisyrinchium striatum*, beneath outcrops of phlomis, santolina, cistus and purple aubrieta; and fine displays from the apricot Tea rose 'Climbing Lady Hillingdon', the buff Noisette rose 'Rêve d'Or', *Lonicera etrusca*, and, in autumn, from the leaves and fruits of stag's horn sumach and numerous berberis, including *B. wilsoniae*.

The Mediterranean and Californian flavour of these upper borders is in response to the sunny, dry conditions, but where the light and soil changes, you meet a different cast. On the cool, shady side of the vegetable garden's brick wall, for example, a National Collection of asters has been assembled: not the mildew-prone *novi-belgii* hybrids, the true Michaelmas daisies, but the various cultivars of the taller, smaller-flowered *A. ericoides* and *A. cordifolius*, which include so many desirable garden plants, interspersed with varieties of short, starry *A. amellus*. They are at their peak in early October. As you reach the lake, water sets a new theme – for this is one of a chain of six former stewponds, formalised by Sir Rushout Cullen, but dating back to medieval times, when the land was held by the Church. The water, fed from a spring on top of Edgehill, collects first in the Monk's Well, south-west of the house, passes through the stewponds and flows eventually into the Thames. The lake you see from the lawn above is part of this, and was given its irregular shape and temple in 1775, when the property was owned by the banker Robert Child. The sunken lawn off to the west is now explained, for as you arrive through the nuttery (another essential in the productive garden), you realise that it too, together with the other water-filled depression now revealed – bordered by rushes and trees, including an impressive hornbeam – is part of the sequence.

Upton's second big surprise is now sprung. For beyond this pond, yet another garden of distinctive character opens up – a water garden of meandering grass paths and sinuous pools, presided over by a Dutch-style banqueting house, now looming between the trees. The building, like the formal framework of the gardens, dates back to the late seventeenth century, but the area was re-landscaped and planted in the 1930s, by which time the stewponds here had become an overgrown marsh. Lush marginal plantings of hostas, rodgersias, ligularias and rheums contrast with the more elegant foliage of ferns, astilbes and the multi-stemmed Katsura trees (*Cercidiphyllum japonicum*), and there are strong flashes of colour from lysichiton, primulas, and irises. Yew terraces, dating from the seventeenth century, lead back up to the main lawn.

This is by no means a complete catalogue of the garden's horticultural attractions. There is Lady Bearsted's limestone rock garden beside the swimming pool on the main lawn; the secret scented garden with its Shrub roses, stocks and sweet peas; the south lake border with its lush foliage; the spectacular delphinium, lupin and peony border; the orchard with its damsons, medlars and greengages; and the Wilderness, where Queen Anne's lace and campion follow the daffodils and bluebells. All contribute to a mood of luscious 1930s country house life.

**FAR LEFT** Lady Bearsted's garden, planted in pinks, whites and mauves, at Upton House. **ABOVE** Garden steps leading from the top terrace down into the gardens, with the mirror pond beyond.

# The Vyne

SHERBORNE ST JOHN, BASINGSTOKE, HAMPSHIRE

**AREA** 5ha (13 acres) • **SOIL** neutral/clay • **ALTITUDE** 61m (200ft)
**AVERAGE RAINFALL** 762mm (30in) • **AVERAGE WINTER CLIMATE** moderate

This composition of spacious pleasure grounds and crisp, clear colours fills a quiet hollow just a few miles from Basingstoke. The house was built for William Sandys, later Lord Chamberlain to Henry VIII, in the early part of the sixteenth century, and modified by Chaloner Chute, Speaker of the House of Commons, after 1653. It is a wide and welcoming building of rose-red brickwork, dressed in stone and decorated with purple header-bricks in diamond pattern (diapering), and when you approach the north façade of the house, it springs the surprise of a white Palladian portico – the earliest known example to adorn an English country house.

The low-lying position makes for a lush, green setting. Towering limes, together with an old horse chestnut and ancient oak, shade the south lawns (flooded with daffodils in spring), and on the north side, a vast expanse of close-mown grass rolls gently down to a lake, flanked by cedars, walnuts, Scots pines and other trees. You can see carp basking in the water and there is much other wildlife besides, including kingfishers, which often dart over the lower lake beyond the weir. A circular walk takes you across two bridges at each end of the lake (the brick piers of which are the remains of a fine Victorian bridge that replaced a Chinese-Gothic structure put up by John Chute in the eighteenth century) and passes through Morgaston Wood, full of bluebells in the spring.

The other, more ornamental wilderness area was developed by Sir Charles Chute in about 1907, following the woodland and meadow gardening ideas of the writer William Robinson. Here, snowdrops, daffodils, anemones and snakeshead fritillaries are naturalised in the grass, accompanied by clumps of geraniums, *Gunnera manicata* and the summer-flowering scented *Philadelphus* 'Beauclerk'. These areas are in contrast to the architectural and more formal touches that John Chute incorporated, or which were reinstated or added in the Victorian and Edwardian eras, when the grounds were reshaped and replanted; they include the gravel walk in front of the house, the narrow avenue of red-twigged limes dating from 1884, and, at its head, the splendid domed brick pavilion, in the shape of a Greek cross, dating from the 1630s.

Standing next to it is one of the oldest oak trees in Hampshire. Nearby, beside the Chapel, you also come upon two evergreen *Phillyrea latifolia*, with ancient twisted trunks.

In summer, the most colourful area of the garden is the small enclosure beside the west front of the house. Here, backed by a yew hedge, is a colourful herbaceous border planted in the 1960s, where violet-blue, purples, pinks, carmines and whites (catmint, *Campanula lactiflora*, acanthus, phlox, sedum, Japanese anemone and others) melt into a scheme of yellows, apricots, creams and scarlets (ligularia, daylilies, macleaya, crocosmia) – all finely associated for height and foliage contrast. I caught this border, designed by the late Graham Stuart Thomas, at its peak in July and it has lodged in my memory as one of the best formal herbaceous schemes I have come across in National Trust gardens. Opposite, the two beds of the fragrant pink Bush rose *Rosa* 'Madame Knorr' (syn. *R.* 'Comte de Chambord') are flanked by a pair of purple vines grown on frames. These are a reference to the house, thought to have been named after *Vin Domus*, or House of Wine, in Roman times.

In recent years the eighteenth-century walled garden has been brought back into production, with large areas of soft fruit, vegetables, and fruit trees, including many historic varieties of apple. You meander through the beds to the soft sound of clucking chickens. The new glasshouse, built on the site of its Victorian predecessor, displays plants such as citrus trees and pelargoniums, which were once grown in the house's Stone Gallery.

**RIGHT** Swans on the main lake at The Vyne, with the north front of the house in the background.

# Waddesdon Manor

**WADDESDON, AYLESBURY, BUCKINGHAMSHIRE**

AREA 67ha (165 acres) • SOIL alkaline/clay, sand • ALTITUDE 76m (250ft)
AVERAGE RAINFALL 864mm (34in) • AVERAGE WINTER CLIMATE cold

Baron Ferdinand de Rothschild rejected the initial design for his country house, intended as a weekend retreat for himself and his guests, as being rather too ambitious. His French architect, Gabriel-Hippolyte Destailleur, told him he would regret his decision, commenting that 'one always builds too small'. 'He prophesied truly,' said the Baron. 'After I had lived in the house for a while I was compelled to add one wing and then another …'

The manor, revealed at the end of a double avenue of trees (recently replanted with young English oak), is a fantastic sight: a broad expanse of Loire château perched on a cold, windy Buckinghamshire hill, bristling with conical towers, high-pitched pavilions, spires and ornament. Accompanying it is sweeping parkland with swirling belts of beech, lime, horse chestnut and other trees – many of which were planted in a semi-mature state, brought to their sites by teams of Percheron horses, specially imported from Normandy.

The tree collection was considerably enriched by Miss Alice de Rothschild after Baron Ferdinand's death in 1898, and is characterised now by its sumptuous stands of specimen exotics, arranged, species by species, for landscape impact. Unfortunately, there were comparatively few subsequent introductions in the years after her death, with the result that a major programme of replacement planting for the future has been required of the Trust, supported and funded by The Alice Trust, the Rothschild charitable trust which manages the property. Horse chestnut, silver lime and Austrian pine are among those you pass as you ascend the curving drive from the village, and at the head of the oak avenue weeping limes drench the air with summer scent around the grand fountain of Triton and Nereids riding on sea monsters.

Coloured-leaved trees, much favoured in the late-Victorian garden, are prominent here on the approach, as elsewhere, with blue Atlas cedar, purple beech and Norway maple (*Acer platanoides* 'Schwedleri') used as highlights among the tapestry of greens.

Golden yew and the golden Lawson cypress 'Stewartii' supply the yellow through the grounds. But the trees are just one element in this composition, which was planned as a series of varied and impressive entertainments for the family and their weekend guests.

The changes in terrain provide some drama, not just the contrast of the levelled areas and the falling hillside, but also the more picturesque additions, in particular the eruptions of rock to the west of the oak avenue. These seem natural, but in fact were made up of stone removed during the creation of the plateau on which the house is built, and are layered with artificial stone, brick and concrete. They were built by the noted rockwork specialists Pulham & Sons and, until the smell became too offensive, were used as shelter by Baron Ferdinand's flock of mountain sheep.

Further down the hill, you come upon a deep gulley (excavated for part of the railway track installed to transport materials for building the house) spanned by a bridge and with its steep sides planted with ferns and bamboo. The grass here is full of bluebells, primroses and daffodils, an echo of the great sloping wildflower and daffodil meadow, planted by Mr and Mrs James de Rothschild as a memorial to Miss Alice, further to the south.

The contrasts of artful gardening and natural landscape, man-made eye-catchers and plant forms play throughout the grounds. Beyond Pulham's rustic rockwork is the most splendid structure of all: a magnificent Rococo ironwork aviary, each compartment housing an assortment of exotic birds. The raucous calls, including those of the dashing white Rothschild's Mynah from Bali, can be heard deep into the park, and on my first visit here, years ago, there was the astonishing sight of macaws flying free over the trees. This policy had to be discontinued because of the damage they inflicted on plants.

The grandest piece of formal gardening, however, is to be found to the south of the house. Here, below the terrace, is the great parterre, designed by the Baron and the arena where he could demonstrate to his guests his gardeners' mastery over plants. With

an ornate fountain displaying Pluto and Proserpine as their centrepiece, and a stone balustrade and clipped hedges of green and golden yew as their frame, the beds heave with many thousands of seasonal bulbs, annuals and tropical dot plants. Across the parterre, there is a panoramic view, past the pink and white-candled chestnuts, down into the Vale of Aylesbury and towards the Rothschild pavilion at Eythrope, near Upper Winchendon, to which Baron Ferdinand would conduct his guests in a procession of landaus on a Sunday afternoon. In the morning, they would have toured Waddesdon's series of show glasshouses and rose, rock and water gardens, all formerly attached to the 2.8ha (7 acre) kitchen garden, which is outside the Trust's boundary and of which nothing much remains.

It was a sumptuous world, and present-day Waddesdon has re-created the spectacular flamboyance of the past with innovation and showmanship – not least in the manor's interiors, which are one of the treasure chests of Europe.

**LEFT** An array of statuary adorns the gardens.
**ABOVE** An impressive spring display of tulips and wallflowers in the great parterre.

# Wakehurst Place

ARDINGLY, HAYWARDS HEATH, WEST SUSSEX

AREA 73ha (180 acres) • SOIL acid to neutral/sandy, clay • ALTITUDE 61–152m (200–500ft)
AVERAGE RAINFALL 889mm (35in) • AVERAGE WINTER CLIMATE moderate

The setting for this mind-boggling collection of trees and shrubs is the unspoilt countryside of the Sussex Weald, with its rolling hills and tracts of ancient woodland. The gardens spill down grassy and rocky slopes below a high plateau, on which stands the Elizabethan mansion, built for Sir Edward Culpeper and restored by the Edwardian architect Sir Aston Webb.

The tall redwoods, formal lawns and small garden lake and rockery that accompany it are part of the nineteenth-century legacy, but it was in 1903 that the exotic planting began in earnest. The estate was bought by Gerald Loder, later Lord Wakehurst, who, following his father and his brother Sir Edmund at nearby Leonardslee and his nephew Giles at The High Beeches, began tapping into the stream of new trees and shrubs becoming available from the Americas, the Far East and Australasia. In 1965, the garden came, by way of a 99-year lease from the National Trust, to the Royal Botanic Garden, Kew, whose influence now shows in the stricter rationalising policy of grouping plants by geographic region and habitat, so that one has a sense of walking through the world's temperate woodlands, among relatively natural associations of leaf and flower.

The great storm of 1987, which tore through Wakehurst with the loss of around 20,000 trees, accelerated this shift in display in various parts of the grounds, including near the house, where sheltered and shady woodland beds were converted overnight into a sunny, exposed hilltop. Replanted with dwarf rhododendrons, junipers, potentillas, and *Daphne bholua*, ground-cover perennials including roscoeas and carpets of *Bergenia ciliata*, and a copse of birch, rowan and maples behind, this now gives a taste of the sub-alpine heathland and scrub of Taiwan, Korea, Japan and the Sino-Himalayas – a region which was of special interest to Tony Schilling, the plant-hunter and former curator.

Such innovations interplay with older and more ornamental features. Around the lawns, white-tiered *Cornus alternifolia* 'Argentea' and golden cypresses share ground with botanical rarities such as *Aesculus wilsonii* and aromatic *Zanthoxylum ailanthoides*. There are displays of autumn colour, and on the other side of the mansion an area has been planted for winter, presenting witch hazels and other flowering shrubs in a scheme of heathers, conifers and white-trunked birches. Nearby are the formal walled gardens, one with an inner enclosure of yew hedges and bedding schemes, and the other with a cottage-garden mood, set by silver-leaved and pastel-flowered shrubs, perennials and roses; the walls shelter many interesting climbers, including a noted specimen of the Chilean coral plant, *Berberidopsis corallina*.

Outside one of the walls, the botanical and geographical themes are picked up again with a pair of borders devoted to bulbs and other monocotyledons, divided according to their Northern or Southern Hemisphere origins. The cast includes some ravishing ginger lilies (*Hedychium*), many of which are hardier than is often supposed. Reputedly tender plants also spring surprises in the Southern Hemisphere Garden by the croquet lawn, where *Banksia integrifolia* subsp. *monticola*, *Hakea*, *Pseudopanax*, *Leptospermum*, and *Telopea* appear among the more familiar genera.

As you walk south, away from the house and the mansion pond, the ground suddenly drops away, and from the semi-circular balustrade of the viewing bastion, you find yourself looking down into a steep glen, known as the Slips, the entrance to one of the two planted valleys that ring the house like a horseshoe. A stream flows down, falling over ledges and feeding into pools of various sizes, bordered by a rich array of moisture-loving perennials, including blue poppies, osmunda fern, arisaemas, and, in well-manured ground, a spectacular colony of the giant Himalayan lily, *Cardiocrinum giganteum*. Magnolias and nyssas thrive on the grassy banks, joined by a range of other garden-worthy trees such as *Stewartia pseudocamellia*, *Trochodendron aralioides* and *Maytenus boaria*. Curving paths, short flights of steps and small bridges over the water beckon this way and that, at one point leading you into the Iris Dell, ringed by a steep bank of Japanese maples and Kurume azaleas. In late June and early July, the numerous forms of *Iris ensata* turn it into a bowl of colour, which you cross by a boardwalk.

The glades and depressions are framed by native oaks and beeches and soaring North American conifers – the western hemlocks and Douglas firs in particular have reached a notable size. There is a concentration of unusual conifers, such as *Picea farreri* and *Keteleeria davidiana*, in the Pinetum. Rhododendrons and azaleas are also a major presence at the head of Westwood Valley, and among the moister pockets and shadier banks, you wander among extensive plantings of the larger-leaved kinds, such as *Rhododendron fulvum*, *R. rex* and the Loderi Group.

To the west, a massive outcrop of weathered grey sandstone is the centrepiece for a wilder and more rugged Himalayan scene, with viewing points down the valley. Here, some of the thickets of *Berberis wilsoniae* have been cleared to expose more of the rock, which is an important habitat for rare mosses, liverworts and lichens, and the native filmy fern, *Hymenophyllum tunbrigense*. In line with Kew's involvement with plant conservation worldwide, much effort is directed towards wildflower and habitat management at Wakehurst, ranging from different mowing and maintenance regimes of the garden's lawn and grass areas to helping in the heathland restoration of Ashdown Forest – visitors are encouraged to inspect the extensive recycling operation on the eastern edge of the garden, where bracken from the Forest is composted.

An extensive sweep of meadows, woods and wetlands in the Loder Valley is also managed as a nature reserve. The public is admitted only by permit, but you get an idea of its content to the south of the garden's lower lake, where an area of swamp, surrounded by woods, has been made accessible by means of a raised wooden walkway, enabling you to pass through reed beds and over watermint and other aquatics, looking down at fish and dragonflies; grebe are usually present, and occasionally you catch a glimpse of a kingfisher. It is a complete change in mood.

Beside Westwood Lake, rhododendrons and other Asian exotics again reappear, and in autumn there is another bonfire of coloured leaves from American species such as *Cotinus obovatus*, *Acer rubrum*, *Oxydendrum arboreum* and liquidambar. The walk back up the western valley takes you through further American forest types, including atmospheric groves of Douglas fir and wellingtonia; a belt of high Arctic species; slopes of Mediterranean pines, oaks and arbutus; a Southern Hemisphere wood of *Nothofagus* (a National Collection) and eucalyptus; and plantings made up of the world's birches (another National Collection). Bluebells, Lent lilies and numerous other wildflowers carpet the banks in spring and summer. This is one of the Trust's largest gardens, and a full day is never long enough.

Opened in 2000, the Millennium Seed Bank is a further addition to the garden. With its laboratories and storage rooms on display through glass panels in a specially designed building, the Bank already conserves 10 per cent of the world's flora, and some 97 per cent of British flora, as an insurance policy against the dangers of extinction in the wild, and to help in the research and restoration of natural ecosystems.

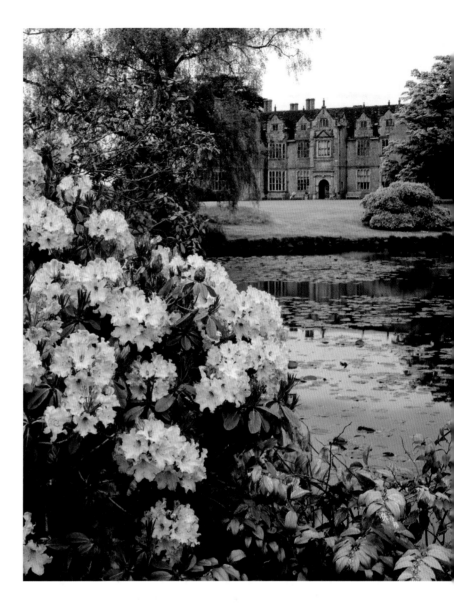

**ABOVE** Wakehurst Place seen from across the lake.

# Wallington

CAMBO, MORPETH, NORTHUMBERLAND

AREA 26ha (65 acres) • SOIL neutral to acid/medium loam • ALTITUDE 152m (500ft)
AVERAGE RAINFALL 838mm (33in) • AVERAGE WINTER CLIMATE moderate to cold

The moorland road from Hexham to Rothbury and Cragside runs through the heart of the Wallington estate, crossing the River Wansbeck over the stone-balustraded bridge designed by James Paine in 1755, and then climbing the wooded hill to skirt the eastern front of the Palladian mansion. Four dragons' heads, embedded in the lawn, grin at you as you pass. Sir Walter Calverley Blackett embarked on the creation of his Georgian idyll some time in the mid-1730s, helped principally by a 'Mr Joyce', and possibly later in the 1760s by Lancelot 'Capability' Brown, whose childhood home was only a mile away.

So, you arrive at Wallington to a taste of the eighteenth century. Either side of the house are the remnants of Sir Walter's elaborately designed plantations: dark walks, straight and serpentine, leading between the beeches, oaks, limes and sycamores, and their laurel and yew understorey, to open pools colonised by waterlily, iris, great water dock and many other native species. Red squirrels still live in these woods, and there is a rich birdlife, including nuthatch, wood warbler and pied flycatcher.

From the house, there is the contrast of sweeping views across the ha-ha, down into the parkland and up over the rolling Northumbrian hills towards Hadrian's Wall and the distant Shaftoe Crags. Urns draw the eye east and west across open lawn, the west view taking you down an avenue of laurel hedges. But there are also more colourful touches, added in Victorian and more recent times: mixed shrubberies of golden yew, golden lonicera, red-purple plum and bronze-purple sloe (*Prunus spinosa* 'Purpurea'); the Bourbon rose 'Madame Isaac Pereire' successfully trained as a climber up the south front of the house, in the company of other roses, sage, rosemary and fuchsia; and, where the entrance drive curves into the clock-tower courtyard, an unexpectedly pretty midsummer partnership of deep violet *Campanula lactiflora*, rich red valerian, moonlight yellow tree lupin and white philadelphus backed by purple sloe.

All this is an appetiser for what awaits in the Walled Garden, 0.8km (½ mile) to the east. The route takes you through the wood, past prospects of Sir Walter's triumphal archway (he had it repositioned here in an upper field, as a folly, after it proved too narrow for coaches to pass through); alongside his handsome, recently restored Portico House, built into the north wall of the original kitchen garden; and then, at the head of the easternmost wilderness pond, to a modest oak gate.

The surprise is sprung. Ahead are stone terraces and curving stairways, lawns and hedges, ponds and rockeries, conservatory and pavilion, ornamental trees and border after border of flowering shrubs, herbaceous plants, roses and bulbs, all backed by views of parkland and woods. The walls and central erect pavilion (the Owl House, now, as formerly, the head gardener's office) were built by Sir Walter to enclose his new kitchen garden, but the internal design is largely the work of Sir George Otto Trevelyan, who inherited in 1886 and gardened here enthusiastically until his death in 1928, at the age of 90. The planting, on the other hand, is almost entirely the work of the Trust, which took over a garden weedy, overgrown and in structural disrepair.

There is a wealth of detail to investigate. The brick, fern-flecked wall of the eighteenth-century upper terrace faces inwards, unlike those at Powis Castle (*qv*), onto a summer border of pastel-tinted Hybrid Musk roses and the almost single-flowered, richly scented 'Souvenir de St Anne's' (a sport of the popular Bourbon rose 'Souvenir de la Malmaison'), accompanied by alliums, eryngiums and a froth of white valerian. *Rosa glauca* (well teamed with black-eyed, magenta *Geranium psilostemon*) terminates the view in a haze of purplish grey. Since 2008, vegetables, soft fruit and herbs have been cultivated in the nuttery within the Walled Garden, as a reminder of the garden's earlier role.

The colour schemes of the Walled Garden are loose, but there is an underlying theme to most of the borders. In front of the conservatory, purple smoke bushes billow over hot plantings of yellow, orange and scarlet. Metal arches of honeysuckle and blue clematis (an echo of the fruit tunnels of the original garden) span beds of blue irises and nepeta, yellow loosestrife, inula and marjoram. White martagon lilies partner golden yews; salmon alstroemerias are teamed with violet campanulas. The wide lower north-facing border is graded from soft to strong colours.

Elsewhere, the planting is dictated more by the nature of the habitat. Dwarf conifers, brooms, potentillas and hebes are grouped along the rocky beds beside the paths and stream, while the damp western fringe of the garden supports large and lush colonies of hostas, water irises and ligularias, accompanied by a comprehensive range of elders.

When bad weather threatens, there is Sir George's conservatory for shelter. The very highest standards of cultivation underpin this splendid Edwardian scene, where pink and red flowers are arrayed against white-painted timberwork and furniture, marble busts and stone-slabbed floor. Pelargoniums and begonias, interspersed with palms, ferns and trailing ivy, fill the display bench with colour. Scent is provided by *Heliotropium arborescens* and a huge lemon verbena, said to pre-date the house.

**LEFT** The Pump House, partly covered by trees and undergrowth, can just be seen behind the China Pond.
**ABOVE** View of the owl house, conservatory and hot border at Wallington.

# Westbury Court Garden

**WESTBURY-ON-SEVERN, GLOUCESTERSHIRE**

AREA 2ha (5 acres) • SOIL alkaline/alluvial silt, clay • ALTITUDE 6m (20ft)
AVERAGE RAINFALL 686mm (27in) • AVERAGE WINTER CLIMATE moderate

The Tall Pavilion offers an elevated vantage point of this handsomely appointed walled garden. The view is of tranquil canals, mown lawns, neat hedges and topiaries, white-painted benches, flashes of flower colour and fruits espaliered against mellow brick. Little seems to have ruffled the scene for 300 years. In fact, when Westbury Court came to the Trust in 1967, it was in an advanced state of dereliction.

Enthusiasm for the major restoration project sprang from the garden's rarity. Very few formal gardens in Britain survived the long era of naturalistic landscaping of the eighteenth century, and among them, Westbury Court was the only example to show a Dutch-style layout from the reign of William of Orange. The low-lying meadows bordering the River Severn make an ideal site for a water garden, but it may also have been the influence of his Dutch neighbour, Catherine Boevey of Flaxley Abbey, that prompted Maynard Colchester to embark on its construction. He began in 1696, with the excavation of the Long Canal, and work continued apace until his death in 1715. The garden was then embellished and altered by his nephew, Maynard Colchester II.

Within the walls, the parallel lines of yew hedges create a series of rectangular framed vistas down the waterways and lawns, with the flowering plants, topiaries and pot plants conveying the Dutch absorption and expertise in the art and craft of horticulture. Some of the hedges themselves sprout yew cones and spheres of holly, while balls and cones of box feature in the flower-filled 'cut parterre' beyond the T-shaped canal. A quincunx of standard trees and clipped evergreens surrounds it, including domes of *Phillyrea angustifolia*, umbrellas of Portugal laurel, and thorns sporting nests of mistletoe (established by pressing the ripe berries into the cracks of branches in late winter).

The espaliered fruit trees, reminders of the garden's important productive role, contribute to the formal patterns. Evocatively named varieties, all in cultivation before 1700, include the apples 'Calville Blanc d'Hiver', 'Catshead' and 'Court Pendu Plat'; the

**TOP OF PAGE** Honeysuckle arch in the walled garden.
**ABOVE** Bed of globe artichokes in June.
**RIGHT** The Tall Pavilion seen from the parterre.

pears 'Beurré Brown', 'Forelle' and 'Bellissime d'Hiver'; and the plums 'Red Magnum Bonum' and 'Catalonia'. Peaches, apricots and Morello cherries are also here. In spring, bulbs make a patchwork of colour between them. The mid-seventeenth century saw the height of 'tulipmania' in Holland, when freakish tulips exchanged hands for vast sums, and although those famous varieties no longer exist, the selection of species and cultivars here evokes that period. Daffodils, anemones, muscari, ranunculus and crown imperials accompany them.

In the small walled enclosure beside the gazebo is a collection of the border perennials grown at the time. Campanulas, astrantia, hellebores, veratrums and meadow sages are among the cast filling the pine-edged beds, and at midsummer they are showered with the scented blooms of old Shrub and Climbing roses. A small collection of dianthus is grown outside the walls, in beds specially raised and gritted. Vegetable plots, as shown in Kip's engraving of about 1707,

have been replanted, and recently the original path layout around the Long Canal, and between the fountain and summerhouse, have been re-established.

The garden is essentially intimate and introspective, but framed views of the countryside are given by the two ironwork grilles, or *clairvoyées*, in the north wall – one surmounted by stone pineapples made in 1704, and the other capped by vases made after 1715. There are some fine trees in the neighbouring fields, including, to the south, a line of rare native black poplars. An avenue of 'Barland' pears, willow and alder shade the glades beyond the canalised stream, which forms the garden's eastern boundary, while within the formal garden itself stands a superb tulip tree and a stupendous evergreen oak, presumed to pre-date the Dutch layout and thought to be one of the largest and oldest specimens in Britain. Recently, a small rabbit warren has also been re-created – the original warren was seven times larger and would have kept the kitchen well supplied with meat.

# West Green House Garden

**WEST GREEN, HARTLEY WINTNEY, HAMPSHIRE**

AREA 2.8ha (7 acres) • SOIL heavy clay • ALTITUDE 69m (225ft) • AVERAGE RAINFALL 762mm (30in) • AVERAGE WINTER CLIMATE moderate

General Henry Hawley is remembered chiefly as 'Hangman Hawley' for his brutality to the defeated Scots Highlanders after the Battle of Culloden – but he shows a different side to his character at West Green, where a tombstone in the garden remembers his dog Monkey, 'The best black spaniell that ere wag'd a taile'. The house that he remodelled in 1750 is a perfect piece of Georgian symmetry, built of warm brick, modest in size, and grandly crowned with pedimented dormers and stone vases. And it sets the tone for the garden around it, which is revealed as a sequence of immaculate walled and hedged enclosures, with crisp lawns, gravel paths and patterns of box. Quite how it evolved is something of a mystery, but by 1773, fourteen years after Hawley's death, there was a complete landscape here, in a formal style that was by then distinctly old-fashioned.

The surviving framework was relished and expanded in the Arts and Crafts style – a *Country Life* article of November 1936 describes 'an idyll of roses, herbaceous borders, vegetables and fruit, croquet on the lawn and tea on the terrace'. Unusually, after coming to the Trust in 1957, the garden has been allowed to respond to the enthusiasms of the house's tenants, who pay for its maintenance, and it has been developed with great gusto, first by Lord McAlpine and, since 1993, by the Australian gardener Marylyn Abbott.

From the approaching country lane, your appetiser is a Memorial Column, one of a number of handsome theatrical follies commissioned by Lord McAlpine from the architect Quinlan Terry. It stands at the head of a young lime avenue. The entrance drive then brings you round past the magnolia-clad south front where, through railings, you look into a polite little parterre of fruit trees, ringed in box.

The main walled garden, however, keeps its secrets until you step through the door. Suddenly, you are in one of the most sumptuous English potagers, a triumphant restoration of Lord McAlpine's architectural design by Marylyn Abbott, overlaid with her own swashbuckling approach to planting. Centred on a fine wrought-iron well-head, narrow box-edged flower borders run alongside the lawns and gravel paths, punctuated by fruit trees and pyramids of clematis. They are packed with annuals as well as perennials and roses, the content constantly changing but always co-ordinated by colour – some areas palely ethereal in lavenders, whites and pinks, others in unusual biscuits, apricots and browns, and still others brooding in burgundy, purple and battleship grey. Quantities of spires and umbels, as from foxgloves, eremurus, verbascums, alliums and pink cow parsley add a dreamy wildness to the mix. A pair of ornamental fruit cages presides over patterns of clipped rosemary, lavender and silver santolina and a spectacular array of hardy and exotic vegetables, which are arranged to a different extravagant theme every year. A new plant house and a red and white *Alice in Wonderland* garden add to the variety.

In the rear wall of the main walled garden, added before 1936, you are led through a moon gate to the *trompe-l'oeil* Nymphaeum, also by Quinlan Terry and modelled on a fountain in the Via Garibaldi in Rome. Restored, fronted by patterned paving, and with its flanking cascading rills splashing down the slope in the company of a new box and yew parterre, this makes a lively change of mood. A sister water garden, a modern interpretation of a paradise garden, has been completed beyond the hedge.

In the adjacent Lake Garden, the formality is exchanged for a miniature Arcadian landscape of water, trees and architectural follies, from Doric gazebo to Chinese bridge, and with a pineapple-topped aviary on the lake's island. An ever-expanding carpet of naturalised bulbs in the grass, from crocuses to massed daffodils and snakeshead fritillaries, accompanies them. Allegorical references to Heaven and Hell were intended, and the cave-like Smoke House, from which visitors were meant to emerge spluttering, symbolised Purgatory. Afterwards, you ascend the Olympian mount to the song of blackbirds, the scent of balsam poplars, and the sway of weeping willows over water.

Equally serene, but formally so, is the Green Theatre to the north of the house, to which the green tiers of lawn descend below an eighteenth-century Orangery adorned with cartouches of painted garden implements. Open-air opera is staged here every summer.

**LEFT**  A view of the lake at West Green House. The still water is surrounded by trees and covered in algae.
**ABOVE**  The parterre of fruit trees, ringed in box.

# West Wycombe Park

**WEST WYCOMBE, BUCKINGHAMSHIRE**

**AREA** 19ha (46 acres) • **SOIL** alkaline • **ALTITUDE** 76m (250ft) • **AVERAGE RAINFALL** 762mm (30in) • **AVERAGE WINTER CLIMATE** cold

The red-blooded passion for life and art held by Sir Francis Dashwood, politician, antiquarian, connoisseur, practical joker, party-giver, founder member of the Society of Dilettanti and of the notorious Hellfire Club, is behind the creation of this Elysian landscape. The mansion, sitting on rising ground and commanding northerly views down its own wooded Chiltern coombe and up to Church Hill opposite, was remodelled by Dashwood over a period of 45 years, from 1735 – by which time he had spent the best part of eleven years on successive cultural tours through Europe and Asia Minor – until his death in 1781. The coombe was landscaped over the same long period.

By 1752, the first phase of Dashwood's redesign of his estate had produced a semi-formal composition, combining straight-edged plantations and avenues with serpentine walks and an irregularly shaped lake, made by damming the River Wye. From 1770, there was a fresh impetus, as Dashwood responded to the current taste for a parkland of more sweeping views and flowing contours. Although this phase – probably directed throughout by Thomas Cook, a pupil of 'Capability' Brown – did much to soften the earlier formality, many of the Baroque and Rococo elements were retained and absorbed, leaving the evolution of the garden clearly exposed.

Little has disturbed the scene since, although a programme of restoration and replanting was much needed by the middle of the last century and was conducted by the Trust and the late 11th Baronet, with assistance from the Historic Buildings Council. The circuit of the park unfolds a succession of composed views and architectural surprises. From the north front of the house, you look down the greensward to the lake, where, on the largest of three islands, a colonnaded music temple by Nicholas Revett shines against the trees. On the hill to the west, above the plantation screening West Wycombe village, stands St Lawrence's church, topped with its gilded sphere.

Past the Palladian east portico, the double colonnades of the south front, the great stone and flintwork arch of the Temple of Apollo, the blue cedars and banks of shrubs, you walk up the slope to find the Round Temple suddenly revealed, a circular dovecote designed by Revett in about 1775. From here, the dog-leg ha-ha draws you between open pastureland above and dark straight-edged plantations of deciduous trees below to the Temple of the Winds, a flint and stuccoed wonder, built in about 1759 and one of the earliest reproductions of an ancient classical monument in the country. The old entrance drive now takes you down to the lakeside and cascade. The early garden's impressive rock arch and accompanying River God were replaced by 1781 with the present simplified structure of piers and reclining nymphs, but the water still gushes over the knobbled steps into the stream. Across the lake, the view is more tranquil, the eye channelled between the islands and down the Broad Walk opposite, the only survivor of the two great avenues shown on the 1752 survey.

Daphne's Temple and Kitty's Lodge mark the original entrance to the park, and from here you skirt the top end of the lake and enter the woods where, by means of little bridges crossing sinuous streams, you pass the eighteenth-century Temple of Venus, cross the Broad Walk, and return to the mansion. But *en route*, the mind must be allowed to wander, conjuring up visions of the Bacchanalian feasts, musical spectacles and other lavish entertainments the park has witnessed.

**ABOVE** The Temple of Music creates a reflection in the lake on this hazy day.

# Wimpole Hall

**ARRINGTON, ROYSTON, CAMBRIDGESHIRE**

**AREA** 24ha (60 acres) • **SOIL** alkaline/clay • **ALTITUDE** 30m (100ft)
**AVERAGE RAINFALL** 584mm (23in) • **AVERAGE WINTER CLIMATE** moderate

A ridge of chalk meets the Cambridgeshire plain to the north and west of Wimpole Hall, giving sudden views of rising woods and grassland, the scene picturesquely animated by flocks of rare antelope-like sheep and herds of hefty (but docile) huge-horned cattle. The approach, however, is across level ground, from which the red-brick Georgian façade ascends imposingly. This is the county's grandest country house, and it is fitting that its park should have been moulded by some of the most famous names in landscape gardening.

A 3.2km (2 mile) long double avenue, conceived by Charles Bridgeman in the 1720s, slices across the flat farmland opposite the south front. Sadly, the original elm trees here, and in the older west avenue, fell victim to Dutch elm disease in the 1970s, but in a major, phased planting project the Trust replaced them with limes, some propagated from ancient trees in the park. Flanked by laid hedges, they are now a fine sight.

From the mid-eighteenth century, the landscaping at Wimpole was essentially directed along more 'natural' lines. The first phase was conducted for the 1st Earl of Hardwicke by Robert Greening, advised by the garden architect Sanderson Miller. It was Miller who produced the design for the Gothic Tower that serves as the distant eye-catcher from the north front of the hall, though it was not built until 1774, and then in a modified form. The broad sweeps of hilly pasture and the clumps and tiers of trees that frame this folly have also been moulded by later designers. For ten years from the mid-1760s, the park was in the hands of 'Capability' Brown and, from 1790, his pupil William Emes. As you walk across the park towards the tower, you will come upon the lakes Brown created from the former fish ponds and enhanced with islands and a Chinese bridge.

The last great name in this extraordinary roll call of designers is Humphry Repton, who came here in 1801. He planned a new approach to the hall from the Cambridge road, filled out Brown's tree clumps, and set out the present formal pattern of neat lawns and paths, exclaiming that: 'It is called natural, but to me it has ever seemed unnatural that a palace shall rise immediately out of sheep pasture.' The parterre is planted with contrasting displays of tulips for spring and some 12,000 pelargoniums and salvias for summer, while in the adjacent Dutch Garden fuchsias follow a mass of blue and white anemones.

Trees are one of Wimpole's chief glories, and while the native oaks, beeches, limes and ashes give the artful backdrop, ornamental varieties, planted over the past two centuries, enhance the foreground. Oriental plane, copper beeches and Indian bean trees are highlights in the formal areas, and in the pleasure grounds, the meandering path to the walled garden takes you past cherries, crab apples and a range of American species, including good specimens of redwood, Cornelian dogwood and a National Collection of walnuts. There was much replanting here in the wake of the 1987 storm, and the cast now includes a generous percentage of conifers, which have proved surprisingly tolerant of the heavy alkaline soil. Western red cedar, Spanish fir, incense cedar and Serbian spruce are among the species added.